Second Edition

Race and Ethnicity in the United States

Richard T. Schaefer
DePaul University

Upper Saddle River, New Jersey 07458

Library of Congress Cataloging-in-Publication Data
Schaefer, Richard T.
Race and ethnicity in the United States / Richard T. Schaefer.—2nd ed.
p. cm.
Includes bibliographical references.
ISBN 0-13-028315-0
1. Minorities—United States. 2. Prejudices—United States. 3. United States—Ethnic relations. 4. United States—Race relations. I. Title.

E184.A1 S25 2001
305.8'00973—dc21

00-032687

VP, Editorial Director: Laura Pearson
AVP, Publisher: Nancy Roberts
Managing Editor: (editorial) Sharon Chambliss
Managing Editor: Ann Marie McCarthy
Production Liaison: Fran Russello
Project Manager: Marianne Hutchinson (Pine Tree Composition)
Prepress and Manufacturing Buyer: Mary Ann Gloriande
Art Director: Jayne Conte
Cover Designer: Kiwi Design
Cover Art: Sergio Baradat/Stock Illustration
Director, Image Resource Center: Melinda Lee Reo
Manager, Rights & Permissions: Kay Dellosa
Image Specialist: Beth Boyd
Photo Researcher: Melinda Alexander

This book was set in 10/12 Garamond light by Pine Tree Composition, Inc., and was printed and bound by Courier Companies, Inc.
The cover was printed by Phoenix Color Corp.

Printed in the United States of America

10 9 8 7 6 5 4 3

ISBN 0-13-028315-0

Prentice-Hall International (UK) Limited, *London*
Prentice-Hall of Australia Pty. Limited, *Sydney*
Prentice-Hall Canada Inc., *Toronto*
Prentice-Hall Hispanoamericana, S.A., *Mexico*
Prentice-Hall of India Private Limited, *New Delhi*
Prentice-Hall of Japan, Inc., *Tokyo*
Pearson Education Asia Pte. Ltd., *Singapore*
Editora Prentice-Hall do Brasil, Ltda., *Rio de Janeiro*

To my students whose questions, answers, and concerns have further enlivened my life over twenty-five years of teaching about race and ethnicity.

Contents

Preface

Race and ethnicity, along with religion and gender, are topics that emerge in every area—politics, law, the economy, entertainment, and sports, to name a few. In addition, we as individuals observe the tension and sometimes violence that emerge in the multicultural nation that is the United States.

This second edition of *Race and Ethnicity in the United States* introduces the reader to the sociological treatment of the topic. I offer the basic perspectives used in the discipline and an overview of the contemporary situation. But as I point out throughout the book and especially in Chapter 6, race and ethnicity are not static. They are changing phenomenon moving to an even more diverse society in terms of race and ethnicity. I equip the reader with the basic intellectual tools to unravel this continuing emotional area of national debate.

A Practical, Useful Introduction

I begin with an introduction on what minority groups are and how assimilation and pluralism function as racial processes. The presentation of the all-important areas of prejudice and discrimination draws on not only sociology but also psychology and economics. The significant role played by immigration—past, present, and future—receives a chapter-length treatment. A discussion of race and ethnicity would not be complete without recognition of both White ethnic groups and the diversity of religious expression today. In the concluding chapters, I seek to stress that intolerance knows no barriers and is experienced even by those minority-group members who have achieved some economic success. I also comment that despite all the discussion of "race relations," we may not all be communicating with the same basic understandings.

Changes in the Second Edition and New Features throughout the Book

Every line, every source, and every number of the first edition have been rechecked for their currency. Throughout the book are additions to improve the pedagogy of the well-received first edition published six years ago:

- Internet exercises at the end of each chapter
- Review questions in addition to critical thinking questions

The second edition includes the following additions and changes:

Dramatic presentation of racial and ethnic change from 1500 to projections for 2050 (Chapter 1)

Listen to Their Voices: *Problem of the Color-Line,* W. E. B. DuBois (Chapter 1)

Section on social construction of race (Chapter 1)

Section on Census 2000's handling of multiracial identification (Chapter 1)

Section titled "Who Am I?" dealing with diversity within individuals (Chapter 1)

Section on resistance and change emphasizing efforts by subordinate groups (Chapter 1)

Section on hate crimes accompanied by map showing state-by-state policies (Chapter 2)

Case study on television as it relates to prejudice (Chapter 2)

Figure illustrating change in racial composition of TV characters (Chapter 2)

Listen to Their Voices: *In Search of Bruce Lee's Grave,* Shanlon Wu (Chapter 2)

Listen to Their Voices: *Of Race and Risk,* Patricia J. Williams (Chapter 3)

Section on glass ceiling's impact in the labor market (Chapter 3)

Section on environmental justice as a form of discrimination (Chapter 3)

Listen to Their Voices: *Roots,* Raffi Ishkanian (Chapter 4)

Section on the economic impact of immigration (Chapter 4)

New tables on benefits and concerns of immigration and on the major policies over the last 130 years (Chapter 4)

"Whiteness" as reflected in the growing consideration of White studies in academe introduced here in the context of ethnicity (Chapter 5)

Listen to Their Voices: *When the Boats Arrived,* Diane Glancy (Chapter 5)

Case example on Italian Americans (Chapter 5)

Section on limits of religious freedom dealing with the Amish (Chapter 5)

The changing workforce in terms of race, ethnicity, and gender (Chapter 6)

Reflecting the changes in virtually every paragraph is the large number of new key terms. By chapter they include the following:

Chapter 1: Afrocentric perspective, ethnic cleansing, fusion, internal colonialism, panethnicity, racial formation, and world systems analysis

Chapter 2: Bogardus scale and hate crimes

Chapter 3: double jeopardy, environmental justice, glass ceiling, glass wall, informal economy (including irregular or underground economy), and reverse discrimination

Chapter 4: refugees, remittances (or migradollars), and sinophobes

Chapter 5: ethnicity paradox and principle of third-generation interest

Acknowledgments

I am very grateful to the many instructors who have used the more comprehensive *Racial and Ethnic Groups* who have assisted me in improving the coverage of the material presented in this more concise volume. In developing this book, I have benefited from my association with Sharon Chambliss and Nancy Roberts of Prentice Hall. I am grateful to the assistance at DePaul University of Department Assistant Melissa Haeffner and Student Assistant Christina Suarez. I would also like to acknowledge the contribution of John Tenuto of the College of Lake County in Illinois for developing the Internet exercises at the conclusion of each chapter. As in all my endeavors, the continuing daily support of my wife, Sandy, and my son, Peter, has been of immeasurable assistance.

Richard T. Schaefer
schaeferrt@aol.com

Understanding Race and Ethnicity

CHAPTER OUTLINE

HIGHLIGHTS

Minority groups are subordinated in terms of power and privilege to the majority, or dominant, group. A minority is defined not by being outnumbered, but by five characteristics: unequal treatment, distinguishing physical or cultural traits, involuntary membership, in-group marriage, and awareness of subordination. Subordinate groups are classified in terms of race, ethnicity, religion, and gender. The social importance of race is significant through a process of racial formation; its biological significance is uncertain. The theoretical perspectives of functionalism, conflict theory, and labeling offer insights into the sociology of intergroup relations. Immigration, annexation, and colonialism are processes that may create subordinate groups. Other processes such as expulsion may remove the presence of a subordinate group. Significant for race and ethnic relations in the United States today is the distinction between assimilation and pluralism. The former demands subordinate-group conformity to the dominant group, and the latter implies mutual respect among diverse groups.

In January 2000, Major League Baseball ordered John Rocker to see a therapist. This demand was not an effort to improve the pitcher's concentration during the game or his curve ball. Rather, it was in response to a series of outrageous statements he made in a published interview the month before. He managed explicitly to blast Asian American women drivers, gays and lesbians, African Americans, and immigrants. With respect to the latter, in exasperation Rocker exclaimed, "How the hell did they get in this country?" His views are hardly rare, but because of concern about the image of baseball, the decision was made that these outbursts were not to be tolerated. Rocker was fined $500, suspended for fourteen days, and ordered to get sensitivity training.

The incident shows the heights that racial and ethnic hatred in the United States can reach today, but the reaction to the expression of prejudice also shows some bitter irony. You see, the team for which Rocker plays is the Atlanta *Braves*. For many years, tribal groups have objected to "Braves" as a name for the mascot of a professional team and everything that goes with it—the sale of rubber tomahawks, the incessant chanting by fans of the team who are trying to imitate some war chant, and the appearance of the faithful in "war paint." Yet the team and organized baseball have remained supportive of "Braves" as a mascot, as have other sports about the "Redskins" or "Blackhawks." The incident with the professional baseball player shows how complex race and ethnicity are in the United States. The nation—through its call-in radio stations, Internet chat rooms, and newspaper editorials—spoke virtually in unison in early 2000 against the racism of one ballplayer. Virtually unmentioned was the corporate-backed name that makes the earliest inhabitants of North America a mascot like some nonhuman animal (Atlanta Braves 2000; Pearlman 1999).

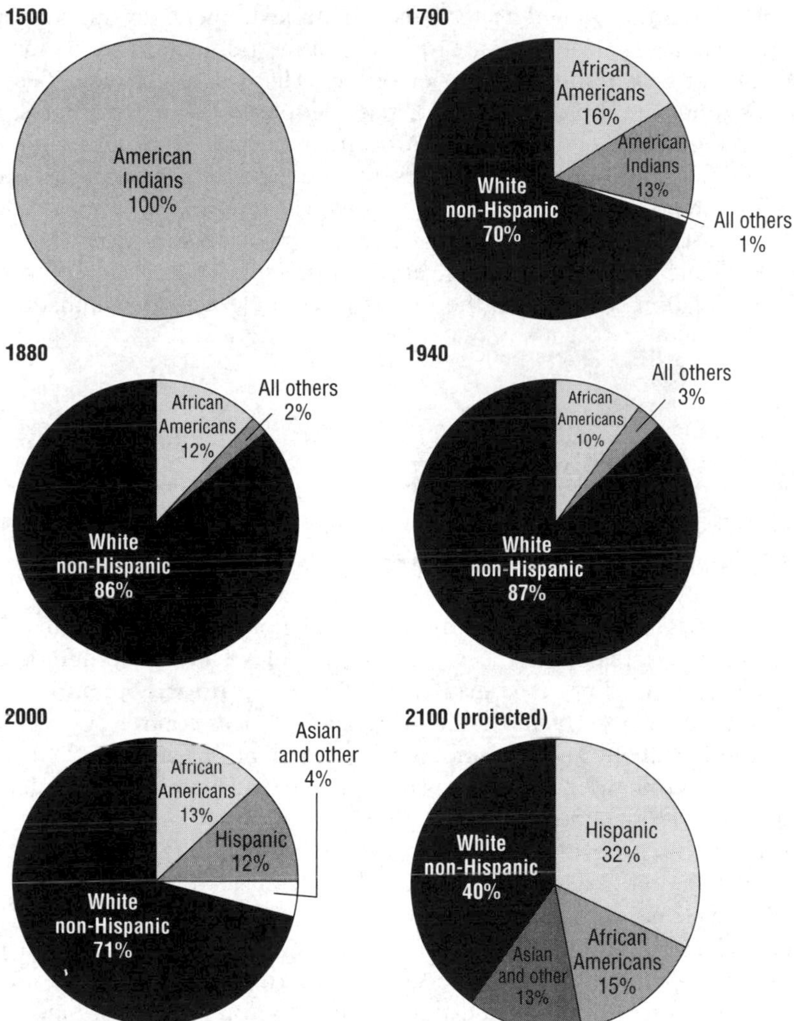

Figure 1.1 Racial and Ethnic Groups in the United States by Race and Ethnicity, 1500 to 2100 (Projected)

According to projections by the U.S. Bureau of the Census, the proportion of residents of the United States who are White and non-Hispanic will decrease significantly by the year 2050. By contrast, there will be a striking rise in the proportion of both Hispanic Americans and Asian Americans.

Source: Author's estimates; U.S. Bureau of the Census 1975, 2000; R. Thornton 1987.

Tensions in the United States arise in an extremely diverse nation, as shown in Figure 1.1. At present, 17 percent of the population are members of racial minorities, and another 12 percent are Hispanic or Latino. These percentages represent more than one of four people in the United States, without counting White ethnic groups. African Americans, Hispanics, and Asian Americans already outnumber Whites in fifteen of the twenty-eight largest cities. The trend is toward even greater diversity by 2100. The population in the United States is expected to rise over the next century from 29 percent Black-Hispanic-Asian-Native American to 60 percent. While the composition of the population is changing, the problems of prejudice, discrimination, and mistrust remain.

What Is a Subordinate Group?

Identifying a subordinate group or a minority in a society would seem to be a simple enough task: groups with fewer members. In the United States, those groups readily identified as minorities—Blacks and Native Americans, for example—are outnumbered by non-Blacks and non–Native Americans. However, minority status is not necessarily the result of being outnumbered. A social minority need not be a mathematical one. A **minority group** is a subordinate group whose members have significantly less control or power over their own lives than do the members of a dominant or majority group. However, minority means the same as subordinate, and dominant is used interchangeably with majority.

Confronted with evidence that a particular minority in the United States is subordinate to the majority, some individuals will respond, "Why not? After all, this is a democracy, and so the majority rules." The subordination of a minority, however, involves more than its inability to rule over society. A member of a subordinate or minority group experiences a narrowing of life's opportunities—for success, education, wealth, the pursuit of happiness—that goes beyond any personal shortcoming he or she may have. A minority group does not share in proportion to its numbers what a given society, such as the United States, defines as valuable.

Being superior in numbers neither guarantees a group the control over its destiny nor assures it of majority status. In 1920, the majority of people in Mississippi and South Carolina were African Americans. Yet African Americans did not have as much significant control over their lives as Whites had, let alone control the states of Mississippi and South Carolina. Throughout the United States today are counties or neighborhoods in which the majority of people are African American, Native American, or Hispanic, but White Americans are the dominant force. Nationally, 51.2 percent of the population are female, but males still dominate positions of authority and wealth well in excess of their numbers. A minority or subordinate group has five characteristics: unequal treatment, distinguishing physical or cultural traits, involuntary membership, awareness of subordination, and in-group marriage (C. Wagley and M. Harris 1958).

1. Members of a minority experience unequal treatment and have less power over their lives than members of a dominant group have over theirs. Prejudice, discrimination, segregation, and even extermination create this social inequality.
2. Members of a minority group share physical or cultural characteristics that distinguish them from the dominant group, such as skin color or language. Each society has its own arbitrary standard for determining which characteristics are most important in defining dominant and minority groups.
3. Membership in a dominant or minority group is not voluntary: people are born into the group. A person does not choose to be an African American or a White.
4. Minority-group members have a strong sense of group solidarity. William Graham Sumner, writing in 1906, noted that individuals make distinctions between members of their own group (the in-group) and everyone else (the out-group). When a group is the object of long-term prejudice and discrimination, the feeling of us versus them can and often does become extremely intense.
5. Members of a minority generally marry others from the same group. A member of a dominant group is often unwilling to join a supposedly inferior minority by marrying one of the latter group's members. In addition, the minority group's sense of solidarity encourages marriage within the group and discourages marriage to outsiders.

Types of Subordinate Groups

There are four types of minority or subordinate groups. All four, except where noted, have the five outlined properties. The four criteria for classifying minority groups are race, ethnicity, religion, and gender.

Racial Groups

The term **racial group** is reserved for those minorities and the corresponding majorities that are classified according to obvious physical differences. Notice the two crucial words in the definition: obvious and physical. What is obvious? Hair color? Shape of an earlobe? Presence of body hair? To whom are these differences obvious, and why? Each society defines what it finds obvious.

In the United States, skin color is one obvious difference. On a cold winter day with clothing covering all but one's head, however, skin color may be less obvious than hair color. Yet people in the United States have learned informally that skin color is important and that hair color is unimportant. We need to say more than that. In the United States, people have traditionally classified and classify themselves as either Black or White. There is no in-between state except for people readily identified as Native Americans or Asian Americans. Later in this chapter we will explore this issue more deeply and see how such assumptions have very complex implications.

Other societies use skin color as a standard but may have a more elaborate system of classification. In Brazil, where hostility among races is less than in the United States, numerous categories identify people on the basis of skin color. In the United States, a person is Black or White. In Brazil, a variety of terms, such as cafuso, mazombo, preto, and escuro, are applied to describe various combinations of skin color, facial features, and hair texture. What makes differences obvious is subject to a society's definition. The designation of a racial group emphasizes physical differences as opposed to cultural distinctions. In the United States, minority races include Blacks, Native Americans (or American Indians), Japanese Americans, Chinese Americans, Arab Americans, Filipinos, Hawaiians, and other Asian peoples. The issue of race and racial differences has been an important one, not only in the United States but throughout the entire sphere of European influence. Later in this chapter we will examine race and its significance more closely. We should not forget that Whites are a race too. As we will consider in Chapter 5, who is White has been subject to change over time as certain European groups were felt historically not to be deserving of being considered White, but as time has passed, partly to compete against a growing Black population, the whiting of some Euro-Americans has occurred.

Ethnic Groups

Ethnic minority groups are differentiated from the dominant group on the basis of cultural differences, such as language, attitudes toward marriage and parenting, and food habits. **Ethnic groups** are groups set apart from others because of their national origin or distinctive cultural patterns.

Ethnic groups in the United States include a grouping that are referred to collectively as Hispanics or Latinos, including Mexican Americans (Chicanos), Puerto Ricans, Cubans, and other Latin Americans in the United States. Latinos can be either Black or White as, for example, in the case of a dark-skinned Puerto Rican who may be taken as Black in central Texas but may be viewed as a Puerto Rican in New York City. The ethnic-group category also includes White ethnics, such as Irish Americans, Polish Americans, and Norwegian Americans.

The cultural traits that make groups distinctive usually originate from their homeland or, for Jews, from a long history of being segregated and prohibited from becoming a part of the host society. An immigrant group, once in the United States, may maintain distinctive cultural practices through associations, clubs, and worship. Ethnic enclaves such as a Little Italy or a Greektown in urban areas also perpetuate cultural distinctiveness. Some of the racial groups discussed in the preceding section may likewise have unique cultural traditions, as we can readily see in the many Chinatowns throughout the United States. For racial groups, however, the physical distinctiveness and not the cultural differences generally prove to be the barrier to acceptance by the host society. For example, Chinese Americans who are faithful Protestants and know the names of all the members of the Baseball Hall of Fame may be bearers of American culture. Yet these Chinese Americans are still part of a minority because they are seen as physically different.

Ethnicity continues to be important, as recent events in Bosnia and other parts of Eastern Europe have demonstrated. By comparison, however, race is even more significant worldwide. Almost a century ago, African American sociologist W. E. B. Du Bois, when addressing an audience in London, called attention to the overwhelming importance of the color line throughout the world. In "Listen to Their Voices," we read the remarks of Du Bois, the first Black person to receive a doctorate from Harvard University, who later helped to organize the National Association for the Advancement of Colored People (NAACP). Du Bois's observances give us a historic perspective on the struggle for equality. We can look ahead—knowing how far we have come and speculating on how much further we have to go.

Religious Groups

Association with a religion other than the dominant faith is the third basis for minority-group status. In the United States, Protestants, as a group, outnumber members of all other religions. Roman Catholics form the largest minority religion. Chapter 5, focusing on Roman Catholics and other minority faiths, details how all five properties of a minority group apply to such faiths in the United States.

Religious minorities include such groups as the Church of Jesus Christ of Latter-Day Saints (the Mormons), Amish, Muslims, and Buddhists. Cults or sects associated with such things as animal sacrifice, doomsday prophecy, demon worship, or the use of snakes in a ritualistic fashion would also constitute minorities. Jews are excluded from this category and placed among ethnic groups. Culture is a more important defining trait for Jewish people worldwide than is religious dogma. Jewish Americans share a cultural tradition that goes beyond theology. In this sense, it is appropriate to view them as an ethnic group rather than as members of a religious faith.

LISTEN TO THEIR VOICES

Problem of the Color-Line

W. E. B. Du Bois

In the metropolis of the modern world, in this the closing year of the nineteenth century, there has been assembled a congress of men and women of African blood, to deliberate solemnly upon the present situation and outlook of the darker races of mankind. The problem of the twentieth century is the problem of the color-line, the question as to how far differences of race—which show themselves chiefly in the color of the skin and the texture of the hair—will hereafter be made the basis of denying to over half the world the right of sharing to their utmost ability the opportunities and privileges of modern civilization. . . .

Let the world take no backward step in that slow but sure progress which has successively refused to let the spirit of class, of caste, of privilege, or of birth, debar from life, liberty and the pursuit of happiness a striving human soul.

Let not color or race be a feature of distinction between white and black men, regardless of worth or ability. . . .

Thus we appeal with boldness and confidence to the Great Powers of the civilized world, trusting in the wide spirit of humanity, and the deep sense of justice of our age, for a generous recognition of the righteousness of our cause.

Source: From *An ABC of Color,* pp. 20–21, 23, by W. E. B. Du Bois. Copyright © 1969 by International Publishers Co. Reprinted by permission.

Gender Groups

Gender is another attribute that creates dominant and subordinate groups. Males are the social majority; females, although more numerous, are relegated to the position of the social minority. Women are considered a minority even though they do not exhibit all the characteristics outlined earlier (there is, for example, little in-group marriage). Women encounter prejudice and discrimination and are physically distinguishable. Group membership is involuntary, and many women have developed a sense of sisterhood. Women who are members of racial and ethnic minorities face a special challenge to achieving equality. They suffer from double jeopardy because they belong to two separate minority groups: a racial or an ethnic group plus a subordinate gender group.

Race

Race has many meanings for many people. Often these meanings are inaccurate and based on theories that were discarded by scientists generations ago. As we will see, race is a socially constructed concept.

Biological Meaning

The way the term *race* has been used by some people to apply to human beings lacks any scientific meaning. We cannot today identify distinctive physical characteristics for groups of human beings in the way that scientists do to distinguish one species of animal from another. The idea of **biological race** is based on the mistaken notion of a genetically isolated group.

Even among proponents that sharp, scientific divisions exist among humans, there have been endless debates over what the races of the world were. Given people's frequent migration, exploration, and invasions, pure genetic types have not existed for some time, if they ever did. There are no mutually exclusive races. Skin color among African Americans varies tremendously, as it does among White Americans. There is even an overlapping of dark-skinned Whites and light-skinned African Americans. If we grouped people by genetic resistance to malaria and by fingerprint patterns, Norwegians and many African groups would be of the same race. If we grouped people by some digestive capacities, some Africans, Asians, and southern Europeans would be of one group and West Africans and northern Europeans of another (R. Leehotz 1995; E. Shanklin 1994). Biologically, there are no pure, distinct races. For example, blood type cannot determine racial groups with any accuracy. Furthermore, applying pure racial types to humans is problematic because of interbreeding. Despite continuing prejudice about Black-White marriages, a large number of Whites have African American ancestry. Scientists, using various techniques, maintain that the proportion of African Americans with White ancestry is between 20 and 75 percent. Despite the extremely wide range of these estimates, the mixed ancestry of today's Blacks and Whites is part of the biological reality of race (M. Herskovits 1930:15; D. Roberts 1955).

Research has been conducted to determine whether personality characteristics such as temperament and nervous habits are inherited among minority groups. Not surprisingly, the question of whether races have different innate levels of intelligence has led to the most explosive controversy.

Typically, intelligence is summarized in an **intelligence quotient,** or IQ, where 100 represents average intelligence and higher scores represent greater intelligence. It should be noted that there is little consensus over just what intelligence is, other than as defined by such IQ tests. Intelligence tests are adjusted for a person's age, so that ten-year-olds take a very different test than someone aged twenty. Although research does show that certain learning strategies can improve a person's IQ, generally IQ remains stable as one ages.

A great deal of debate continues over the accuracy of these tests. Are they biased toward people who come to the tests with knowledge similar to that of the test writers? Consider the following two questions used on standard tests:

1. Runner: Marathon (A) envoy: embassy, (B) oarsman: regatta, (C) martyr: massacre, (D) referee: tournament.
2. Your mother sends you to a store to get a loaf of bread. The store is closed. What should you do? (A) return home, (B) go to the next store, (C) wait until it opens, (D) ask a stranger for advice.

Both correct answers are B. But is a lower-class youth likely to know, in the first question, what a regatta is? Skeptics argue that such test questions do not truly measure intellectual potential. Inner-city youths have been shown often to respond with A to the second question, since the closed store may be the only one with which the family has credit. Youths in rural areas, where the next store may be miles away, are also unlikely to respond with the designated correct answer. The issue of culture bias in tests remains an unresolved concern. The most recent research shows that differences in intel-

Given the diversity in the nation, the workplace is increasingly a place where intergroup tensions may develop.

ligence scores between Blacks and Whites are virtually eliminated when adjustments are made for social and economic characteristics (J. Brooks-Gunn et al. 1996; R. Herrnstein and C. Murray 1994:30; J. Kagan 1971).

The second issue, trying to associate these results with certain subpopulations such as races, also has a long history. In the past, a few have contended that, as a group, Whites have more intelligence on average than Blacks. All researchers agree that within-group differences are greater than any speculated differences among groups. The range of intelligence among, for example, Korean Americans is much greater than any average difference between them as a group and Japanese Americans.

The third issue relates to the subpopulations themselves. If Blacks or Whites are not mutually exclusive biologically, how can there be measurable differences? Many Whites and most Blacks have mixed ancestry that complicates the inheritance issue. Both groups reflect a rich heritage of very dissimilar populations from Swedes to Slovaks and Zulus to Tutsis.

In 1994, an 845-page book unleashed a new national debate on the issue of IQ. The latest research effort of psychologist Richard J. Herrnstein and social scientist Charles Murray (1994), published in *The Bell Curve,* concluded that 60 percent of IQ is inheritable and that racial groups offer a convenient means to generalize about any differences in intelligence. Unlike most other proponents of the race-IQ link, the authors offer policy suggestions that include ending welfare to discourage births among low-IQ poor women, and changing immigration laws so that the IQ pool in the United States is not diminished. Herrnstein and Murray made generalizations even about IQ levels among Asians and Hispanics in the United States—groups subject to even more intermarriage. It is not possible to generalize about absolute differences between groups, such as Latinos versus Whites, when close to half of Latinos in the United States marry non-Hispanics. Years later, the mere mention of "the bell curve" signals to many the belief in a racial hierarchy that has Whites toward the top and Blacks near the bottom. The research present then and repeated today points to the difficulty in definitions: what is intelligence, and what constitutes a racial group, given generations, if not centuries, of intermarriage? How can we speak of definitive inherited racial differences if there has been intermarriage between people of every color? Furthermore, as people on both sides of the debate have noted, regardless of the findings, we would still want to strive to maximize the talents of each individual. All research shows that the differences within a group are much greater than any alleged differences between group averages (F. Cullen et al. 1997; C. Jencks and M. Phillips 1998).

All these issues and controversial research have led to the basic question of what difference it would make even if there were significant differences. No researcher believes that race can be used to predict one's intelligence. Also, there is a general agreement that certain intervention strategies can improve scholastic achievement and even intelligence as defined by standard tests. Should we mount efforts to upgrade the abilities of those alleged to be below average? These debates tend to contribute to a sense of hopelessness among some policy makers who think that biology is destiny, rather than causing them to rethink the issue or to expand positive intervention efforts (E. Dionne 1995).

Why does such IQ research reemerge if the data are subject to different interpretations? The argument that "we" are superior to "them" is very appealing to the dominant group because it justifies receiving opportunities that are denied to others. For example, the authors of *The Bell Curve* argue that intelligence significantly determines the poverty problem in the United States. We can anticipate that the debate over IQ and the allegations of significant group differences will continue. Policy makers need to acknowledge the difficulty in using race in any biologically significant manner.

Social Construction of Race

If race does not distinguish humans from one another biologically, why does it seem to be so important? It is important because of the social meaning that people have attached to it. The 1950 UNESCO Statement on Race maintains that "for all practical social purposes 'race' is not so much a biological phenomenon as a social myth" (A. Montagu 1972:118). Adolf Hitler expressed concern over the "Jewish race" and translated this concern into Nazi death camps. Winston Churchill spoke proudly of the "British race" and used that pride to spur a nation to fight. Evidently, race was a useful political tool for two rather different leaders in the 1930s and 1940s.

People could speculate that if human groups have obvious physical differences, then they could have corresponding mental or personality differences. No one disagrees that people differ in temperament, potential to learn, and sense of humor. In its social sense, race implies that groups that differ physically also bear distinctive emotional and mental abilities or disabilities. These beliefs are based on the notion that humankind can be divided into distinct groups. We have already seen the difficulties associated with pigeonholing people into racial categories. Despite these difficulties, belief in the inheritance of behavior patterns and in an association between physical and cultural traits is widespread. This belief is called **racism** when it is coupled with the feeling that certain groups or races are inherently superior to others. Racism is a doctrine of racial supremacy, stating that one race is superior to another (see also E. Bonilla-Silva 1996). We questioned the biological significance of race in the previous section. In modern complex industrial societies, we find little adaptive utility in the presence or absence of prominent chins, epicanthic folds of the eyelids, or the comparative amount of melanin in the skin. What is important is not that people are genetically different but that they approach one another with dissimilar perspectives. It is in the social setting that race is decisive. Race is significant only because people have given it significance.

Race definitions are crystallized through what Michael Omi and Howard Winant (1994) called **racial formation.** Racial formation is a sociohistorical process by which racial categories are created, inhabited, transformed, and destroyed. Those in power define groups of people in a certain way that depends on a racist social structure. The Native Americans and the creation of the reservation system in the latter 1800s would be an example of this racial formation. From previously distinctive tribes, the federal American Indian policy created a single group where one had not existed before. No one—absolutely no one—escapes the extent and frequency to which we are subjected to racial formation.

In the South of the United States, the social construction of race was known as the "one-drop rule." This tradition stipulated that if a person had even a single drop of "Black blood," that person was defined and viewed as Black. Today the children of biracial or multiracial marriages try to build their own identity in a United States that seems intent on placing them in some single traditional category (S. Love 1996; R. Schaefer 1996). A particularly sobering aspect of racial formation is that the United States is exporting this development. Just as this nation promotes tastes in music and television, the racial identities in the United States are being internationalized. Although the United States is certainly not responsible for racial, ethnic, and religious tensions, we have been contributing to the defining of racial awareness (H. Winant 1994:20).

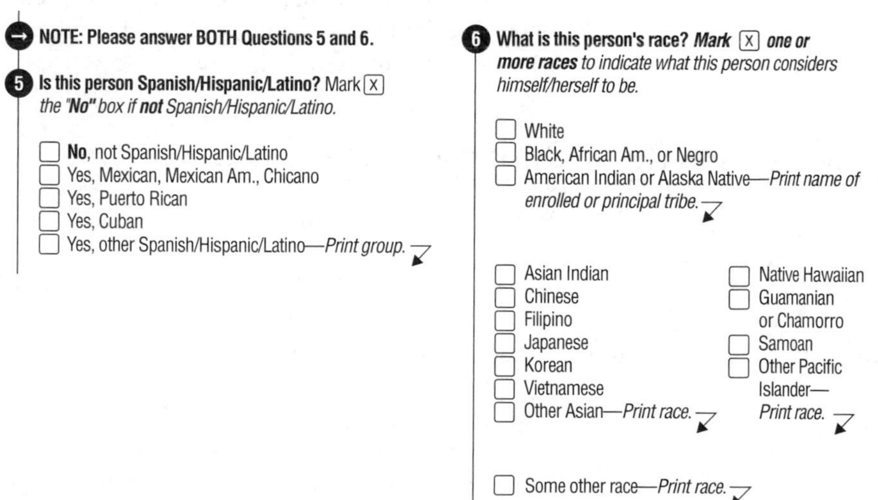

→ **NOTE: Please answer BOTH Questions 5 and 6.**

5 **Is this person Spanish/Hispanic/Latino?** Mark [X] *the "**No**" box if **not** Spanish/Hispanic/Latino.*

- ☐ **No**, not Spanish/Hispanic/Latino
- ☐ Yes, Mexican, Mexican Am., Chicano
- ☐ Yes, Puerto Rican
- ☐ Yes, Cuban
- ☐ Yes, other Spanish/Hispanic/Latino—*Print group.*

6 **What is this person's race?** ***Mark*** [X] ***one or more races*** *to indicate what this person considers himself/herself to be.*

- ☐ White
- ☐ Black, African Am., or Negro
- ☐ American Indian or Alaska Native—*Print name of enrolled or principal tribe.*

- ☐ Asian Indian
- ☐ Chinese
- ☐ Filipino
- ☐ Japanese
- ☐ Korean
- ☐ Vietnamese
- ☐ Other Asian—*Print race.*
- ☐ Native Hawaiian
- ☐ Guamanian or Chamorro
- ☐ Samoan
- ☐ Other Pacific Islander—*Print race.*

- ☐ Some other race—*Print race.*

Figure 1.2 Census 2000 Questions on Race and Ethnicity
Source: U.S. Bureau of the Census 1998a.

Census 2000

Only six questions are asked of every person in the United States on Census Day, April 18, 2000—and two of them deal with ethnicity and race. As you can see in the reproduction from official Census materials in Figure 1.2 on p. 13, people were first asked to indicate whether they are Spanish/Hispanic/Latino, and if they are, what specific Hispanic group they are. Then, in the next question, people again were asked to check off one or more racial groups. In the longer questionnaire form given to a sample of about one-sixth of the entire population, a series of five questions asked people to indicate in what country they were born, to provide their citizenship status, and to identify their ancestry or ethnic origin (for example, Italian, Jamaican, and so on).

For the first time, in Census 2000, respondents were allowed to indicate a multiracial identity, an event that can be viewed as another step in racial formation. The 1990 Census and most earlier ones required people to indicate whether they were Black or White or American Indian or Asian, and the censuses did not allow one to indicate multiple identities. There was great debate over this wording, as many felt that it was unfair to ask people, especially the children of interracial marriages, to pick a single group. Some actually lobbied the government to include the category "multiracial," but instead a compromise was reached allowing people to select several categories while still working within the confines of traditionally used terms for racial groups. Sociologists and others are speculating on the likely outcome. How many tens of millions of people may identify themselves with multiple identities? The discussion over identifying people's race or ethnicity shows that race is socially defined. If it were relatively unambiguous, as age is, such a debate would not occur. Later in this chapter we will give consideration to the issue of "Who am I?" in terms of racial and ethnic identity.

Sociology and the Study of Race and Ethnicity

Before proceeding further with our study of racial and ethnic groups, let us consider several sociological perspectives that provide insight into dominant-subordinate relationships. **Sociology** is the systematic study of social behavior and human groups, and therefore is aptly suited to enlarge our understanding of intergroup relations. There is a long, valuable history of the study of race relations in sociology. Admittedly, it has not always been progressive and, indeed, it has at times reflected the prejudice and discrimination of society. There have been examples in the past whereby scholars who are members of racial, ethnic, and religious minorities, as well as women, have not been permitted to make to the field the kind of contributions of which they are capable.

Stratification by Class and Gender

All societies are characterized by members having unequal amounts of wealth, prestige, or power. Sociologists observe that entire groups may be assigned to have less or more of what a society values. The hierarchy that emerges is called stratification. **Stratification** is the structured ranking of entire groups of people that perpetuates unequal rewards and power in a society.

Much discussion of stratification identifies the **class,** or social ranking, of people who share similar wealth, according to sociologist Max Weber's classic definition. Mobility from one class to another is not necessarily easy. Movement into classes of greater wealth may be particularly difficult for subordinate-group members faced with lifelong prejudice and discrimination (H. Gerth and C. Mills 1958).

Recall that the first property of subordinate-group standing is unequal treatment by the dominant group in the form of prejudice, discrimination, and segregation. Stratification is intertwined with the subordination of racial, ethnic, religious, and gender groups. Race has implications for the way people are treated; so does class. One also has to add the effects of race and class together. For example, being poor and Black is not the same as being either one by itself. A wealthy Mexican American is not the same as an affluent Anglo or as Mexican Americans as a group.

The monumental 1992 South-Central Los Angeles riots that followed the acquittal of four White police officers charged with beating African American Rodney King illustrated the power of both race and class. The most visible issue was White brutality against Blacks; yet during the riot, the concentrated attack on Korean American merchants, whose economic role placed them in a very vulnerable social position, underscored the role of race in defining how we see others. The multiracial character of the looting involving Hispanics and Whites was a response not only to the judicial system but also to poverty. Frequently, public discussion of issues such as housing or public assistance is disguised as discussion of class issues when in fact the issues are based primarily on race. Similarly, some topics such as the poorest of poor or the working poor are addressed in terms of race, when the class component should be explicit. Nonetheless, the link between race and class in society is abundantly clear (H. Winant 1994).

Another stratification factor that we need to consider is gender. How different is the situation for women as contrasted to men? Returning again to that first property of minority groups—unequal treatment and less control—treatment for women is not equal to that received by men. Whether it is jobs or poverty, education or crime, the experience of women typically is more difficult. In addition, the situation faced by women in such areas as health care and welfare raises different concerns than it does for men. Just as we need to consider the role of social class better to understand race and ethnicity, we also need to consider the role of gender.

Theoretical Perspectives

Sociologists view society in different ways. Some see the world basically as a stable and ongoing entity. They are impressed by the endurance of a Chinatown, the relative sameness of male-female roles over time, and other aspects of intergroup relations. Other sociologists see society as composed of many groups in conflict, competing for scarce resources. Within this conflict, some people or even entire groups may be labeled or stigmatized in a way that blocks their access to what a society values. We will examine three theoretical perspectives that are widely used by sociologists today: the functionalist, conflict, and labeling perspectives.

Functionalist Perspective In the view of a functionalist, a society is like a living organism in which each part contributes to the survival of the whole. The **functionalist perspective** emphasizes how the parts of society are structured to maintain its stability. According to this approach, if an aspect of social life does not contribute to a society's stability or survival, it will not be passed on from one generation to the next. It would seem reasonable to assume that bigotry between races offers no such positive function, and so, we ask, why does it persist? The functionalist, although agreeing that racial hostility is hardly to be admired, would point out that it does serve some positive functions from the perspective of the racists. We can identify five functions that racial beliefs have for the dominant group:

1. Racist ideologies provide a moral justification for maintaining a society that routinely deprives a group of its rights and privileges.
2. Racist beliefs discourage subordinate people from attempting to question their lowly status; to do so is to question the very foundations of the society.
3. Racial ideologies not only justify existing practices but also serve as a rallying point for social movements, as seen in the rise of the Nazi Party.
4. Racist myths encourage support for the existing order. The argument is used that if there were any major societal change, the subordinate group would suffer even greater poverty and the dominant group would suffer lower living standards (M. Nash 1962).
5. Racist beliefs relieve the dominant group of the responsibility to address the economic and educational problems faced by subordinate groups.

As a result of these beliefs, racial ideology grows when a value system (for example, that underlying a colonial empire or slavery) is being threatened.

There are also definite dysfunctions caused by prejudice and discrimination. **Dysfunctions** are elements of society that may disrupt a social system or tend to decrease its stability. There are six ways in which racism is dysfunctional to a society, including to its dominant group:

News media treat Asian Americans, such as Olympic figure skater Michele Kwan, a Chinese American, as if they were foreigners. The cable news network MSNBC, an affiliate of the NBC network, covered the 1996 Olympics when Tara Lipinski defeated Kwan and then proclaimed "American Beats out Kwan."

1. A society that practices discrimination fails to use the resources of all individuals. Discrimination limits the search for talent and leadership to the dominant group.
2. Discrimination aggravates social problems such as poverty, delinquency, and crime, and places the financial burden of alleviating these problems on the dominant group.
3. Society must invest a good deal of time and money to defend the barriers that prevent the full participation of all members.

4. Racial prejudice and discrimination undercut goodwill and friendly diplomatic relations between nations. They also negatively affect efforts to increase global trade.
5. Social change is inhibited, because change may contribute to assisting a subordinate group.
6. Discrimination promotes disrespect for law enforcement and for the peaceful settlement of disputes.

That racism has costs for the dominant group as well as the subordinate group reminds us that intergroup conflict is exceedingly complex (B. Bowser and R. Hurst 1996; J. Feagin and H. Vera 1995; A. Rose 1951).

Conflict Perspective In contrast to the functionalists' emphasis on stability, conflict sociologists see the social world as being in continual struggle. The **conflict perspective** assumes that the social structure is best understood in terms of conflict or tension among competing groups. Specifically, society is a struggle between the privileged (the dominant group) and the exploited (the subordinate groups). Such conflicts need not be physically violent and may take the form of immigration restrictions, real estate practices, or disputes over cuts in the federal budget.

The conflict model is often selected today when one is examining race and ethnicity because it readily accounts for the presence of tension between competing groups. The competition, according to the conflict perspective, takes place between groups with unequal amounts of economic and political power. The minorities are exploited or, at best, ignored by the dominant group. The conflict perspective is viewed as more radical and activist than functionalism because conflict theorists emphasize social change and the redistribution of resources. Functionalists are not necessarily in favor of such inequality; rather, their approach helps us to understand why such systems persist.

Those who follow the conflict approach to race and ethnicity have remarked repeatedly that the subordinate group is criticized for its low status. That the dominant group is responsible for the subordination is often ignored. William Ryan (1976) calls this an instance of "blaming the victim": portraying the problems of racial and ethnic minorities as their fault rather than recognizing society's responsibility. This idea is not new. Gunnar Myrdal, a Swedish social economist of international reputation, headed a project that produced the classic 1944 work on Blacks in the United States, *The American Dilemma*. Myrdal concluded that the plight of the subordinate group is the responsibility of the dominant majority. It is not a Black problem but instead is a White problem. Similarly, we can use the same approach and note that it is not a Hispanic problem or a Haitian refugee problem, but a White problem. Myrdal and others since then have reminded the public and policy makers alike that the ultimate responsibility for society's problems must rest with those who possess the most authority and the most economic resources (D. Southern 1987; see also J. Hochschild 1995).

Labeling Approach Related to the conflict perspective and its concern over blaming the victim is labeling theory. **Labeling theory,** a concept introduced by sociologist Howard Becker, is an attempt to explain why certain people are viewed as different from or less worthy than others. Students of crime and deviance have relied heavily on labeling theory. A youth who misbehaves, according to labeling theory, may be considered and treated as a delinquent if she or he comes from the "wrong kind of family." Another youth, from a middle-class family, who commits the same sort of misbehavior might be given another chance before being punished.

The labeling perspective directs our attention to the role that negative stereotypes play in race and ethnicity. The image that prejudiced people maintain of a group toward which they hold ill feelings is called a stereotype. **Stereotypes** are exaggerated images of the characteristics of a particular group. The warrior image of American Indian people is perpetuated by the frequent use of tribal names or even terms like "Indians" and "Redskins" as sports team mascots. In Chapter 2, we will review some of the research on the stereotyping of minorities. This labeling is not limited to racial and ethnic groups, however. Age, for instance, can be used to exclude a person from an activity in which he or she is actually qualified to engage. Groups are subjected to stereotypes and discrimination in such a way that their treatment resembles that of social minorities. Social prejudice exists toward ex-convicts, gamblers, alcoholics, lesbians, gays, prostitutes, people with AIDS, and people with disabilities, to name a few.

The labeling approach points out that stereotypes, when applied by people in power, can have very negative consequences for people or groups identified falsely. A crucial aspect of the relationship between dominant and subordinate groups is the prerogative of the dominant group to define society's values. American sociologist William I. Thomas (1923), an early critic of racial and gender discrimination, saw that the "definition of the situation" could mold the personality of the individual. In other words, Thomas observed that people respond not only to the objective features of a situation (or person) but also to the meaning these features have for them. So, for example, a lone walker seeing a young Black male walking toward him may perceive the situation differently than if the oncoming person is an elderly woman. In this manner, we can create false images or stereotypes that become real in their consequences.

In certain situations, we may respond to negative stereotypes and act on them, with the result that false definitions become accurate. This reaction is known as a **self-fulfilling prophecy.** A person or group described as having particular characteristics begins to display the very traits attributed to them. Thus, a child who is praised for being a natural comic may focus on learning to become funny in order to gain approval and attention.

Self-fulfilling prophecies can be devastating for minority groups (see Figure 1.3 on p. 20). Such groups often find that they are allowed to hold only low-paying jobs with little prestige or opportunity for advancement. The rationale of the dominant society is that these minority individuals lack the abil-

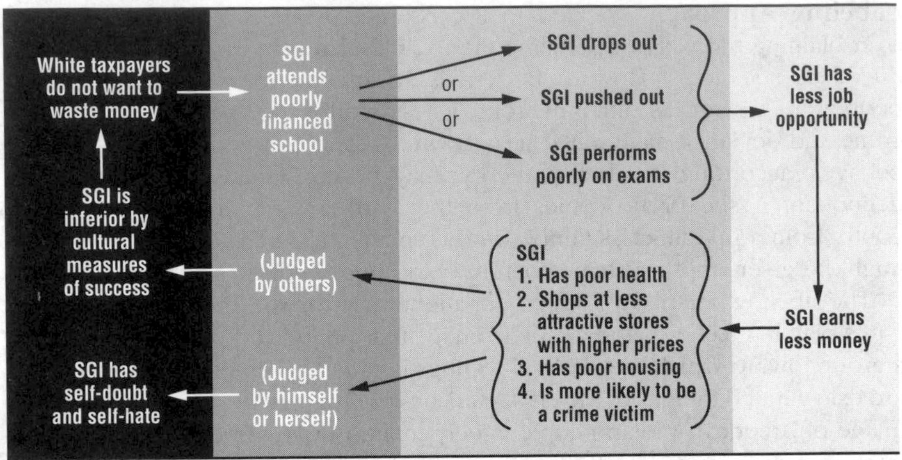

Figure 1.3 Self-fulfilling Prophecy
The self-validating effects of dominant-group definitions are shown in this figure. The subordinate-group individual (SGI) attends a poorly financed school and is left unequipped to perform jobs that offer high status and pay. He or she then gets a low-paying job and must settle for a standard of living far short of society's standards. Since the person shares these societal standards, he or she may begin to feel self-doubt and self-hatred.

ity to perform in more important and lucrative positions. Training to become scientists, executives, or physicians is denied to many subordinate-group individuals, who are then locked into society's inferior jobs. As a result, the false definition becomes real. The subordinate group has become inferior because it was defined at the start as inferior and was therefore prevented from achieving the levels attained by the majority.

Because of this vicious circle, a talented subordinate-group individual may come to see the worlds of entertainment and professional sports as his or her only hope for achieving wealth and fame. Thus, it is no accident that successive waves of Irish, Jewish, Italian, African American, and Hispanic performers and athletes have made their mark on culture in the United States. Unfortunately, these very successes may convince the dominant group that its original stereotypes were valid—that these are the only areas of society in which subordinate-group members can excel. Furthermore, athletics and the arts are highly competitive areas. For every Michael Jordan and Gloria Estefan who make it, many, many more will end up disappointed.

The Creation of Subordinate-Group Status

Three situations are likely to lead to the formation of a subordinate-group–dominant-group relationship. A subordinate group emerges through (1) migration, (2) annexation, and (3) colonialism.

Migration

People who immigrate to a new country often find themselves a minority in that new country. Cultural or physical traits or religious affiliation may set the immigrant apart from the dominant group. Immigration from Europe, Asia, and Latin America has been a powerful force in shaping the fabric of life in the United States. **Migration** is the general term used to describe any transfer of population. **Emigration** (by emigrants) describes leaving a country to settle in another; **immigration** (by immigrants) denotes coming into the new country. From Vietnam's perspective, the "boat people" were emigrants from Vietnam to the United States, but in the United States, they were counted among this nation's immigrants.

Although people may migrate because they want to, leaving the home country is not always voluntary. Conflict or war has displaced people throughout human history. In the twentieth century, we saw huge population movements caused by two world wars; revolutions in Spain, Hungary, and Cuba; the partition of British India; conflicts in Southeast Asia, Korea, and Central America; and the confrontation between Arabs and Israelis.

In all types of movement, even the movement of an American family from Ohio to Florida, two sets of forces operate: push factors and pull factors. Push factors discourage a person from remaining where she or he lives. Religious persecution and economic factors such as dissatisfaction with employment opportunities are possible push factors. Pull factors, such as a better standard of living, the previous emigration of friends and relatives, and a promised job, attract an immigrant to a particular country.

Although generally we think of migration as a voluntary process, much of the population transfer that has occurred in the world has been involuntary. The forced movement of people into another society guarantees a subordinate role. Involuntary migration is no longer common; although enslavement has a long history, all industrialized societies today prohibit such practices. Of course, many contemporary societies, including the United States, bear the legacy of slavery.

Annexation

Nations, particularly during wars or as a result of war, incorporate or attach land. This new land is contiguous to the nation, as in the German annexation of Austria and Czechoslovakia in 1938 and 1939 and in the United States' Louisiana Purchase of 1803. The Treaty of Guadalupe Hidalgo that ended the Mexican-American War in 1848 gave the United States the area that would become California, Utah, Nevada, most of New Mexico, and parts of Arizona, Wyoming, and Colorado. The indigenous peoples in some of this huge territory were dominant in their society one day, only to become minority-group members the next. When annexation occurs, the dominant power generally suppresses the language and culture of the minority. Such was the practice of Russia with the Ukrainians and Poles, and of Prussia with the Poles. Minorities try to maintain their cultural integrity despite annexation. Poles inhabited an area divided into territories ruled by three countries but maintained their own culture across political boundaries.

Colonialism

Colonialism has been the most frequent way for one group of people to dominate another. **Colonialism** is the maintenance of political, social, economic, and cultural domination over people by a foreign power for an extended period (W. Bell 1991). Colonialism is rule by outsiders but, unlike annexation, does not involve actual incorporation into the dominant people's nation. The long control exercised by the British Empire over much of North America, parts of Africa, and India is an example of colonial domination. Societies gain power over a foreign land through military strength, sophisticated political organization, and the massive use of investment capital. The extent of power may also vary according to the dominant group's scope of settlement in the colonial land. Relations between the colonial nation and the colonized people are similar to those between a dominant group and exploited

A demonstration in San Juan urges voters to participate in a referendum on Puerto Rico's future relationship with the United States. Puerto Rico's relationship to the United States is very similar to that of a colony.

subordinate groups. The colonial subjects are generally limited to menial jobs and the wages from their labor. However, the natural resources of their land benefit the members of the ruling class.

By the 1980s, colonialism, in the sense of political rule, had become largely a phenomenon of the past, yet industrial countries of North America and Europe still dominated the world economically and politically. Sociologist Immanuel Wallerstein (1974, 1979, 1996), drawing on the conflict perspective, views the global economic system today as much like the height of colonial days. Wallerstein has advanced the **world systems analysis,** which views the global economic system as divided between nations that control wealth and those that provide natural resources and labor. Many of the ethnic, racial, and religious conflicts around the world are exacerbated by the limited economic resources available in developing nations.

A significant exception to the end of foreign political rule is Puerto Rico, whose territorial or commonwealth status with the United States is basically that of a colony. The more than 2 million people on the island are U.S. citizens but are unable to vote in presidential elections unless they migrate to the mainland. In 1998, 58 percent of Puerto Ricans on the island voted for options favoring continuation of commonwealth status, 47 percent favored statehood, and less than 5 percent voted for independence. Despite their poor showing, pro-independence forces are very vocal and enjoy the sympathies of others concerned about the cultural and economic dominance of the U.S. mainland (M. Navarro 1998; L. Saad 1998).

Colonialism is domination by outsiders. Relations between the colonizer and the colony are similar to those between the dominant and subordinate peoples within the same country. This distinctive pattern of oppression is called **internal colonialism.** Among other cases, it has been applied to the plight of Blacks in the United States and to Mexican Indians in Mexico, who are colonial peoples in their own country. Internal colonialism covers more than simple economic oppression. Nationalist movements in African colonies struggled to achieve political as well as economic independence from Europeans. Similarly, African Americans also call themselves nationalists in trying to gain more autonomy over their lives (R. Blauner 1969, 1972).

The Consequences of Subordinate-Group Status

There are several consequences for a group of subordinate status. These differ in their degree of harshness, ranging from physical annihilation to absorption into the dominant group. In this section, we will examine six consequences of subordinate-group status: extermination, expulsion, secession, segregation, fusion, and assimilation. Figure 1.4 on p. 24 illustrates how these consequences can be defined.

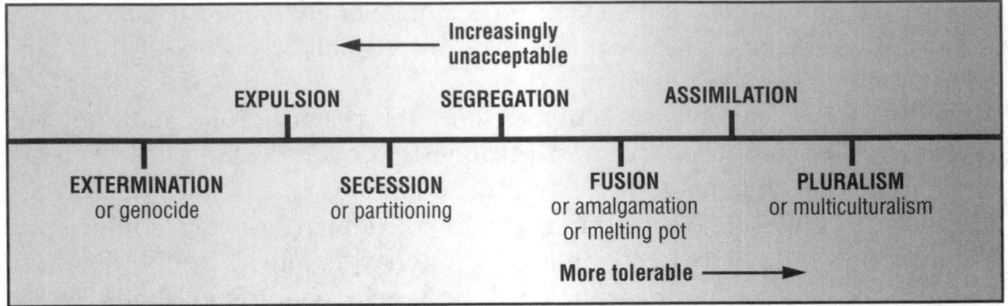

Figure 1.4 Intergroup Relations Continuum
The social consequences of being in a subordinate group can be viewed along a continuum ranging from extermination to forms of mutual acceptance such as pluralism.

Extermination

The most extreme way of dealing with a subordinate group is to eliminate it. One historical example is the British destruction of the people of Tasmania, an island off the coast of Australia. There were 5,000 Tasmanians in 1800, but because they were attacked by settlers and forced to live on less habitable islands, the last full-blooded Tasmanian died in 1876. A human group had become extinct, totally eliminated. Today the term **genocide** is used to describe the deliberate, systematic killing of an entire people or a nation. This term is frequently used in reference to the Holocaust—Nazi Germany's extermination of 12 million European Jews and other ethnic minorities during World War II. The term **ethnic cleansing** was introduced into the world's vocabulary as ethnic Serbs instituted a policy intended to "cleanse"—eliminate—Muslims from parts of Bosnia. More recently, a genocidal war between the Hutu and the Tutsi peoples in Rwanda left 300,000 school-age children orphaned.

Genocide, however, also appropriately describes White policies toward Native Americans in the nineteenth century. In 1800, the American Indian population in the United States was about 600,000; by 1850, it had been reduced to 250,000 through warfare with the U.S. Army, disease, and forced relocation to inhospitable environments.

Expulsion

Dominant groups may choose to force a specific subordinate group to leave certain areas or even to vacate a country. Expulsion is therefore another extreme consequence of minority-group status. European colonial powers in North America and eventually the U.S. government itself drove virtually all Native Americans out of their tribal lands into unfamiliar territory.

More recently, Vietnam in 1979 expelled nearly 1 million ethnic Chinese from the country, partly as a result of centuries of hostility between the two Asian neighbors. These "boat people" were abruptly eliminated as a minority within Vietnamese society. This expulsion meant, though, that they were now uprooted and became a new minority group in many nations, including Australia, France, the United States, and Canada. Thus expulsion may remove a minority group from one society; however, the expelled people merely go to another nation, where they are again a minority group.

Secession

A group ceases to be a subordinate group when it secedes to form a new nation or moves to an already established nation where it becomes dominant. After Great Britain withdrew from Palestine, Jewish people achieved a dominant position in 1948, attracting Jews from throughout the world to the new state of Israel. In a similar fashion, Pakistan was created in 1947 when India was partitioned. The predominantly Muslim areas in the north became Pakistan, making India predominantly Hindu. Throughout the last one hundred years, minorities have repudiated dominant customs. In this spirit, the Estonian, Latvian, Lithuanian, and Armenian peoples, for example, not content merely to be tolerated by the majority, all seceded to form independent states following the demise of the Soviet Union in 1991. In 1999, ethnic Albanians fought bitterly for their cultural and political recognition in the Kosovo region of Yugoslavia.

Some African Americans have called for secession. Suggestions dating back to the early 1700s supported the return of Blacks to Africa as a solution to racial problems. The settlement target of the American Colonization Society was Liberia, but proposals were also advanced to establish settlements in other areas. Territorial separatism and the emigrationist ideology were recurrent and interrelated themes among African Americans from the late nineteenth century well into the 1980s. The Black Muslims, or Nation of Islam, once expressed the desire for complete separation in their own state or territory within the present borders of the United States. Although a secession of Blacks from the United States has not taken place, it has been considered and even proposed in the past (J. Bracey, A. Meier, and E. Rudwick 1970; F. Butterfield 1986).

Segregation

Segregation refers to the physical separation of two groups in residence, workplace, and social functions. Generally, the dominant group imposes segregation on a subordinate group. Segregation is rarely complete, however; intergroup contact inevitably occurs even in the most segregated societies.

The extent of racial and ethnic isolation in the United States is staggering. Two-thirds of all Blacks attend schools in which more than half of the students are either Black or Hispanic. Almost three-fourths of all Hispanics attend predominantly Hispanic and Black schools (G. Orfield 1993; see also D. Massey and N. Denton 1993).

Although the word *segregation* usually evokes images of urban neighborhoods and schools, the isolation of reservations is yet another illustration of the legacy of past segregation. Shown here is the Hopi reservation in Arizona.

Residential segregation is also pervasive in the United States. Cities, suburbs, and even small towns have neighborhoods dominated by certain racial and ethnic groups. Residential patterns may change, but segregation persists.

The focus on metropolitan areas should not cause us to ignore the continuing legally sanctioned segregation of Native Americans on reservations. Although the majority of this nation's first inhabitants do live outside these tribal areas, the reservations play a prominent role in the identity of Native Americans. They face the difficult choice that, although it is easier to maintain tribal identity on the reservation, economic and educational opportunities are more limited in these areas that are segregated from the rest of society. Residential segregation patterns are not unique to the United States. In Germany today, people speak of Ghettoisierung (or "ghettoization") as concentrations of Turkish immigrants are emerging. Social scientists in Sweden have used the concept of segregation to document the isolation of Greek, Chilean, and Turkish immigrants from the rest of the population. Segregation is present in virtually all multiracial societies.

Fusion

Fusion describes the result when a minority and a majority group combine to form a new group. This combining can be expressed as A+B+C→D, where A, B, and C represent the groups present in a society, and D signifies the result, a cultural-racial group unlike any of the initial groups. Theoretically, fusion does not require intermarriage, but it is very similar to **amalgamation,** or the cultural and physical synthesis of various groups into a new people. In everyday speech, the words *fusion* and *amalgamation* are rarely used, but the concept is expressed in the notion of a human **melting pot,** in which diverse racial or ethnic groups form a new creation, a new cultural entity (W. Newman 1973).

The analogy of the cauldron—the "melting pot"—was first used to describe the United States by the French observer Crèvecoeur in 1782 (see P. Gleason 1980:33). The phrase dates back to the Middle Ages, when alchemists attempted to change less valuable metals into gold and silver. Similarly, the idea of the human melting pot implied that the new group would represent only the best qualities and attributes of the different cultures contributing to it. The belief in the United States as a melting pot became widespread in the first part of the twentieth century. This belief suggested that the United States had an almost divine mission to destroy artificial divisions and to create a single kind of human. The dominant group, however, had indicated its unwillingness to welcome such groups as Native Americans, Blacks, Hispanics, Jews, Asians, and Irish Roman Catholics into the melting pot. It is a mistake to think of the United States as an ethnic mixing bowl. Although there are superficial signs of fusion, as in a cuisine that includes sauerkraut and spaghetti, virtually all contributions of subordinate groups are ignored.

Marriage patterns indicate the resistance to fusion. People are unwilling, in varying degrees, to marry out of their own ethnic, religious, and racial groups. Surveys still show that 20 to 50 percent of various White ethnic groups report single ancestry. When White ethnics do cross boundaries, they tend to marry within their religion and social class. For example, Italians are more likely to marry Irish, who are still Roman Catholic, than they are to marry Protestant Swedes.

There is only modest evidence in the United States of a fusion of races. Racial intermarriage has been increasing, and the number of interracial couples immigrating to the United States has also grown. 1970 showed 678,000 interracial couples, but by 1998 the figure stood at over 3 million. Taken together, such marriages across racial lines represent about 5 percent of all couples. The growth of mixed marriages can be seen in the growing presence of children of biracial parentage (M. Lind 1998; Z. Qian 1997; U.S. Bureau of the Census 1999a:58).

Assimilation

Assimilation is the process by which a subordinate individual or group takes on the characteristics of the dominant group and is eventually accepted as part of that group. Assimilation is a majority ideology in which A+B+C→A. The majority (A) dominates in such a way that the minorities (B and C) become indistinguish-

Faced with new laws restricting rights of noncitizens, coupled with a desire to assimilate, 10,000 people representing 113 countries participate in naturalization ceremonies in Texas.

able from the dominant group. Assimilation dictates conformity to the dominant group, regardless of how many racial, ethnic, or religious groups are involved (H. Bash 1979; M. Gordon 1964, 1996; C. Hirschman 1983; W. Newman 1973:53).

To be complete, assimilation must entail an active effort by the minority-group individual to shed all distinguishing actions and beliefs and must include the total, unqualified acceptance of that individual by the dominant society. In the United States, dominant White society encourages assimilation. The assimilation perspective tends to devalue alien culture and to treasure the dominant. For example, assimilation assumes that whatever is admirable among Blacks was adapted from Whites and that whatever is bad is inherently Black. The assimilation solution to Black-White conflict is the development of a consensus around White American values (L. Broom 1965:23).

Assimilation is difficult. The individual must forsake his or her cultural tradition to become part of a different, often antagonistic, culture. Members of the subordinate group who choose not to assimilate look on those who do so as deserters. Many Hindus in India complained of their compatriots who copied the traditions and customs of the British. Those who assimilate must break entirely with the past. Australian Aborigines who become part of dominant society conceal their origin by ignoring darker-skinned relatives, including their immediate family. As one assimilated Aborigine explained, "Why should I have anything to do with them? I haven't anything in common with them, and I don't even like most of them." These conflicting demands leave an individual torn between two value systems (R. Berndt and B. Berndt 1951; B. McCully 1940).

Assimilation does not occur at the same pace for all groups or for all individuals in the same group. Assimilation tends to take longer under the following conditions, in which

1. the differences between the minority and the majority are large;
2. the majority is not receptive, or the minority retains its own culture;
3. the minority group arrives in a short period of time;
4. the minority-group residents are concentrated rather than dispersed; and
5. the arrival is recent, and the homeland is accessible.

Assimilation is not a smooth process (W. Warner and L. Srole 1945).

Assimilation is viewed by many as "unfair" or even "dictatorial." However, most see it as reasonable that people shed their distinctive cultural traditions. In public discussions today, assimilation is the ideology of the dominant group in forcing people how to act. Consequently, the social institutions in the United States, such as the educational system, economy, government, religion, and medicine, all push toward assimilation, with occasional references to the pluralist approach.

The Pluralist Perspective

Thus far we have concentrated on how subordinate groups cease to exist (removal) or take on the characteristics of the dominant group (assimilation). The alternative to these relationships between the majority and the minority is pluralism. **Pluralism** implies that various groups in a society have mutual respect for one another's culture, a respect that allows minorities to express their own culture without suffering prejudice or hostility. Whereas the assimilationist or integrationist seeks the elimination of ethnic boundaries, the pluralist believes in maintaining many of them (see also R. Manning 1995).

There are limits to cultural freedom. A Romanian immigrant to the United States could not expect to avoid learning English and still move up the occupational ladder. In order to survive, a society must have a consensus among its members on basic ideals, values, and beliefs. Nevertheless, there is still plenty of room for variety. Earlier, fusion was described as A+B+C→D and assimilation as A+B+C→A. Using this same scheme, we can think of pluralism as A+B+C→A+B+C, where groups coexist in one society (W. Newman 1973; J. Simpson 1995.)

In the United States, cultural pluralism is more an ideal than a reality. Though there are vestiges of cultural pluralism—in the various ethnic neighborhoods in major cities, for instance—the rule has been for subordinate groups to assimilate. The cost of cultural integrity has been high. The various Native American tribes have succeeded to a large extent in maintaining their heritage, but the price has been bare subsistence on federal reservations.

In the United States, there is a reemergence of ethnic identification by groups that had previously expressed little interest in their heritage. Groups that make up the dominant majority are also reasserting their ethnic heritage. Various nationality groups are rekindling interest in almost forgotten languages, customs, festivals, and traditions. In some instances, this expression of the past has taken the form of a protest against exclusion from the dominant society. Chinese youths, for example, chastise their elders for forgetting the old ways and accepting White American influence and control. The most visible controversy about pluralism is the debate surrounding bilingualism. **Bilingualism** is the use of two or more languages in places of work or education, with each language being treated as equally legitimate.

According to a report released by the U.S. Bureau of the Census, almost 32 million residents of the United States—or about one of every seven people—speak a native language other than English. Indeed, fifty different languages are spoken by at least 30,000 residents of this country. Over the period 1980–1990, there was a 38 percent increase in the number of people in the United States whose native language was not English (M. Usdansky 1993).

The passionate debate under way in the United States over bilingualism frequently acknowledges the large number of people who do not speak English at home. In education, bilingualism has seemed to be one way of assisting millions of people who want to learn English in order to function more efficiently within the United States. In the 1990s, bilingualism became an increasingly controversial political issue. For example, a proposed constitutional amendment has been introduced that designates English as the "official language of the nation." A major force behind the proposed amendment and other efforts to restrict bilingualism is "U.S. English," a nationwide organization that views the English language as the "social glue" that keeps the nation together. This organization supports assimilation. By contrast, Hispanic leaders see the U.S. English campaign as a veiled expression of racism.

Who Am I?

When Tiger Woods appeared on the *Oprah Winfrey Show,* he was asked whether it bothered him, the only child of a Black American father and a Thai mother, to be called an African American, he replied, "It does. Growing up, I

Children of biracial or multiracial couples face special challenges in the United States, where there is a strong desire to place everyone in just a few categories. Few of these children move into adulthood enjoying the kind of acclaim experienced by professional golfer Tiger Woods, whose parentage embraces White, Asian, African American, and American Indian roots.

came up with this name: I'm a 'Cablinasian'" (J. White 1997:34). This is a self-crafted acronym to reflect that Tiger Woods is one-eighth Caucasian, one-fourth Black, one-eighth American Indian, one-fourth Thai, and one-fourth Chinese roots. While we acknowledge his diversity in background, soon after he achieved professional stardom, another golfer was strongly criticized for making racist remarks based on seeing Woods only as African American. If Tiger Woods were not so famous, would most people, on meeting him, see him as anything but an African American? Probably not. Tiger Woods's problem is really the problem of a diverse society that continues to try to place people in a few socially constructed racial and ethnic boxes.

The diversity in the United States today has made it more difficult for many people to view themselves clearly on the racial and ethnic landscape. This difficulty reminds us that racial formation continues to take place. Obviously, the racial and ethnic "landscape," as we have seen, is constructed not naturally but socially and is therefore subject to change and different interpretations. Although our focus is on the United States, virtually every nation faces the same dilemmas.

Within little more than a generation, we have witnessed changes in labeling subordinate groups from Negroes to Blacks to African Americans, from American Indians to Native Americans or Native Peoples. However, more Native Americans prefer the use of their tribal name, such as Seminole, instead of a collective label. The old 1950s statistical term of people with a Spanish surname has long been discarded, yet there is disagreement over a new term: Latino or Hispanic. As with Native Americans, Hispanic Americans avoid such global terms and prefer the use of their native names, such as Puerto Rican or Cuban. People of Mexican ancestry indicate preferences for a variety of names, such as Mexican American, Chicano, or simply Mexican.

Some advocates for racial and ethnic groups consider names a very important issue with great social significance. If nothing else, others argue, changes in names reflect that people are taking over the power to choose their name. Still others do not see this as an issue; as editor Anna Maria Arias of *Hispanic* magazine termed the debate, "It's stupid. There are more important issues we should be talking about" (P. Bennett 1993:A10; see also A. Portes and D. MacLeod 1996).

In the United States and other multiracial, multiethnic societies, panethnicity has emerged. **Panethnicity** is the development of solidarity among ethnic subgroups. The coalition of tribal groups as Native Americans or American Indians to confront outside forces, notably the federal government, is one example of panethnicity. The coalition of Hispanics or Latinos and Asian Americans are other examples of panethnicity. Although it is rarely recognized by dominant society, the very term Black or African American represents the descendants of many different ethnic or tribal groups, such as Akamba, Fulani, Hausa, Malinke, and Yoruba (D. Lopez and Y. Espiritu 1990; N. Onishi 1996).

Is panethnicity a convenient label for "outsiders" or a term that reflects a mutual identity? Certainly, many people outside the group are unable or unwilling to recognize ethnic differences and prefer "umbrella" terms such as Asian Americans. For some small groups, combining with other groups is emerging as a useful way to make themselves heard, but there is always a fear that their own distinctive culture will become submerged. Although many Hispanics share the Spanish language and many are united by Roman Catholicism, only one in four native-born people of Mexican, Puerto Rican, or Cuban descent prefers a panethnic label over nationality or ethnic identity. Yet the growth of a variety of panethnic associations among many groups, including Hispanics, continues into the twenty-first century (de la Garza et al. 1992; Y. Espirito 1992).

There is even less agreement about how to identify oneself in racially conscious America if one is of mixed ancestry. Roberto Chong, who immigrated to the United States, has a Chinese father and a Peruvian mother. He considers himself Hispanic, but others view him as Asian or Latino Asian American. As discussed earlier, there are relatively few intermarriages in America, and social attitudes discourage them, but such unions are on the increase. Interracial births doubled from 63,700 in 1978 to 133,200 in 1992. In a race-conscious society, how are we going to respond to these multiracial children? As noted by the mother of one such child, Hannah Spangler, how is the mother to complete the school form as Hannah starts first grade in Washington, D.C.? Hannah's father is White, and her mother is half Black and half Japanese. We may be slowly recognizing that the United States is a multiracial society, but we are not yet prepared to respond to such a society (S. Kalish 1995).

The Office of Management and Budget has established an Interagency Committee for the Review of the Racial and Ethnic Standards. This panel was created to address the effect of having a multiracial category among the list of races in the Census to be taken in the year 2000. Although results showed that relatively few (1.5 percent) chose the multiracial category, the consideration of a new category did mark a recognition that a segment of the population exists for whom old categories may not work. We are witnessing by such efforts the official recognition of the social construction of race and another phase of racial formation.

Add to this cultural mix the many peoples with clear social identities who are not yet generally recognized in the United States. Arabs are a rapidly growing segment whose identity is heavily subject to stereotypes or, at best, is still ambiguous. Haitians and Jamaicans affirm that they are Black but rarely accept the identity of African American. Brazilians, who speak Portuguese, often object to being called Hispanic, because of that term's association with Spain. Similarly, there are White Hispanics and non-White Hispanics, some of the latter being Black, and others, like Roberto Chong, Asian (P. Bennett 1993; M. Omi and H. Winant 1994:162).

Another challenge to identity is **marginality,** the status of being between two cultures, as in the case of an individual whose mother is a Jew and whose father is a Christian. Incomplete assimilation also results in marginality. Although a Filipino woman migrating to the United States may take on the characteristics of her new host society, she may not be fully accepted and may therefore feel neither Filipino nor American. The marginal person finds himself or herself being perceived differently in different environments, with varying expectations (J. Billson 1988; R. Park 1928; E. Stonequist 1937).

As we seek to understand diversity in the United States, we must be mindful that ethnic and racial labels are just that: labels that have been socially constructed. Yet these social constructs can have a powerful impact, whether self-applied or applied by others.

Resistance and Change

By virtue of wielding power and influence, the dominant group may define the terms by which all members of society operate. This process is particularly evident in a slave society, but even in contemporary industrialized nations, the dominant group has a disproportionate role in shaping immigration policy, the curriculum of the schools, and the content of the media. For example, *Time,* in a 1996 cover story, proclaimed "back to segregation" and "the end of integration" over failed attempts in school busing to achieve racial balance. Such headlines suggest that the United States has never come close to being integrated or to truly overcoming segregation, whether in the schools, housing, health care, or religious worship. Yet the notion that we are giving up on integration is framed in such a way as to exaggerate the amount of change that has been accomplished, implying that we need only go a little further. Similarly, a book entitled *Alien Nation* attacked immigration and declared that the country is changing for the worse (P. Brimelow 1996; J. Kunen 1996). Subordinate groups simply have not accepted and do not accept the definitions and ideology proposed by the dominant group. A continuing theme in dominant-subordinate relations is the minority group's challenging their subordination. We will see throughout this book the resistance of subordinate groups as they seek to promote change that will bring them more rights and privileges, if not true equality (F. Moulder 1996).

Resistance can be seen in efforts by racial and ethnic groups to maintain their identity through newspapers, organizations, and, in today's technological age, cable stations and Internet sites. Resistance manifests itself in social movements such as the civil rights movement, the feminist movement, and gay rights efforts. The passage of such legislation as the Age Discrimination Act or the Americans with Disabilities Act marks the organization of the oppressed group to lobby on its behalf.

Resistance efforts may begin through small actions. For example, members of a reservation population question a second toxic waste dump being located on their land. Although it may bring in money, they question the wisdom of such a move. Their concerns lead to further investigations of the extent to which American Indian lands are used disproportionately for the housing of dangerous materials. This action in turn leads to a broader investigation of the way that minority-group people often find themselves "hosting" dumps and incinerators. As we will discuss later, these local efforts led eventually to the Environmental Protection Agency's monitoring the disproportionate placement of toxic facilities among or near racial and ethnic minority people's communities. There is little reason to expect that such reforms would have occurred if we had relied on traditional decision-making processes alone.

An even more basic form of resistance is to question societal values. In this book, we avoid the use of the term "American" to describe people of the United States, since in our geographical sense, Brazilians, Canadians, and El Salvadorans are Americans as well. It is very easy to overlook how our understanding of today has been shaped by the way institutions and even the very telling of history has been presented by members of the dominant group. African American studies scholar Molefi Kete Asante (1992, 1996) has called for an **Afrocentric perspective** that emphasizes the customs of African cultures and the way that they have pervaded the history, culture, and behavior of Blacks in the United States and around the world. Afrocentrism counters Eurocentrism and works toward a multiculturalist or pluralist orientation in which no viewpoint is suppressed. The Afrocentric approach could become part of our school curriculum, which has not adequately acknowledged the importance of this heritage.

The Afrocentric perspective has attracted considerable attention in colleges. Opponents view it as a separatist view of history and culture that distorts both past and present. Its supporters counter that African peoples everywhere can come to full self-determination only when they are able to overthrow "White" or Eurocentric intellectual interpretations (G. Early 1994).

In considering the inequalities present today, as we will in the chapters that follow, it is easy to forget how much change has taken place. Much of the resistance to prejudice and discrimination in the past, whether to slavery or to women's prohibition from voting, took the active support of members of the dominant group. The indignities still experienced by subordinate groups continue to be resisted as subordinate groups and their allies among the dominant group seek further change.

Conclusion

One hundred years ago sociologist and activist W. E. B. Du Bois took another famed Black activist, Booker T. Washington, to task for saying that the races could best work together apart, like fingers on a hand. Du Bois felt that Black people had to be a part of all social institutions and not to create their own. Today among African Americans, Whites, and other groups, the debate persists as to what form society should take. Should we seek to bring everyone together into an integrated whole, considering the assimilation that process will require? Or do we strive to maintain as much of our group identities as possible while working cooperatively as necessary?

In this first chapter, we have attempted to organize our approach to subordinate-dominant relations in the United States. We observed that subordinate groups do not necessarily contain fewer members than the dominant group. Subordinate groups are classified into racial, ethnic, religious, and gender groups. Racial classification has been of interest, but scientific findings do not explain contemporary race relations. Biological differences of race are not supported by scientific data. Yet as the continuing debate over the Bell Curve demonstrates, attempts to establish a biological meaning of race have not been swept entirely into the dustbin of history. The social meaning given to physical differences, however, is very significant. People have defined racial differences in such a way as to encourage or discourage the progress of certain groups.

The confinement of certain people to subordinate groups may function to serve some people's vested interests. This denial of opportunities or privileges to an entire group, however, leads only to conflict between dominant and subordinate groups. Societies such as the United States develop ideologies to justify that privileges are given to some and that opportunities are denied to others. These ideologies may be subtle, such as assimilation (that is, "You should be like us"), or overt, such as racist thought and behavior.

Subordinate groups generally emerge in one of three ways: migration, annexation, or colonialism. Once a group is given subordinate status, it does not necessarily keep it indefinitely. Extermination, expulsion, secession, segregation, fusion, and assimilation remove the status of subordination, although inequality may persist. Subordinate-group members' reactions include the seeking of an alternate avenue to acceptance and success: "Why should we forsake what we are to be accepted by them?" In response to this question, there has been a resurgence of ethnic identification. Pluralism describes a society in which several different groups coexist, with no dominant or subordinate groups. The hope for such a society remains unfulfilled, except perhaps for isolated exceptions.

Subordinate groups have not and do not always accept passively their second-class status. They may protest, organize, revolt, and resist society as defined by the dominant group. Patterns of race and ethnic relations are changing, not stagnant. Furthermore, in many nations, including the United States, the nature of race and ethnicity changes through migration. Indicative of the changing landscape, biracial and multiracial children present us with new definitions of identity emerging through a process of racial formation, reminding us that race is socially constructed.

The two significant forces that are absent in a truly pluralistic society are prejudice and discrimination. In an assimilation society, prejudice disparages out-group differences, and discrimination financially rewards those who shed their past. In the next two chapters, we will explore the nature of prejudice and discrimination in the United States.

Key Terms

Afrocentric perspective 34
amalgamation 27
assimilation 27
bilingualism 30
biological race 9
class 15
colonialism 22
conflict perspective 18
dysfunction 16
emigration 21
ethnic cleansing 24
ethnic group 6
functionalist perspective 16
fusion 26
genocide 24
immigration 21
intelligence quotient 9
internal colonialism 23
labeling theory 19
marginality 33
melting pot 27
migration 21
minority group 4
panethnicity 32
pluralism 29
racial formation 13
racial group 5
racism 12
segregation 25
self-fulfilling prophecy 19
sociology 14
stereotypes 19
stratification 15
world systems analysis 23

Review Questions

1. In what ways have you seen issues of race and ethnicity emerge? Identify groups that have been subordinated for reasons other than race, ethnicity, or gender.
2. How can a significant political or social issue (such as bilingual education) be viewed in assimilationist and pluralistic terms?

3. How does the concept of racial formation relate to the issue of "Who am I?"

Critical Thinking

1. How diverse is your city? Can you see evidence that some group is being subordinated? What social construction of categories do you see that may be different in your community as compared with elsewhere?
2. In 1996, Denny Mendéz was crowned Miss Italy, but many people protested her selection because they said she did not reflect the appropriate physical image of the Italian people. Mendéz had moved to Italy from the Dominican Republic when her mother married an Italian and has since become a citizen. What does this controversy around a beauty pageant tell us about the social construction of race? What similar situations have you witnessed where it seems that race and ethnicity can be seen only in their social context?
3. Identify some protest and resistance efforts by subordinated groups in your area. Have they been successful? Why are some people who say that they favor equality uncomfortable with such efforts? How can people unconnected with such efforts either help or hinder such protests?

Internet Exercises

1. The struggle for civil rights in the United States is chronicled within the photography of Charles Moore on the web page Powerful Days (http://www.civilrightsphotos.com/Pages/index2.html). Activate your sociological imagination while viewing the pictures and captions so that you can answer the following questions: Who was James Meredith? Who was Medgar Evers? What contributions did Dr. Martin Luther King, Jr., make to the civil rights movement? What events occurred at the University of Mississippi in 1962 and in Birmingham in 1963? Why were these events important? What specific causes and issues mobilized the protesters and marchers featured on the web site? What symbols and labels were used during this era by law enforcement, by businesses, and by those who were for and against desegregation? How would you characterize the interactions between the various groups featured in the photos? Consider the discussion in this chapter on "The Consequences of Subordinate-Group Status." Which of the consequences detailed in that section are most reflected within the images and experiences of the people photographed by Moore? How did the pictures make you feel? Which picture affected you the most, and why?

2. In this chapter, you learned about the types of subordinate groups studied by sociologists. Engage in web-based cultural emersion by directing your Internet browser to (http://dir.yahoo.com/Society_and_Culture/Cultures_and_Groups/Cultures/American__United States_/). Here you will view an extensive list of racial and ethnic groups

found in the United States today. Choose three of the groups from the list, and then visit web sites dedicated to your selections. Compare and contrast your selections by exploring the following questions for each group: What is the name of the group? What is the history behind the group's arrival in the United States? Is there a religion or religions frequently associated with the group? Are there specific holidays associated with the group? Is so, which ones? What are the origins of these celebrations? What symbols, rituals, and traditions are expressed during these holidays? Foods, music, dancing, and other cultural contributions have been made by all racial and ethnic groups in the United States. What cultural contributions has each of your selected groups made? What new information did you learn about each group? In what ways are the three groups similar? In what ways are they different? Why did you choose the three groups that you did?

3. This first chapter offers an examination of the theoretical perspectives that will be the foundation for your sociological study of racial and ethnic groups. To learn more about sociology, visit SocioSite on the Internet at (http://www.pscw.uva.nl/sociosite/index.html). Be sure to spend time in the "Subject Areas" and "Sociologists" sections, paying special attention to the information on Howard Becker, Émile Durkheim, and Karl Marx. Read about these three thinkers, and also select two more from the web site to expand your understanding of sociology and its founders. You can link to pictures, original writings, and biographical information. When did the five people whom you have researched live? Which of the theoretical perspectives from the chapter is each thinker most associated with? What are some of the important terms and concepts proffered by these sociologists? How might these ideas be important to the study of racial and ethnic groups? What are some other subject areas of human interaction studied by sociologists? Can you see a connection between these other areas in general and the study of racial and ethnic groups in particular? How so? Which theoretical perspective intrigues you the most, and why?

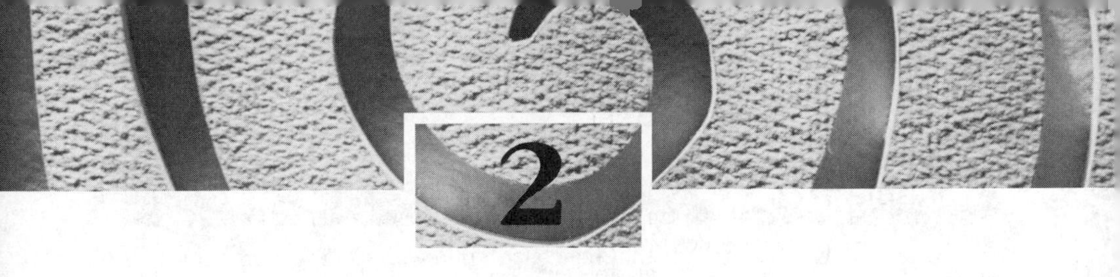

Prejudice

CHAPTER OUTLINE

HIGHLIGHTS

Prejudice is a negative attitude that rejects an entire group; discrimination is behavior that deprives a group of certain rights or opportunities. Prejudice does not necessarily coincide with discrimination, as is made apparent by a typology developed by sociologist Robert Merton. Several theories have been advanced to explain prejudice. The explanations are scapegoating, authoritarian personality, exploitation, and normative factors. These explanations examine prejudice in terms of content (negative stereotypes) and extent. Prejudice is not limited to the dominant group; subordinate groups often dislike one another. The attitudes in the United States toward Arab Americans and American Muslims illustrate the development of stereotypes and scapegoating. The mass media seem to be of limited value in reducing prejudice and may even intensify ill feeling. Equal-status contact and the shared-coping approach may reduce hostility among groups.

Virtually the entire nation was stunned by events outside Jasper, Texas, in 1998. James Byrd, Jr., a 39-year-old African American, accepted a ride with three White men as he walked along a street. The next morning his mutilated body was found after he had been dragged behind the truck by his ankles for two miles. The three men's hatred for Blacks had been documented, and one of the men sported tattoos reading "Aryan Pride" and displaying a Nazi SS symbol. Townspeople were so shocked by such blatant racism within their midst that within a week, Whites and Blacks joined in a prayer vigil in front of the town's courthouse, singing "Amazing Grace."

In another case, in 1994, the general public as well as law-enforcement officials were quick to accept the story of a South Carolina White woman who reported that a Black man had kidnapped her two children. Only later was it learned that no Black man had been involved; in fact, the woman had killed her own children by strapping them into their car seats and rolling the car into a lake.

From a web site on the Internet called Nazism Now, it is only a mouse click to reach the I Hate Jews—The Anti-Semetic (note the misspelling of "Semitic") Homepage, Knights of the Ku Klux Klan, and the White Nationalist Resources Page.

These are just a few examples of the ill feelings and overt hostility expressed between groups in the United States. Sometimes the expression of prejudice may be explicit, as in these examples, but it can also be found in a more subtle, indirect manner. In 1993, looking for a night's entertainment in the movie *Falling Down,* people cheered the Michael Douglas character Bill "D-Fens" Foster as he went over the edge, assaulting a Korean immigrant who owned a convenience store because of the owner's poor English and the price of a soda. In another situation, it took the combined effort of Native Americans and several

African American artist Jacob Lawrence portrays the separate facilities typical of the treatment received by Blacks in the earlier part of the twentieth century.

large church groups to block the sale of a malt liquor named "Crazy Horse." It was argued that the name of the alcoholic beverage was offensive to the honored position that Crazy Horse has as a political and religious leader in Oglala Lakota history. And for those who are too young for liquor but not too old for video games, one finds that Asian characters appear in video games only in martial arts games, such as E. Honda in "Street Fighter" or Liu Kang in "Mortal Kombat II States" (Anti-Defamation League 1996; Jenness 1995; National Asian Pacific American Legal Consortium 1996; F. Robles and L. Casimir 1996).

Prejudice is so prevalent that it is tempting to consider it inevitable or, even more broadly, just part of human nature. Such a view ignores its variability from individual to individual and from society to society. People must learn prejudice as children before they exhibit it as adults; therefore, prejudice is a social phenomenon, an acquired characteristic. A truly pluralistic society would lack unfavorable distinctions made through prejudicial attitudes among racial and ethnic groups.

Ill feeling among groups may result from ethnocentrism. **Ethnocentrism** is the tendency to assume that one's culture and way of life are superior to all others. The ethnocentric person judges other groups and other cultures by the standards of his or her own group. This attitude leads people quite easily to view other cultures as inferior.

Hate Crimes

Although prejudice is certainly not new in the United States, it is receiving increased attention as it manifests itself in neighborhoods, at meetings, and on college campuses. The Hate Crime Statistics Act, which became law in 1990, directs the Department of Justice to gather data on hate or bias crimes. The government defines a **hate crime** as

> *a criminal offense committed against a person, property, or society which is motivated, in whole or in part, by the offender's bias against a race, religion, sexual orientation, or ethnic/national origin group. (U.S. Department of Justice 1999:57)*

This law created a national mandate to identify such crimes, whereas previously only twelve states had monitored hate crimes. In 1994, the act was amended to include disabilities, both physical and mental, as factors that could be considered a basis for hate crimes. The manner in which hate crimes are defined for prosecution varies dramatically from state to state, as shown in Figure 2.1.

In 1999, law-enforcement agencies released hate crime data submitted by police agencies covering 79 percent of the United States. There were reports for 1998 of over 7,700 hate crimes and bias-motivated incidents. Race was the apparent motivation for the bias in 58 percent of the reports, and religion, sexual

Figure 2.1 Hate Crime Laws in the United States in 2000

Source: National Gay and Lesbian Task Force 2000.

orientation, or ethnicity appeared to be the motivation for the bias in about 10 to 16 percent of the reports. Although vandalism and intimidation were the most common offenses, 30 percent of all offenses against people involved assault and even rape or murder (U.S. Department of Justice 1999:58–60).

National legislation and publicity have made *hate crime* a meaningful term, and we are beginning to recognize the victimization associated with such incidents. There is a proposal that would make a violent crime into a federal crime if it is motivated by racial or religious bias. Even though passage is uncertain, the serious consideration of the proposal indicates the willingness to consider a major expansion of federal jurisdiction. Currently, federal law prohibits crimes motivated by race, color, religion, or national origin only if they involve violation of a federally guaranteed right, such as voting (B. Jacobs and K. Potter 1998).

Victimized groups are not merely observing these events. Watchdog organizations play an important role in documenting bias-motivated violence—among such groups are the Anti-Defamation League (ADL), the National Institute Against Prejudice and Violence, the Southern Poverty Law Center, and the National Gay and Lesbian Task Force. Established hate groups have even set up propaganda sites on the World Wide Web, thereby creating opportunities for previously unknown haters and hate groups to promote themselves. However, hate crimes legislation does not affect such outlets because of legal questions involving freedom of speech (ADL 1996; Jenness 1995).

What causes people to dislike entire groups of other people? Is it possible to change attitudes? This chapter tries to answer these questions about prejudice. In Chapter 3, the focus is on discrimination.

Prejudice and Discrimination

Prejudice and *discrimination* are related concepts but are not the same. **Prejudice** is a negative attitude toward an entire category of people. The two important components in this definition are *attitude* and *entire category*. Prejudice involves attitudes, thoughts, and beliefs, not actions. Frequently, prejudice is expressed through the use of **ethnophaulisms,** or ethnic slurs, which include derisive nicknames such as *honkie, gook,* or *wetback*. Ethnophaulisms also include speaking about or to members of a particular group in a condescending way—"José does well in school for a Mexican American"—or referring to a middle-aged woman as "one of the girls."

A prejudiced belief leads to categorical rejection. Prejudice is not disliking someone you meet because you find his or her behavior objectionable. It is disliking an entire racial or ethnic group, even if you have had little or no contact with that group. A college student who requests a room change after three weeks of enduring his roommate's sleeping all day, playing loud music all night, and piling garbage on his desk is not expressing prejudice. He is displaying prejudice, however, if he requests a change on arriving at school and learning from his roommate's luggage tags that his new roommate is of a different nationality.

Prejudice is a belief or an attitude; discrimination is action. **Discrimination** involves behavior that excludes all members of a group from certain rights, opportunities, or privileges. As with prejudice, the behavior must be categorical. If an employer refuses to hire as a typist an Italian American who is illiterate, the refusal is not discrimination. If an employer refuses to hire any Italian Americans because he or she thinks they are incompetent and does not make the effort to see whether an applicant is qualified, that refusal is discrimination.

Prejudice does not necessarily coincide with discriminatory behavior. Sociologist Robert Merton (1949, 1976), in exploring the relationship between negative attitudes and negative behavior, identified four major categories (see Figure 2.2). The label added to each of Merton's categories may more readily identify the type of individual being described. These types are

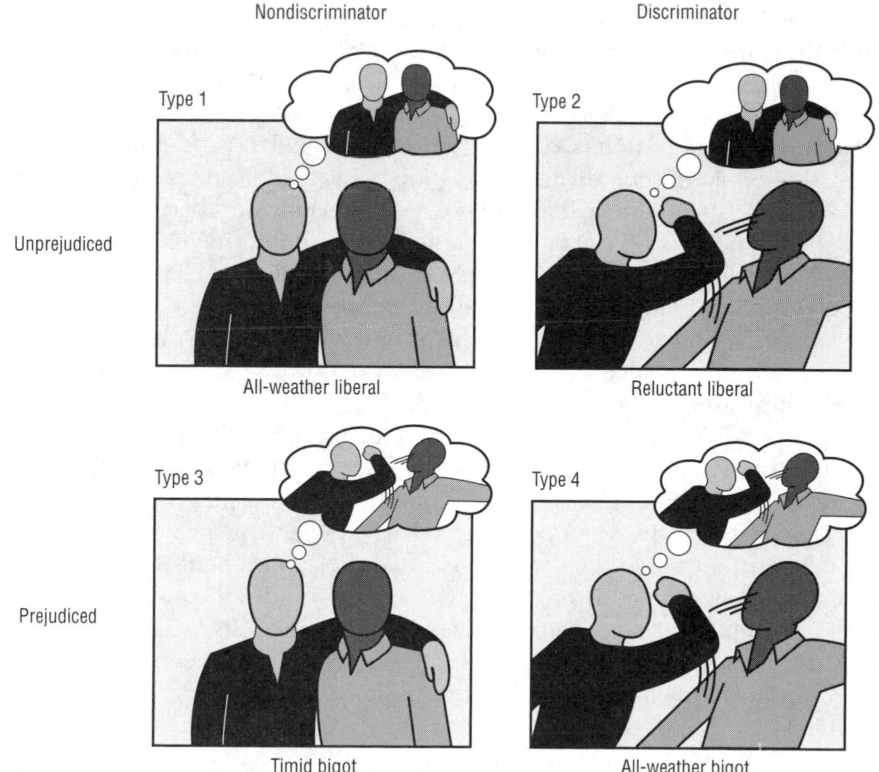

Figure 2.2 Prejudice and Discrimination
As sociologist Robert Merton's formulation shows, prejudice and discrimination are related to each other but are not the same.

1. The unprejudiced nondiscriminator: all-weather liberal
2. The unprejudiced discriminator: reluctant liberal
3. The prejudiced nondiscriminator: timid bigot
4. The prejudiced discriminator: all-weather bigot

Liberals, as the term is employed in types 1 and 2, are committed to equality among people. The all-weather liberal believes in equality and practices it. Merton was quick to observe that all-weather liberals may be far removed from any real competition with subordinate groups such as African Americans or women. Furthermore, such people may be content with their own behavior and may do little to change themselves. The reluctant liberal is not even this committed to equality among groups. Social pressure may cause such a person to discriminate. Fear of losing employees may lead a manager to avoid promoting women to supervisory capacities. Equal-opportunity legislation may be the best way to influence the reluctant liberals.

Types 3 and 4 do not believe in equal treatment for racial and ethnic groups, but they vary in their willingness to act. The timid bigot, type 3, will not discriminate if discrimination costs money or reduces profits or if he or she is pressured by peers or by the government not to discriminate. The all-weather bigot unhesitatingly acts on the prejudiced beliefs that she or he holds.

Merton's typology points out that attitudes should not be confused with behavior. People do not always act as they believe. More than half a century ago, Richard LaPiere (1934, 1969) exposed the relationship between racial attitudes and social conduct. From 1930 to 1932, LaPiere traveled throughout the United States with a Chinese couple. Despite an alleged climate of intolerance of Asians, LaPiere observed that the couple was treated courteously at hotels, motels, and restaurants. He was puzzled by the good reception they received; all the conventional attitude surveys showed extreme prejudice by Whites toward the Chinese.

Was it possible that LaPiere had been fortunate during his travels and consistently stopped at places operated by the tolerant members of the dominant group? To test this possibility, he sent questionnaires asking the very establishments at which they had been served whether the owner would "accept members of the Chinese race as guests in your establishment." More than 90 percent responded no, even though LaPiere's Chinese couple had been treated politely at all the establishments. How can this inconsistency be explained? Those people who returned questionnaires in which they reflected prejudice were unwilling to act on the basis of those asserted beliefs: they were timid bigots.

The LaPiere study is not without flaws. First, he had no way of knowing whether the respondent to the questionnaire was the same person who had served him and the Chinese couple. Second, whereas he had accompanied the couple, the questionnaire suggested that the arrival would be unescorted (and in the minds of some, uncontrolled) and perhaps would consist of many Chinese individuals. Third, personnel may have changed between the time of the visit and the mailing of the questionnaire (I. Deutscher et al. 1993).

The LaPiere technique has been replicated with similar results. This technique raises the question of whether attitudes are important if they are not completely reflected in behavior. But if attitudes are not important in small matters, they are important in other ways: lawmakers legislate and courts may reach decisions on the basis of what the public thinks.

This is not just a hypothetical possibility. Legislators in the United States are often persuaded to vote in a certain way by what they perceive as changed attitudes toward immigration, affirmative action, school busing, abortion, and prayer in public schools. Sociologists Jack and William C. Levin (1982) enumerated some of prejudice's functions. For the majority group, it serves to maintain privileged occupations and more power for its members. Levin and Levin go on to point out that prejudice may be viewed as having some functions even for subordinate groups. These functions include maintaining in-group solidarity and reducing competition in some areas of employment, admittedly in those areas with lower status or smaller rewards.

The following sections examine the theories of why prejudice exists and discuss the content and extent of prejudice today.

Theories of Prejudice

Prejudice is learned. Friends, relatives, newspapers, books, movies, and television all teach it. Awareness begins at an early age that there are differences among people that society judges to be important. Several theories have been advanced to explain the rejection of certain groups in a society. We will examine four theoretical explanations—first, two explanations (scapegoating and authoritarian personality) that tend to be psychological, emphasizing why a particular person harbors ill-feelings. Then we will turn to two that are more sociological (exploitation and normative), which view prejudice in the context of our interaction in larger society.

Scapegoating Theory

Scapegoating theory says that prejudiced people believe that they are society's victims. Exploitation theory maintains that intolerant individuals abuse others, whereas scapegoaters feel that they themselves are being abused. The term **scapegoat** comes from a biblical injunction telling the Hebrews to send a goat into the wilderness symbolically to carry away the people's sins. Similarly, the theory of scapegoating suggests that an individual, rather than accepting guilt for some failure, transfers the responsibility for failure to some vulnerable group. In the major, tragic twentieth-century example, Adolf Hitler used the Jews as the scapegoat for all German social and economic ills in the 1930s. This premise led to the passage of laws restricting Jewish life in pre–World War II Germany and eventually escalated into the mass extermination of many of Europe's Jews.

Studies of prejudice in the United States have found that the downwardly economic mobile are usually more prejudiced. People who lose a job and are forced to accept a lower-status occupation experience increased tension and anxiety. Who is responsible, they ask, for their misfortune? At this time, a scapegoat, such as a racial, an ethnic, or a religious group, may enter the picture (B. Bettelheim and M. Janowitz 1964).

Like exploitation theory, scapegoating theory adds to our understanding of why prejudice exists, but it does not explain all the facets of prejudice. For example, scapegoating theory offers little explanation of why a specific group is selected or why frustration is not taken out on the real culprit whenever possible. Also, both the exploitation and the scapegoating theories suggest that every individual sharing the same general experiences in society would be equally prejudiced, but that is not the case. Prejudice varies among individuals who would seem to benefit equally from the exploitation of a subordinate group or who have experienced equal frustration. In an effort to explain these personality differences, social scientists developed the concept of the authoritarian personality.

Authoritarian Personality Theory

A number of social scientists do not see prejudice as an isolated trait that anyone can have. Several efforts have been made to detail the prejudiced personality, but the most comprehensive effort culminated in a volume entitled *The Authoritarian Personality* (T. Adorno et al. 1950). Using a variety of tests and relying on more than 2,000 respondents, ranging from middle-class Whites to inmates of San Quentin State Prison in California, the authors claimed that they had isolated the characteristics of the authoritarian personality. In these authors' view, the basic characteristics of the **authoritarian personality** were adherence to conventional values, uncritical acceptance of authority, and concern with power and toughness. With obvious relevance to the development of intolerance, the authoritarian personality was also characterized by aggressiveness toward people who did not conform to conventional norms or did not obey authority. According to the authors, this personality type developed from an early childhood of harsh discipline. A child with an authoritarian upbringing obeyed and then later treated others as he or she had been raised. This study has been widely criticized, but the very existence of such wide criticism indicates the influence of the study. Critics have attacked the study's equation of authoritarianism with right-wing politics (though liberals can also be rigid); the study's failure to see that prejudice is more closely related to other individual traits, such as social class, than to authoritarianism as it was defined; and the research methods employed. Graham Kinloch (1974), discussing personality research, added a fourth criticism: the authors concentrated on factors behind extreme racial prejudice, rather than on more common expressions of hostility.

Exploitation Theory

Racial prejudice is frequently used to justify keeping a group in a subordinate position, such as a lower social class. Conflict theorists in particular stress the role of racial and ethnic hostility as a way for the dominant group to keep intact its position of status and power. Indeed, this approach maintains that even the less affluent White working class uses prejudice to minimize competition from upwardly mobile minorities.

This **exploitation theory** is clearly part of the Marxist tradition in sociological thought. Karl Marx emphasized exploitation of the lower class as an integral part of capitalism. Similarly, the exploitation or conflict approach explains how racism can stigmatize a group as inferior so that the exploitation of that group can be justified. As developed by Oliver Cox (1942), exploitation theory saw prejudice against Blacks as an extension of the inequality faced by the entire lower class.

The exploitation theory of prejudice is persuasive. Japanese Americans were the object of little prejudice until they began to enter occupations that brought them into competition with Whites. The movement to keep Chinese out of the country became strongest during the latter half of the nineteenth century, when Chinese immigrants and Whites fought over dwindling numbers of jobs. Both the enslavement of African Americans and the removal westward of Native Americans were to a significant degree economically motivated.

Related to the exploitation theory is the **caste approach** to race relations in the United States. The term *caste* describes a system of social inequality in which status is inherited and people have little, if any, opportunity to change their social position. As we have seen through exploitation theory, economic subordination benefits the dominant group's financial interests. The caste approach, however, does not rely on Marxist theory for theoretical support. The caste explanation for racial subordination sees race and social class as closely related because Blacks and other non-Whites are destined by the social structure to occupy a castelike position. Membership in the subordinate group is inherited and permanent.

The caste approach is basically descriptive and not very analytical; for example, sociologists using it make less effort to explain why caste relations originated than do those working within the exploitation approach of Oliver C. Cox. The caste approach, although acknowledging the importance of social class, argues that race is more important, whereas Cox's general exploitation theory sees racial discrimination as merely an example of class differences. The caste explanation seems somewhat limited. In a caste system, as strictly defined, the lower castes accept the system and their low status. But the increased numbers of Blacks in high-paying occupations and the continuous struggle for equal rights indicate that African Americans have not acquiesced and do not acquiesce (G. Berreman 1973).

Although some cases support the exploitation theory, it is too limited to explain prejudice in all its forms. First, not all minority groups are exploited economically to the same extent. Second, many groups that have been the victims of prejudice have not been persecuted for economic reasons—for example, the Quakers. Nevertheless, as Gordon Allport (1979) concludes, the exploitation theory correctly points a finger at one of the factors in prejudice, that is, the rationalized self-interest of the upper classes.

Normative Approach

Although personality factors are important contributors to prejudice, normative or situational factors must also be given serious consideration. The **normative approach** takes the view that prejudice is influenced by societal norms and situations that serve to encourage or discourage the tolerance of minorities.

Analysis reveals how societal influences shape a climate for tolerance or intolerance. Societies develop social norms that dictate not only what foods are desirable (or forbidden) but also what racial and ethnic groups are to be favored (or despised). Social forces operate in a society to encourage or discourage tolerance. The force may be widespread—for example, the pressure on White Southerners to oppose racial equality while there was slavery or segregation. The influence of social norms may be limited—for example, one male who finds himself becoming more sexist as he competes with three females for a position in a prestigious law firm.

Social psychologist Thomas Pettigrew (1958, 1959) collected data that substantiated the importance of such social norms in developing a social climate conducive to the expression of prejudice. Pettigrew found that Whites in the South were more anti-Black than Whites in the North, and that Whites in the United States were not as prejudiced as Whites in the Republic of South Africa.

Personality alone cannot account for such differences. Pettigrew's research revealed no significant variation between the two societies in the proportion of authoritarian individuals. This finding has been confirmed by research showing that as people moved from the North to the South and as others moved from the South to the North during the 1980s and early 1990s, attitudes changed, adapting to the new social environment. This changing is particularly true when it comes to racial public policies such as fair housing, busing, and federal money aimed at assisting Blacks. We can conclude that structural factors explain differences in the levels of prejudice between these two regions (J. Glaser and M. Gilens 1997).

We should not view the four approaches to prejudice summarized in Table 2.1 as mutually exclusive. Social circumstances provide cues for people's attitudes; personality determines the extent to which people follow social cues and the likelihood that they will encourage others to do the same. Societal norms may promote or deter tolerance; personality traits suggest the degree to which people will conform to norms of intolerance.

The Content of Prejudice: Stereotypes

It is the year 2000, and a last-minute shopper wants to take advantage of the latest technology. Desiring to buy a gift for a young cousin, the shopper turns to Etoy.com. Unsure of what to buy for the six-year old, the shopper takes advantage of "last minute gift ideas." There on the web are ideas for boys such as Daytona 500 Superspeedway Set, Dic Golf, and Deep Sea Explorer Playset. For a six-year-old girl, the ideas are quite different and include Barbie Dream Bed and Bath, a zither, and Patty Playground. Where do these images come from, and what influence can they have over our daily lives?

In Chapter 1, we saw that stereotypes play a powerful role in how people come to view dominant and subordinate groups. Numerous scientific studies have been made of these exaggerated images. This research has shown the willingness of people to attribute positive and negative traits to entire groups of people, which are then used to generalize particular individuals. Stereotyp-

Table 2.1 Theories of Prejudice

There is no one explanation of why prejudice exists, but several approaches taken together offer insight.

Theory	*Proponent*	*Explanation*	*Example*
Scapegoating	Bruno Bettelheim Morris Janowitz	People blame others for their own failures.	An unsuccessful applicant assumes that a minority member or a woman got "his" job.
Authoritarian personality	Adorno and associates	Childrearing leads one to develop intolerance as an adult.	The rigid personality type dislikes people who are "different."
Exploitation	Oliver C. Cox Marxist theory	People utilize others unfairly for economic advantage.	A minority member is hired at a lower wage level.
Normative	Thomas Pettigrew	Peer and social influences encourage tolerance or intolerance.	A person from an intolerant household is more likely to be openly prejudiced.

ing causes people to view Blacks as superstitious, Whites as uncaring, and Jews as shrewd. Over the last seventy years of such research, social scientists have found that people are less willing to express such views openly but, as we will see later, that prejudice persists (C. Macrae et al. 1996).

If stereotypes are exaggerated generalizations, why are they so widely held, and why are some traits more often assigned than others? Evidence for traits may arise out of real conditions. For example, more Puerto Ricans live in poverty than Whites, and so the prejudiced mind associates Puerto Ricans with laziness. According to the New Testament, some Jews were responsible for the crucifixion of Jesus, and so, to the prejudiced mind, all Jews are Christ-killers. Some activists in the women's movement are lesbians, and so, the thinking is, all feminists are lesbians. From a kernel of fact, faulty generalization creates a stereotype. Stereotyping of both women and men is well documented; however, little research has been done on the stereotyping of women of color. Rose Weitz (1992), surveying White undergraduates, found a definite willingness to characterize African American women as "loud" and "argumentative," Mexican American women as "lazy" and "quick-tempered," and Jewish women as "spoiled" and "shrewd." "American white women" were seen as "intelligent," "materialistic," and "sophisticated"—quite a contrast to the labeling of women of color.

Labels take on such strong significance that people often ignore facts that contradict their previously held beliefs. People who believe many Italian Americans to be members of the Mafia disregard law-abiding Italian Americans. Muslims are regularly portrayed in a violent, offensive manner that contributes to their being misunderstood and distrusted. We will consider later in the chapter how this stereotype has become widespread since the mid-1970s.

In the last thirty years, we have become more and more aware of the power of the mass media to introduce stereotypes into everyday life. Television is a prime example. Almost all television roles showing leadership feature Whites. Even urban-based programs such as *Seinfeld* and *Friends* prospered without any major Black or Hispanic or Asian American characters. A 1998 national survey of boys and girls aged 10 to 17 that asked a very simple question came up with some disturbing findings. The children were asked, "How often do you see your race on television?" The results showed that 71 percent of White children said "very often," compared with only 42 percent of African Americans, 22 percent of Latinos, and 16 percent of Asian Americans. Even more troubling is that generally the children view the White characters as affluent and well educated, whereas they see the minority characters as "breaking the law or rules," "being lazy," and "acting goofy." Later in this chapter we will consider the degree to which the media have changed in presenting stereotyped images (Children Now 1998).

The labeling of individuals has strong implications for the self-fulfilling prophecy besides fostering a negative racial climate. Studies show that people are all too aware of the negative images other people have of them. When asked to estimate the prevalence of hard-core racism among Whites,

Many would regard this statue of colonist Hannah Duston in Massachusetts as perpetuating stereotypes about American Indians. She is honored for killing and scalping ten Abenaki Indians in 1697 while defending her family. Believed to be the first woman ever honored in the United States with a monument, she is portrayed here holding a hatchet.

1 in 4 Blacks agrees that more than half "personally share the attitudes of groups like the Ku Klux Klan toward Blacks"; only 1 Black in 10 says "only a few" share such views. Not only do stereotypes influence how people feel about themselves but, perhaps of equal importance, they also affect how people interact with others. If people feel that others hold incorrect, if not also extremely disparaging, attitudes, that perception undoubtedly will make it difficult to have harmonious relations (L. Sigelman and S. Tuch 1997).

Are stereotypes held only by dominant groups about subordinate groups? The answer is clearly no. White Americans believe generalizations even about themselves, although admittedly these are usually positive. Subordinate groups also hold exaggerated images of themselves. Studies before World War II showed a tendency for Blacks to assign to themselves many of the same negative traits assigned to them by Whites. Today stereotypes of themselves are largely rejected by African Americans, Jews, Asians, and other minority groups, although subordinate groups will to some degree stereotype each other. The nature of the subordinate group's self-image is explored later in this chapter. The subordinate group also develops stereotyped images of the dominant group. Anthony Dworkin (1965) surveyed Mexican Americans and found that the majority agreed that White non-Hispanics were prejudiced, snobbish, hypocritical, tense, anxious, and neurotic, and that they had little family loyalty. Stereotyping, like prejudice itself, is widespread.

The Extent of Prejudice

Interest in developing theories of prejudice or studying its concept has been exceeded only by interest in measuring it. From the outset, efforts to measure prejudice have suffered from disagreement over exactly what constitutes intolerance and whether there is such a phenomenon as no prejudice at all. Add to these uncertainties the methodological problems of attitude measurement, and the empirical study of prejudice becomes an undertaking fraught with difficulty.

The extent of prejudice can be measured only in relative, rather than absolute, differences. We cannot accurately say, for example, that prejudice toward Puerto Ricans is four times greater than that toward Portuguese Americans. We can conclude that prejudice is greater toward one group than toward the other; we just cannot quantify how much greater. The social distance scale is especially appropriate to assess differences in prejudice.

The Social Distance Scale

Robert Park and Ernest Burgess first defined *social distance* as the tendency to approach or withdraw from a racial group (1921:440). A few years later, Emory Bogardus (1968) conceptualized a scale that could measure social distance empirically. His social distance scale is so widely used that it is frequently referred to as the **Bogardus scale.**

The scale asks people how willing they would be to interact with various racial and ethnic groups in specified social situations. The situations describe different degrees of social contact or social distance. The seven items used, with their corresponding distance scores, follow. People are asked whether they would be willing to admit each group

- To close kinship by marriage (1.00)
- To my club as personal chums (2.00)
- To my street as neighbors (3.00)
- To employment in my occupation (4.00)
- To citizenship in my country (5.00)
- As only visitors to my country (6.00)
- Or would exclude from my country (7.00)

A score of 1.00 for any group would indicate no social distance and therefore no prejudice. The social distance scale has been administered to many different groups in other countries as well. Despite some minor flaws and certain refinements needed in the scale, the results of these studies are useful and can be compared.

The data in Table 2.2 summarize the results of studies using the social distance scale in the United States at three points in time over a sixty-five-year period. In the top third of the hierarchy are White Americans and northern Europeans. In the middle are eastern and southern Europeans, and generally near the bottom are racial minorities. This prestige hierarchy resembles the relative proportions of the various groups in the population. The similarity in the hierarchy during the sixty-five years was not limited to White respondents. Several times, the scale was administered to Jewish, Mexican American, Asian, Puerto Rican, Black African, and Black American groups. These groups generally shared the same hierarchy, although they placed their own group at the top. The extent of prejudice as illustrated in the ranking of racial and ethnic groups seems to be widely shared. Studies have also been performed in other societies and show that they have a racial and ethnic hierarchy as well.

A tentative conclusion that we can draw from these studies is that the extent of prejudice is decreasing. At the bottom of Table 2.2 is the arithmetic mean of the racial reactions on a scale of 1.0 to 7.0. Although the change was slight from survey to survey, it is generally downward. Many specific nationalities and races, however, experienced little change. The spread in social distance (the difference between the top- and bottom-ranked groups) also decreased or held steady from 1926 to 1991, a finding indicating that fewer distinctions were being made. This result was also confirmed empirically in research on stereotypes (S. Crull and B. Bruton 1985; C. Owen et al. 1981).

Table 2.2 Changes in Social Distance

The social distance scale developed by Emory Bogardus has been a useful measure of people's feelings of hostility toward different racial and ethnic groups.

1926		*1966*		*1991*	
1. English	1.06	1. Americans (U.S. White)	1.07	1. Americans (U.S. White)	1.00
2. Americans (U.S. White)	1.10	2. English	1.14	2. English	1.08
3. Canadians	1.13	3. Canadians	1.15	3. French	1.16
4. Scots	1.13	4. French	1.36	4. Canadians	1.21
5. Irish	1.30	5. Irish	1.40	5. Italians	1.27
6. French	1.32	6. Swedish	1.42	6. Irish	1.30
7. Germans	1.46	7. Norwegians	1.50	7. Germans	1.36
8. Swedish	1.54	8. Italians	1.51	8. Swedish	1.38
9. Hollanders	1.56	9. Scots	1.53	9. Scots	1.50
10. Norwegians	1.59	10. Germans	1.54	10. Hollanders	1.56
11. Spanish	1.72	11. Hollanders	1.54	11. Norwegians	1.66
12. Finns	1.83	12. Finns	1.67	12. Native Americans	1.70
13. Russians	1.88	13. Greeks	1.82	13. Greeks	1.73
14. Italians	1.94	14. Spanish	1.93	14. Finns	1.73
15. Poles	2.01	15. Jews	1.97	15. Poles	1.74
16. Armenians	2.06	16. Poles	1.98	16. Russians	1.76
17. Czechs	2.08	17. Czechs	2.02	17. Spanish	1.77
18. Native Americans	2.38	18. Native Americans	2.12	18. Jews	1.84
19. Jews	2.39	19. Japanese Americans	2.14	19. Mexicans (U.S.)	1.84
20. Greeks	2.47	20. Armenians	2.18	20. Czechs	1.90
21. Mexicans	2.69	21. Filipinos	2.31	21. Americans (U.S. Black)	1.94
22. Mexican Americans	—	22. Chinese	2.34	22. Chinese	1.96
23. Japanese	2.80	23. Mexican Americans	2.37	23. Filipinos	2.04
24. Japanese Americans	—	24. Russians	2.38	24. Japanese (U.S.)	2.06
25. Filipinos	3.00	25. Japanese	2.41	25. Armenians	2.17
26. Negroes	3.28	26. Turks	2.48	26. Turks	2.23
27. Turks	3.30	27. Koreans	2.51	27. Koreans	2.24
28. Chinese	3.36	28. Mexicans	2.56	28. Mexicans	2.27
29. Koreans	3.60	29. Negroes	2.56	29. Japanese	2.37
30. Indians (from India)	3.91	30. Indians (from India)	2.62	30. Indians (from India)	2.39
Arithmetic mean	2.14	Arithmetic mean	1.92	Arithmetic mean	1.76
Spread in distance	2.85	Spread in distance	1.56	Spread in distance	1.39

Source: Emory S. Bogardus, "Comparing Racial Distance in Ethiopia, South Africa, and the United States," *Sociology and Social Research, 52* (January 1968). Copyright, University of Southern California, 1968. All rights reserved; and Tae-Hyon Song, "Social Contact and Ethnic Distance between Koreans and the U.S. Whites in the United States," paper, Macomb, Western Illinois University, 1991. Reprinted by permission.

Attitude Change

We hold certain images or stereotypes of each other, and we also may be more prejudiced toward some groups of people than toward others. However, is prejudice less than it used to be? The evidence we will see is mixed, with some indications of willingness to give up some old prejudices, while at the same time new negative attitudes emerge.

Over the years, nationwide surveys have consistently shown growing support by Whites for integration, even during the Southern resistance and Northern turmoil of the 1960s. National opinion surveys conducted from the 1950s through the 1990s, with few exceptions, show an increase in the number of Whites responding positively to hypothetical situations of increased contact with African Americans. For example, 30 percent of the Whites sampled in 1942 felt that Blacks should not attend separate schools, but by 1970, 74 percent supported integrated schools, and fully 93 percent responded in that manner in 1991 (J. Davis and T. Smith 1996).

Attitudes are still important, however, apart from behavior. A change of attitude may create a context in which legislative or behavioral change can occur. Such attitude changes leading to behavior changes did, in fact, occur in some areas during the 1960s. Changes in intergroup behavior mandated by law in housing, schools, public places of accommodation, and the workplace appear to be responsible for making some new kinds of interracial contact a social reality. Attitudes translate into votes, peer pressure, and political clout, each of which can facilitate efforts to undo racial inequality. However, attitudes can work in the opposite direction. In the mid-1990s, surveys showed resistance to affirmative action and immigration. Policy makers quickly developed new measures to respond to these concerns that were voiced largely by Whites.

When surveying White attitudes toward African Americans, two conclusions are inescapable. First, attitudes are subject to change, and in periods of dramatic social upheaval, dramatic shifts can occur within one generation. Second, less progress was made in the last part of the twentieth century than was made in the 1950s and 1960s. Researchers have variously termed these subtle forms of prejudice *symbolic racism,* or *modern racism,* or *laissez-faire racism.* People today may not be as openly racist or prejudiced as in the past in expressing the notion that they are inherently superior to others. Yet much of the opposition to policies related to eradicating poverty or immigration are often a smoke screen that hides the dislike of entire groups of racial and ethnic minorities (L. Bobo et al. 1997; J. McConahay and J. Hough 1976; D. Sears and D. Kinder 1971). In the 1990s, White attitudes hardened still further as issues such as affirmative action, immigration, and crime provoked strong emotions among members of this dominant group as well as among members of subordinate groups. Economically less successful groups, such as African Americans and Hispanics, have been credited with negative traits to such a

Despite efforts to block the move, Missouri reluctantly had to grant permission for a local chapter of the Ku Klux Klan to clean up a mile of that state's interstate highway. Eventually Missouri had to remove the sign because it kept being vandalized or stolen.

point that issues like welfare and crime are now viewed as "race issues." Besides making the resolution of very difficult social issues even harder, these views introduce another instance of blaming the victim. These perceptions come at a time when the willingness of government to address domestic ills is limited by increasing opposition to new taxes. Although there is some evidence that fewer Whites are consistently prejudiced on all issues from interracial marriage to school integration, it is also apparent that many Whites continue to endorse some anti-Black statements and that negative images are widespread as they relate to the major domestic issues of the 1990s (M. Gilens 1996; M. Hughes 1998; R. Schaefer 1996).

The Mood of the Subordinate Group

Sociologist W. E. B. Du Bois relates an experience from his youth in a largely White community in Massachusetts. He tells how, on one occasion, the boys and girls were exchanging cards and how everyone was having a lot of fun. One girl, a newcomer, refused his card as soon as she saw that Du Bois was Black. He wrote,

> *Then it dawned upon me with a certain suddenness that I was different from others . . . shut out from their world by a vast veil. I had therefore no desire to tear down that veil, to creep through; I held all beyond it in common contempt and lived above it in a region of blue sky and great wandering shadows (W. Du Bois 1903:2).*

In using the image of a "veil," Du Bois describes how members of subordinate groups learn that they are being treated differently. In his case and that of many others, this treatment leads to feelings of contempt toward all Whites that continue for a lifetime.

Opinion pollsters have been interested in White attitudes on racial issues longer than they have measured the views of subordinate groups. This neglect of minority attitudes reflects, in part, the bias of the White researchers. It also stems from the contention that the dominant group is more important to study because it is in a better position to act on its beliefs. The results of nationwide surveys conducted in the United States in 1999 offer insight into the sharply different attitudes of African Americans and of Whites (see Table 2.3).

Racial attitudes were also reassessed in the aftermath of the 1992 Los Angeles riots, one of the worst civil disturbances in the twentieth century—possibly the worst. With 53 dead and 2,300 injured, this outbreak gave racism front-page attention. The riots were precipitated by a jury's failure to find four Los Angeles police officers guilty of beating a Black man, Rodney King. Since the beating had been videotaped and replayed numerous times on television, most people felt that the police were guilty. In fact, a survey taken after the rioting began found that 100 percent of African Americans and 86 percent of Whites believed that the jury's verdict was wrong. Five years later, a survey showed that most Whites, Blacks, Hispanics, and Asians felt that Los Angeles had remained about the same since the riots. Of interest is that all four groups also were likely to see Whites as getting more economic power and to perceive Blacks and Hispanics as experiencing the most discrimination. Although the people of Los Angeles, regardless of racial and ethnic group, gen-

Table 2.3 Views of the United States, 1999

	Blacks	*Whites*
Black Americans will eventually be able to earn as much money as Whites.	42%	71%
A big problem today for Black families is:		
Not enough jobs paying a decent wage	68%	48%
Crime in their neighborhoods	60%	60%
Racism in society in general	56%	31%
Public schools not providing a good education	54%	42%

Source: From "Feeling Better About the Future." *Newsweek,* June 7, 1999.

erally felt that the city was healing emotionally from the terrible violence, it did not seem that there was much feeling of positive change. However, there was somewhat more disagreement on other issues. Two-thirds of Whites, compared with four-fifths of Blacks, saw the Rodney King beating as evidence of widespread racism. Blacks definitely saw race relations worsening in the wake of the riots. Fully 43 percent felt that relations were poor, compared with 17 percent of the Whites questioned (M. Baumann 1992; J. Merl 1997).

We have focused so far on what usually comes to mind when we think about prejudice: one group's hating another group. But there is another form of prejudice: a group may come to hate itself. Members of groups held in low esteem by society may, as a result, have low self-esteem themselves. Many social scientists once believed that members of subordinate groups hated themselves or, at least, had low self-esteem. Similarly, they argued that Whites had high self-esteem. *High self-esteem* means that an individual has fundamental respect for himself or herself, appreciates his or her own merits, and is aware of personal faults and will strive to overcome them. The research literature of the 1940s through the 1960s emphasized the low self-esteem of minorities. Usually, the subject was African Americans, but the argument has also been generalized to include any subordinate racial or ethnic group (J. Porter 1985; M. Rosenberg and R. Simmons 1971:9). This view is no longer accepted. Leonard Bloom (1971:68–69) cautions against assuming that minority status influences personality traits in either a good or a bad way. First, Bloom says, such assumptions may create a stereotype. We cannot describe a Black personality any more accurately than we can a White personality. Second, characteristics of minority-group members are not entirely the result of subordinate racial status; such characteristics are also influenced by low incomes, poor neighborhoods, and so forth. Third, many studies of personality imply that certain values are normal or preferable but that the values chosen are those of dominant groups.

If, as Bloom suggests, assessments of a subordinate group's personality are so prone to misjudgments, why has the belief in low self-esteem been so widely held? Much of the research rests on studies with preschool-age Black children asked to express preferences among dolls with different facial colors. Indeed, one such study, by psychologists Kenneth and Mamie Clark (1947), was cited in the arguments before the U.S. Supreme Court in the landmark 1954 case, *Brown* v. *Board of Education*. The Clarks' study showed that Black children preferred White dolls, a finding suggesting that the children had developed a negative self-image. Although subsequent doll studies (D. Powell-Hopson and D. Hopson 1988) have sometimes shown Black children's preference for white-faced dolls, other social scientists contend that this preference shows a realization of what most commercially sold dolls look like rather than a documentation of low self-esteem.

Because African American children, as well as other subordinate groups' children, can realistically see that Whites have more power and resources and therefore rate Whites higher does not mean that they personally feel inferior. Indeed, studies, even with children, show that when the self-images of middle-class or affluent African Americans are measured, their feelings of self-esteem are more positive than those of comparable Whites (W. Cross 1991; M. Hughes and D. Demo 1989; R. Martinez and R. Dukes 1991; C. Raymond 1991).

Identity is a major issue for people who are defined as being in a subordinate group. For young Asian Americans, in particular, life in the Untied States is often a struggle for one's identity. Sometimes that struggle means finding a role in White America, other times finding a place among Asian Americans collectively and then locating oneself within one's own racial or ethnic community. In Listen to Their Voices, we become acquainted with Shanlon Wu, a Chinese American who literally searched the United States for Chinese American heroes.

LISTEN TO THEIR VOICES

In Search of Bruce Lee's Grave

Shanlon Wu

It's Saturday morning in Seattle, and I am driving to visit Bruce Lee's grave. I have been in the city for only a couple of weeks and so drive two blocks past the cemetery before realizing that I've passed it. I double back and turn through the large wrought-iron gate, past a sign that reads: "Open to 9 p.m. or dusk, whichever comes first."

It's a sprawling cemetery, with winding roads leading in all directions. I feel silly trying to find his grave with no guidance. I think that my search for his grave is similar to my search for Asian heroes in America.

I was born in 1959, an Asian-American in Westchester County, N.Y. During my childhood there were no Asian sports stars. On television I can recall only that most pathetic of Asian characters, Hop Sing, the Cartwright family houseboy on "Bonanza." But in my adolescence there was Bruce.

I was 14 years old when I first saw "Enter the Dragon," the granddaddy of martial-arts movies. Bruce had died suddenly at the age of 32 of cerebral edema, an excess of fluid in the brain, just weeks before the release of the film. Between the ages of 14 and 17, I saw "Enter the Dragon" 22 times before I stopped counting. During those years I collected Bruce Lee posters, putting them up at all angles in my bedroom. I took up Chinese martial arts and spent hours comparing my physique with his. . . .

My parents, who immigrated to America and had become professors at Hunter College, tolerated my behavior, but seemed puzzled at my admiration of an "entertainer." My father jokingly tried to compare my obsession with Bruce to his boyhood worship of Chinese folk-tale heroes.

"I read them just like you read American comic books," he said.

But my father's heroes could not be mine; they came from an ancient literary tradition, not comic books. He and my mother had grown up in a land where they belonged to the majority. I could not adopt their childhood and they were wise enough not to impose it upon me.

Although I never again experienced the kind of blind hero worship I felt for Bruce, my need to find heroes remained strong.

In college, I discovered the men of the 442d Regimental Combat Team, a United States Army all-Japanese unit in World War II. Allowed to fight only against Europeans, they suffered heavy casualties while their families were put in internment camps. Their motto was "Go for Broke."

I saw them as Asians in a Homeric epic, the protagonists of a Shakespearean tragedy; I knew no Eastern myths to infuse them with. They embodied my own need to prove myself in the Caucasian world. I imagined how their American-born flesh and muscle must have resembled mine: epicanthic folds set in strong faces nourished on milk and beef. I thought how much they had proved where there was so little to prove.

After college, I competed as an amateur boxer in an attempt to find my self-image in the ring. It didn't work. My fighting was only an attempt to copy Bruce's movies. What I needed was instruction on how to live. I quit boxing after a year and went to law school.

I was an anomaly there: a would-be Asian litigator. I had always liked to argue and found I liked doing it in front of people even more. When I won the first-year moot court competition in law school, I asked an Asian classmate if he thought I was the first Asian to win. He laughed and told me I was probably the only Asian to even compete.

The law-firm interviewers always seemed surprised that I wanted to litigate. "Aren't you interested in Pacific Rim trade?" they asked.

"My Chinese isn't good enough," I quipped.

My pat response seemed to please them. It certainly pleased me. I thought I'd found a place of my own—a place where the law would insulate me from the pressure of defining my Asian maleness. I sensed the possibility of merely being myself. . . .

The hunger is eased this gray morning in Seattle. After asking directions from a policeman—Japanese—I easily locate Bruce's grave. The headstone is red granite with a small picture etched into it. The picture is very Hollywood—Bruce wears dark glasses—and I think the calligraphy looks a bit sloppy. Two tourists stop but leave quickly after glancing at me.

I realize I am crying. Bruce's grave seems very small in comparison to his place in my boyhood. So small in comparison to my need for heroes. Seeing his grave, I understand how large the hole in my life has been, and how desperately I'd sought to fill it.

I had sought an Asian hero to emulate. But none of my choices quite fit me. Their lives were defined through heroic tasks—they had villains to defeat and wars to fight—while my life seemed merely a struggle to define myself.

But now I see how that very struggle has defined me. I must be my own hero even as I learn to treasure those who have gone before.

Source: Shanlon Wu in *New York Times Magazine,* April 15, 1990.

Intergroup Hostility

Prejudice is as diverse as the nation's population. It exists not only between dominant and subordinate peoples but also among specific subordinate groups. Unfortunately, until recently there was little research on this subject except for a few social distance scales administered to racial and ethnic minorities.

A 1993 national survey conducted for the National Conference of Christians and Jews (1994) revealed that, like Whites, many African Americans, Hispanic Americans, and Asian Americans held prejudiced and stereotypical views of other racial and ethnic minority groups. The survey made the following findings:

- Majorities of Black, Hispanic, and Asian American respondents agreed that Whites are "bigoted, bossy, and unwilling to share power." Majorities of these non-White groups also believed that they had less opportunity than Whites to obtain a good education, a skilled job, or decent housing.
- Forty-six percent of Hispanic Americans and 42 percent of African Americans agreed that Asian Americans are "unscrupulous, crafty, and devious in business."
- Sixty-eight percent of Asian Americans and 49 percent of African Americans believed that Hispanic Americans "tend to have bigger families than they are able to support."
- Thirty-one percent of Asian Americans and 26 percent of Hispanic Americans agreed that African Americans "want to live on welfare."

Officials of the National Conference of Christians and Jews expressed concern about the extent to which subordinate-group members agreed with negative stereotypes about other subordinate groups. At the same time, the survey also revealed positive views of major racial and ethnic minorities:

- More than 80 percent of respondents admired Asian Americans for "placing a high value on intellectual and professional achievement" and "having strong family ties."
- A majority of all groups surveyed agreed that Hispanic Americans "take deep pride in their culture and work hard to achieve a better life."
- Large majorities from all groups stated that African Americans "have made a valuable contribution to American society and will work hard when given a chance."

Many people are surprised to see ill feelings expressed between subordinate groups. From the dominant-group perspective, these feelings can be very functional. For example, in the aftermath of the 1992 Los Angeles riots, much of the discussion focused on relations between Korean American merchants and their African American and Hispanic clientele. Also, attention was focused on economic competition for jobs between Hispanics and African Americans. In some respects, as these discussions continued, they served to direct attention away from the issues that precipitated the riots in the first place—the treatment by the criminal-justice system of Black people as displayed by the acquittal of four White police officers following the Rodney King beating (J. Merl 1997; J. Miles 1992).

Reducing Prejudice

Focusing on how to eliminate prejudice involves an explicit value judgment: prejudice is wrong and causes problems both for those who are prejudiced and for their victims. The obvious way to eliminate prejudice is to eliminate its causes: the desire to exploit, the fear of being threatened, and the need to blame others for one's own failure. These causes might be eliminated by personal therapy, but therapy, even if it worked for every individual, is no solution for a society. Such a program would not be feasible because of its prohibitive cost and because it would have to be compulsory, which would violate civil rights. Furthermore, many of those in need of such therapy would not acknowledge their problem—the first step in effective therapy.

The answer appears to rest with programs directed at society as a whole. Prejudice is attacked indirectly when discrimination is attacked. Despite prevailing beliefs to the contrary, we can legislate against prejudice; statutes and decisions do affect attitudes. In the past, people firmly believed that laws could not overcome norms, especially racist ones. Recent history, especially after the civil rights movement began in 1954, has challenged that common wisdom. Laws and court rulings that have equalized the treatment of Blacks and Whites have led people to reevaluate their beliefs about what is right and wrong. The increasing tolerance by Whites during the civil rights period from 1954 to 1965 seems to support this conclusion.

Much research has been done to determine how to change negative attitudes toward groups of people. The most encouraging findings point to the mass media, education, and intergroup contact.

Mass Media and Education

The research on the mass media and education consists of two types: (1) research performed in artificially (experimentally) created situations and (2) studies examining the influence on attitudes of motion pictures, television, and advertisements. Leaflets, radio commercials, comic books, billboards, and classroom posters bombard people with the message of racial harmony. Television audiences watch a public service message that for thirty seconds shows smiling White and African American infants reaching out toward each other. Law-enforcement and military personnel attend in-service training sessions that preach the value of a pluralistic society. Does this publicity do any good? Do these programs make any difference?

Most but not all studies show that well-constructed programs do have some positive effect in reducing prejudice, at least temporarily. The reduction is rarely as much as one might wish, however. The difficulty is that a single program is insufficient to change lifelong habits, especially if little is done to reinforce the program's message once it ends. Persuasion to respect other groups does not operate in a clear field because, in their ordinary environments, individuals are still subjected to situations that promote prejudicial feelings. Children and adults are encouraged to laugh at Polish jokes, or a Black adolescent may be discouraged by peers from befriending a White youth. All this behavior serves to undermine the effectiveness of prejudice-reduction programs (G. Allport 1979). Study results indicate the influence of educational programs designed specifically to reduce prejudice. For example, a special program in a small country town in Australia helped to reduce negative stereotypes of Aborigines, that nation's native people (R. Donovan and S. Levers 1993). However, studies consistently document that increased formal education, regardless of content, is associated with racial tolerance. Research data show that more highly educated people are more likely to indicate respect and liking for groups different from themselves. Why should more years of schooling have this effect? It could be that more education gives a broader outlook and makes a person less likely to endorse myths that sustain racial prejudice. Formal education teaches the importance of qualifying statements and the need at least to question rigid categorizations, if not to reject them altogether. Another explanation is that education does not actually reduce intolerance but simply makes individuals more careful about revealing it. Formal education may simply instruct individuals in the appropriate responses, which in some settings could even be prejudiced views. Despite the lack of a clear-cut explanation, either theory suggests that the continued trend toward a better-educated population will contribute to a reduction in overt prejudice.

However, the education experience at the college level may not reduce prejudice uniformly. For example, some White students will come to hold the belief that minority students did not earn their admission into college. Students may feel threatened to see large groups of people of different racial and cultural backgrounds congregating together and forming their own groups. Racist confrontations do occur outside the classroom and, even if they do involve only a few people, the events themselves will be watched by many. Therefore, there are aspects of the college experience that may only foster the "we" and "they" attitude (R. Schaefer 1986, 1996).

Education is not limited to formal schooling; increasingly, many forms of instruction are offered in the workplace. Remedies for intolerance can be taught there as well. With the entry of women and minority men into nontraditional work settings, training and support programs take on increased importance. Generally, when minorities enter an organization, they are thinly represented. Education programs have been introduced so that management does not treat these pioneers as golden (can do no wrong) or as hopeless cases doomed to failure (T. Pettigrew and M. Martin 1987).

The mass media, like schooling, may reduce prejudice without the need for specially designed programs. Television, radio, motion pictures, newspapers, and magazines present only a portion of real life, but what effect do they have on prejudice if the content is racist or antiracist, sexist or antisexist? As with measuring the influence of programs designed to reduce prejudice, coming to strong conclusions on the mass media's effect is hazardous, but the evidence points to a measurable effect. The 1915 movie *The Birth of a Nation* depicts African Americans unfavorably and glorifies the Ku Klux Klan. A study of Illinois schoolchildren has shown that watching the movie made them more unfavorably inclined toward African Americans than they had been, a negative effect that persisted even five months later when the children were retested. Conversely, the 1947 movie *Gentleman's Agreement,* which takes a strong stand against anti-Semitism, appears to have softened the anti-Semitic feelings of its audience (Commission on Civil Rights 1977, 1980).

Recent research has examined the influence of television because it commands the widest viewing audience among children and adolescents. A 1988 study found that almost a third of high school students felt that television entertainment was "an accurate representation" of African American "real life" (S. Lichter and L. Lichter 1988). Many programs, such as *Amos n' Andy,* or films with "dumb Injuns," which depict subordinate groups in stereotyped, demeaning roles, are no longer shown. Blacks and members of other subordinate groups are now more likely than before to appear in programs and commercials. As a result of the networks' greater sensitivity to the presentation of minority groups, people now see more balanced portrayals.

Television programs showing positive African American family life, as in *Family Matters, Living Single,* and *The Cosby Show,* have been quite a change from *Diff'rent Strokes* and *Webster,* which promoted the notion that African American orphans are best off in White homes. How far have the mass media really come? We will consider that question in a case study in the next section.

Television: A Case Study of the Media

How does television today approach race and ethnicity, and how do the races approach television? For one thing, we know that Whites and Blacks watch different programs. Of the top twenty television programs watched in Black households in the 1999 television season, only six were on the top fif-

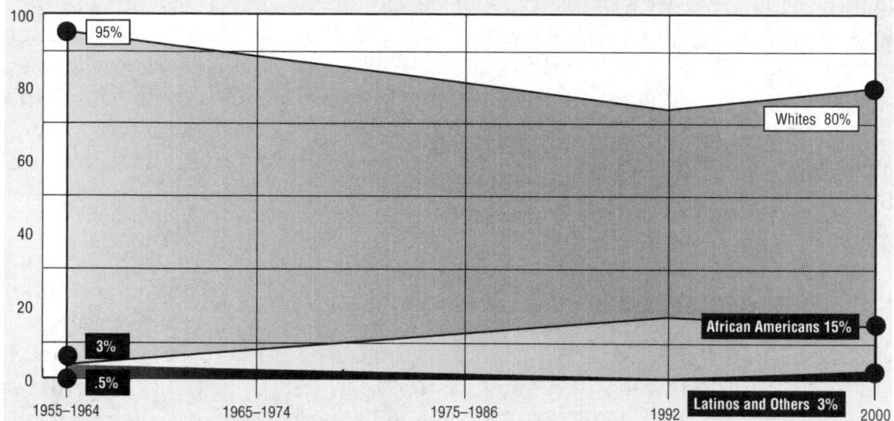

Figure 2.3 Television's Ethnic Portrayals
An analysis of prime-time entertainment (excluding reality-based syndicated series) shows an actual decline in the representation of Hispanics and an increase in the representation of African Americans.

Source: From "Portrayals of Latinos on TV Regressing" by Rick DuBrow. T*he Los Angeles Times,* September 7, 1994. Reprinted by permission.

teen list of all households—programs such as *Monday Night Football* and *Sixty Minutes.* As Figure 2.3 shows, there has been very uneven progress in the appearance of African Americans and other minorities over the last forty-five years. The overwhelming majority of Black actors on prime-time television are employed in comedic roles or as criminals; no Black dramatic series has lasted a season, and very few are even given a chance. Asians and Hispanics have an even greater image problem in contemporary television (G. Levin 1999).

In late spring 1999, as the television networks prepared their schedules for the 1999–2000 season, an article in the *Los Angeles Times* hit the broadcasting industry like a bombshell. In every new prime-time series—twenty-six of them—set to debut in the coming season, the *Times* reported, all the leading characters, as well as the vast majority of the supporting casts, would be White. The public response was immediate. The NAACP, alarmed by the "virtual whitewash in programming," threatened a lawsuit, and a national coalition of Latino groups urged viewers to boycott network TV (G. Braxton 1999:F10).

Why the underreperesentation? Incredibly, network executives seemed surprised by the news of the all-White season. Producers, writers, executives, and advertisers blamed each other for the oversight. In recent years, the rise of both cable TV and the Internet has fragmented the broadcast entertainment market, siphoning viewers away from the general-audience sitcoms and dramas of the past. With the proliferation of cable channels such as Black Entertainment Television (BET) and the Spanish-language Univision, and web sites that cater to every imaginable taste, there no longer seems a need for broadly popular series such as *The Cosby Show*, whose tone and content appealed to Whites as well as Blacks in a way that the newer series do not. The result of these sweeping technological changes has been a sharp divergence in viewer preferences.

While BET and Univision were grabbing minority audiences and offering new outlets for minority talent, network executives and writers remained overwhelmingly White. It is not surprising that these mainstream writers and producers, most of whom live far from ethnically and racially diverse inner-city neighborhoods, tend to write and prefer stories about people like themselves. Marc Hirschfeld, an NBC executive, claims that some White producers have told him they don't know how to write for Black characters. Steven Bochko, producer of *NYPD Blue,* is a rare exception. Bochko's series, *City of Angels,* has a cast that is mostly non-White, like the people Bochko grew up with in an inner-city neighborhood.

The networks' first response to the bad press was to move some token Black or ethnic characters into the casts of the all-White series set for the fall season. In the long run, industry observers believe, the networks will need to integrate their ranks before they achieve true diversity in programming. Adonis Hoffman, director of the Corporate Policy Institute, has urged network executives to open up their studios and boardrooms to minorities. Hoffman thinks such a move would empower Black writers and producers to present a true-to-life portrait of African Americans. Why should it matter that minority groups aren't visible on network television, if they are well represented on BET and Univision? The answer is that if they are not, Whites as well as minorities will see a distorted picture of their society every time they turn on network TV. The color line that W. E. B. Du Bois spoke of persists well into the twenty-first century and on television (A. Hoffman 1997; also see B. Lowry et al. 1999; D. Wood 2000).

Equal-Status Contact

An impressive number of research studies have confirmed the **contact hypothesis,** a hypothesis that states that intergroup contact between people of equal status in harmonious circumstances will cause them to become less prejudiced and to abandon previously held stereotypes. Most studies indicate that such contact also improves the attitude of subordinate-group members. The importance of equal status in the interaction cannot be stressed enough. If a Puerto Rican is abused by his employer, little interracial harmony is promoted. Similarly, the situation in which contact occurs must be pleasant, making a positive evaluation likely for both individuals. Contact between two

Copley News Service/Cartoonist, Michael Ramirez

nurses, one Black and the other White, who are competing for one vacancy as a supervisor, may lead to greater racial hostility (R. Schaefer 1976).

The key factor in reducing hostility in addition to equal-status contact is the presence of a common goal. If people are in competition, as already noted, contact may heighten tension. However, bringing people together to share a common task has been shown to reduce ill feeling when these people belong to different racial, ethnic, or religious groups. A 1994 study of Mexican and El Salvadoran immigrants in Houston found that contact with African Americans generally improved relations, and the absence of contact tended to foster ambivalent, even negative, attitudes (S. McCollom 1996; M. Sherif and C. Sherif 1969; R. Slavin 1985).

In a 1992 study of housing integration, researchers examined the harassment, threats, and fears that Blacks face in White schools in which low-income Black students are in the minority. Did these African American youth experience acceptance, friendships, and positive interactions with their White classmates? The researchers interviewed youth who had moved to the suburbs and those who had relocated within the city of Chicago under the auspices of a federally funded program. In this program, low-income Black families received housing subsidies that allowed them to move from inner-city housing projects into apartment buildings occupied largely by middle-income Whites and located in middle-income, mostly White suburbs. The study found that these low-income Black youth did experience some harassment and some difficulty in gaining acceptance in the suburban schools, but the findings also suggested that they eventually experienced great success in social integration and that they felt they fit into their new environments (J. Rosenbaum and P. Meaden 1992).

As African Americans and other subordinate groups slowly gain access to better-paying and more responsible jobs, the contact hypothesis takes on greater significance. Usually, the availability of equal-status interaction is taken for granted, yet in everyday life intergroup contact does not conform to the equal-status idea of the contact hypothesis as often as we are assured by researchers who hope to see a lessening of tension. Furthermore, in a highly segregated society such as the United States, contact, especially between Whites and minorities, tends to be brief and superficial (W. Ford 1986; Sigelman et al. 1996).

Conclusion

This chapter has examined theories of prejudice and measurements of its extent. Prejudice should not be confused with discrimination. The two concepts are not the same: prejudice refers to negative attitudes, and discrimination refers to negative behavior toward a group.

Several theories try to explain why prejudice exists. Some emphasize economic concerns (the exploitation and scapegoating theories), whereas other approaches stress personality or normative factors. No one explanation is sufficient. Surveys conducted in the United States over the past sixty years point to a reduction of prejudice as measured by the willingness to express stereotypes or maintain social distance. Survey data also show that many Whites and Blacks are still intolerant of each other. Prejudice involving Hispanic groups, Asian Americans, and relatively large recent immigrant groups such as Arab Americans and Muslim Americans is well documented. Issues such as immigration and affirmative action reemerge and cause bitter resentment. Furthermore, ill feelings exist among subordinate groups in schools, in the streets, and in the workplace.

Equal-status contact may reduce hostility among groups. However, in a highly segregated society defined by inequality, such opportunities are not typical. The mass media can be of value in reducing discrimination but have not done enough and may even intensify ill feeling by promoting stereotypical images. Although strides are being made in increasing the appearance of minorities in positive roles in television and films, one would not realize how diverse our society is by sampling advertisements, programs, or movies. Even though we can be encouraged by the techniques available to reduce intergroup hostility, there are still sizable segments of the population who do not want to live in integrated neighborhoods, who do not want to work for or be led by someone of a different race, and who certainly object to the idea of their relatives' marrying outside their own group. People still harbor stereotypes toward one another, and this tendency includes racial and ethnic minorities having stereotypes about one another (C. Herring and C. Amissah 1997).

Chapter 3 outlines the effects of discrimination. Discrimination's costs are high to both dominant and subordinate groups. With that fact in mind, we will examine some techniques for reducing discrimination.

Key Terms

authoritarian personality 48
Bogardus scale 55
caste approach 49
contact hypothesis 68
discrimination 45
ethnocentrism 42
ethnophaulism 44
exploitation theory 49
hate crime 42
normative approach 50
prejudice 44
scapegoat 47

Review Questions

1. How are prejudice and discrimination both related and unrelated to each other?
2. How do theories of prejudice relate to different expressions of prejudice?
3. Besides Arab Americans and American Muslims, identify other groups recently subjected to prejudice, perhaps in your own community.
4. Why does prejudice develop even towards groups with whom people have little contact?

Critical Thinking

1. Identify stereotypes associated with a group of people such as the elderly or people with physical handicaps.
2. What social issues do you think are most likely to engender hostility along racial and ethnic lines?
3. Consider the television programs you have watched the most. In terms of race and ethnicity, how well do the programs you watch tend to reflect the diversity of the population in the United States?

Internet Exercises

1. This chapter details the connection between the mass media and education, particularly comparing the limitations and possibilities of television as a tool for reducing prejudice. A new attempt to achieve such a goal is being offered in part by the Public Broadcasting System, entitled "Television Race Initiative" (TRI). Visit the web site for PBS at (http://www.pbs.org/pov/tvraceinitiative/) to critically assess this initiative. What are the long-term goals of TRI? What approaches and strategies are being used? What topics are covered by the nearly dozen programs airing as part of the initiative? (You can also link to each television program's individual web page for more information.) Which of these stories/documentaries do you find the most interesting? Why? Can you think of a current or historical event that would be well suited to TRI? If you had to choose, which

one of the dozen programs would you select as having the most potential for education and for reducing prejudice? Why this selection? Considering what you have learned in this chapter, what are the potential challenges and limitations of initiatives like TRI? How would a functionalist view the use of television as a tool for reducing prejudice? How would a conflict theorist view the same issue? Do you believe that television can be used to promote equality and understanding? Why, or why not?

2. Hate crimes are a violent manifestation of prejudice along racial, religious, ethnic, and sexual orientation lines. To expand your understanding of the social facts regarding hate crimes, read the article by Ricco Villanueva Siasoco and the links/statistics found at infoplease.com (http://www.infoplease.com/spot/hatecrimes.html). What are hate crimes? What are the goals of the Hate Crimes Prevention Act of 1999? How does this act change already existing hate crime legislation? What are some of the key arguments made by those who are in opposition to hate crime legislation? What are some of the key arguments offered by those who are in support of such laws? Where do you stand on the issue, and why? How is the Internet being used by hate groups? Next, utilize the "White House Initiative on Hate Crimes" and "Summary of Hate Crime Statistics" links on the page to answer the following: What is the President's One America initiative? What are the policies and goals of this plan? What is the current "Face of America" according to the White House site, and how will the demographic character of the United States change by the year 2050? Do you think One America can help reduce the frequency of hate crimes? Why, or why not? Which racial group and which religious group are most often the victims of hate crimes? Why do you think that this is the case? What can be done to alleviate this social problem?

3. The American Civil Liberties Union Freedom Network (http://www.aclu.org/profiling) offers an examination of the issue of racial profiling. What is racial profiling, and what do the initials DWB refer to? Reflect on the stories found in the "Tales of DWB" section and the information provided in the "ACLU's Special Report on Racial Profiling" by David A. Harris. Which story surprised you the most? How would you react if you were the victim of a similar situation? What myths and stereotypes about crime and drug trafficking does the special report seek to dismiss? Which key court cases are listed in the special report? What events and issues do these cases revolve around? What statistics and data are used in the special report to support its conclusions? Read "The Personal and Societal Costs" section of the report. What are some of the consequences—to both individuals and the wider society—of racial profiling according to the report? What has been the variety of responses by law enforcement officials to charges of racial profiling? What evidence is used to support their responses? In what ways does the discussion of stereotypes in this chapter apply to racial profiling? What realistic and specific suggestions would you make to help solve this problem? How do your ideas compare with the five suggestions listed in the special report? What is your opinion of those suggestions on the web site?

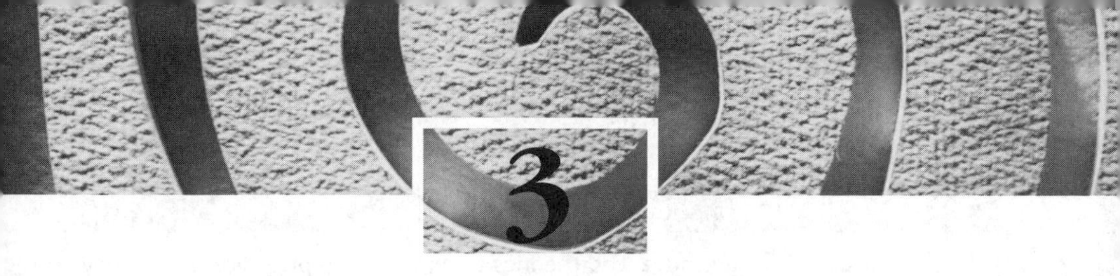

3

Discrimination

CHAPTER OUTLINE

HIGHLIGHTS

Just as social scientists have advanced theories to explain why prejudice exists, they have also presented explanations of why discrimination occurs. Social scientists look more and more at the manner in which institutions, not individuals, discriminate. Institutional discrimination describes a pattern in social institutions that produces or perpetuates inequalities, even if individuals in the society do not intend to be racist or sexist. Income data document that gaps do exist among racial and ethnic groups. Historically, attempts have been made to reduce discrimination, usually as a result of strong lobbying efforts by minorities themselves. Patterns of total discrimination make solutions particularly difficult for people in the informal economy or the underclass. Affirmative action was designed to equalize opportunity but has encountered significant resentment by those who charge that it constitutes reverse discrimination. Despite many efforts to end discrimination, glass ceilings and glass walls remain in the workplace.

Discrimination can take many forms. As the next two incidents indicate, discrimination can be direct, or it can be the result of a complex combination of factors. It can lead to indignities or to death.

Lawrence Otis Graham (1995) had "arrived" by the standards of most people in the United States. He was a graduate of Harvard Law School, was married, and had become a well-regarded member of a Manhattan law firm. But he was also Black. Despite his success in securing clients for himself and his firm, Graham had noticed that White attorneys seemed to get a jump on him because of their associations with corporate leaders at private clubs. By tradition, the clubs were exclusively White. Graham decided to take time out from his law firm to learn more about the workings of these private clubs that allowed some Whites to mingle in an informal atmosphere and so contributed to their establishing networks. These networks in turn allowed people to establish contacts that advanced their success in the business world. Rather than present himself as a successful Ivy League college graduate to become a member, he presented himself as a working-class African American seeking a job as a waiter. From the vantage point of a server, Graham figured he could observe the network of these predominantly White country-club members. This was not to be the case. At club after club, he was not able to get a job. Despite all sorts of encouragement when he talked to employers over the phone, he was denied a job when he presented himself and the employers saw that this articulate, well-mannered young man was Black. Eventually he obtained a job as a busboy, clearing tables in a club where the White servers commented that he could do their job better than they could.

Cynthia Wiggins was also African American, but she lived in a different world from that of Lawrence Otis Graham. She was a seventeen-year-old sin-

Harvard-educated lawyer Lawrence Otis Graham sought a position as a waiter in exclusive clubs to learn more about contemporary discrimination.

gle mother struggling to make a living. She had sought jobs near her home but had found no employment opportunities. Eventually she found employment as a cashier at a mall food mart, but it was far from her home, and she could not afford a car. Still, she was optimistic and looked forward to marrying the man to whom she was engaged. In 1995, she made the fifty-minute bus ride from her predominantly Black neighborhood in Buffalo, New York, to her job at the Galleria, a fancy suburban shopping mall. Every day, charter buses unloaded shoppers from as far away as Canada, but city buses were not allowed on mall property. The bus Wiggins rode was forced to stop across the lot and across a seven-lane highway without sidewalks. On a December day, with the roadway lined with 8 feet of snow, she tried to cross the highway, only to be struck by a dump truck. She died three weeks later. Subsequently, investigation showed that the bus company had been trying to arrange for the bus to stop in the mall parking lot but that the shopping center authorities had blocked the move. Prior to the incident, the mall said they would consider allowing in suburban buses but not public buses from the city. As one mall store owner put it, "You'll never see an inner-city bus on the mall premises" (E. Barnes 1996:33).

Discrimination has a long history, right up to the present, of taking its toll on people. For some, like Lawrence Otis Graham, discrimination meant being reminded that even when you do try to seek employment, you may be treated like a second-class citizen. For others, like Cynthia Wiggins, discrimination meant suffering for the unjust decisions made in a society that quietly discriminated. Wiggins lost her life not because anyone actually intended to kill her but because certain decisions made it more likely that an inner-city resident would be an accident victim. Despite legislative and court efforts to eliminate discrimination, members of dominant and subordinate groups pay a price for continued intolerance.

Understanding Discrimination

Discrimination is the denial of opportunities and equal rights to individuals and groups because of prejudice or for other arbitrary reasons. Some people in the United States find it difficult to see discrimination as a widespread phenomenon. "After all," it is often said, "these minorities drive cars, hold jobs, own their homes, and even go to college." Regardless of this observation, discrimination is not rare. An understanding of discrimination in modern industrialized societies such as the United States must begin by distinguishing between relative and absolute deprivation.

Relative versus Absolute Deprivation

Conflict theorists have said correctly that it is not absolute, unchanging standards that determine deprivation and oppression. It is crucial that, although minority groups may be viewed as having adequate or even good incomes, housing, health care, and educational opportunities, it is the position of minority groups relative to that of some other group that offers evidence of discrimination.

The term **relative deprivation** is defined as the conscious feeling of a negative discrepancy between legitimate expectations and present actualities. After settling in the United States, immigrants often enjoy better material comforts and more political freedom than it was possible to have in their old country. If they compare themselves with most other people in the United States, however, they will feel deprived, because, even though their standard has improved, the immigrants still perceive relative deprivation.

Absolute deprivation, on the other hand, implies a fixed standard based on a minimum level of subsistence below which families should not be expected to exist. Discrimination does not necessarily mean absolute deprivation. A Japanese American who is promoted to a management position may still be a victim of discrimination, if she or he had been passed over for years because of corporate reluctance to place an Asian American in a highly visible position.

Dissatisfaction is also likely to arise from feelings of relative deprivation. Those members of a society who feel most frustrated and disgruntled by the social and economic conditions of their lives are not necessarily worse off in an objective sense. Social scientists have long recognized that what is most significant is how people perceive their situations. Karl Marx pointed out that, although the misery of the workers was important in reflecting their oppressed state, so, too, was their position relative to that of the ruling class. In 1847, Marx wrote that

> *Although the enjoyment of the workers has risen, the social satisfaction that they have has fallen in comparison with the increased enjoyment of the capitalist. (Marx and Engels 1955:94)*

This statement explains why the groups or individuals who are most vocal and best organized against discrimination are not necessarily in the worst economic and social situation. They are likely, however, to be those who most strongly perceive that, relative to others, they are not receiving their fair share. Resistance to perceived discrimination, rather than the actual amount of absolute discrimination, is the key.

Total Discrimination

Social scientists—and increasingly policy makers—have begun to use the concept of total discrimination. **Total discrimination,** as shown in Figure 3.1, refers to current discrimination operating in the labor market *and* past discrimination. Past discrimination experienced by an individual includes the relatively poorer education and job experience of racial and ethnic minorities compared with that of many White Americans. When one is considering discrimination, therefore, it is not enough to focus only on what is being done to people now. Sometimes a person may be dealt with fairly but may still be at a disadvantage. These disadvantages may stem from poorer health care, inferior counseling in the school system, less access to books and other educational materials, or a poor job record resulting from absences to take care of brothers and sisters.

In Listen to their Voices, we find that Patricia Williams, a nationally recognized legal scholar, was the object of discrimination herself, as she sought to secure housing. Little wonder, given that national studies show that Whites are seven times as likely to receive conventional mortgages as African Americans and Latinos (ACORN 1998). We find another variation of this past-in-present discrimination when apparently nondiscriminatory present practices have negative effects because of prior intentionally biased practices. Although unions that purposely discriminated against minority members in the past may no longer do so, some people are still prevented from achieving higher

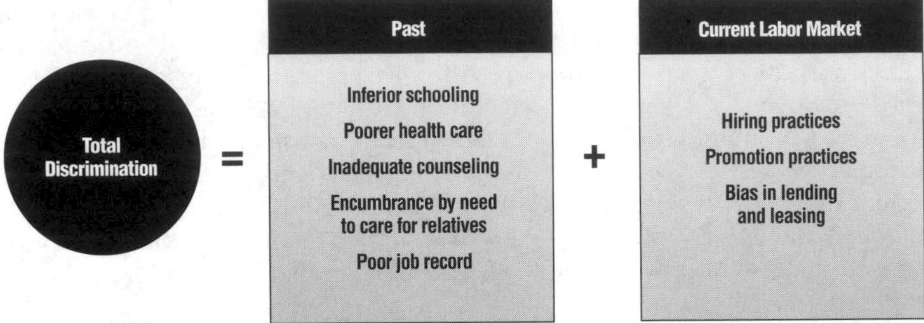

Figure 3.1 Total Discrimination

levels of seniority because of those past practices. Personnel records include a cumulative record that is vital in promotion and selection for desirable assignments. Blatantly discriminatory judgments and recommendations in the past, however, remain part of a person's record.

Institutional Discrimination

Individuals practice discrimination in one-to-one encounters, whereas institutions practice discrimination through their daily operations. Indeed, a consensus is growing today that this institutional discrimination is more significant than that committed by prejudiced individuals.

Social scientists are particularly concerned with the ways in which patterns of employment, education, criminal justice, housing, health care, and government operations maintain the social significance of race and ethnicity. **Institutional discrimination** refers to the denial of opportunities and equal rights to individuals and groups that results from the normal operations of a society.

Civil rights activist Stokely Carmichael and political scientist Charles Hamilton are credited with introducing the concept of *institutional racism*. Individual discrimination refers to overt acts of individual Whites against individual Blacks; Carmichael and Hamilton reserved the term *institutional racism* for covert acts committed collectively against an entire group. From this perspective, discrimination can take place without an individual's intending to deprive others of privileges and even without the individual's being aware that others are being deprived (K. Ture and C. Hamilton 1992).

How can discrimination be widespread and unconscious at the same time? The following represent a few documented examples of institutional discrimination:

1. Standards for assessing credit risks work against African Americans and Hispanics seeking to establish businesses, because many lack conventional credit references. Businesses in low-income areas where these groups often reside also have much higher insurance costs.

LISTEN TO THEIR VOICES

Of Race and Risk

Patricia J. Williams

Several years ago, at a moment when I was particularly tired of the unstable lifestyle that academic careers sometimes require, I surprised myself and bought a real house. Because the house was in a state other than the one where I was living at the time, I obtained my mortgage by telephone. I am a prudent little squirrel when it comes to things financial, always tucking away stores of nuts for the winter, and so I meet the criteria of a quite good credit risk. My loan was approved almost immediately.

A little while later, the contract came in the mail. Among the papers the bank forwarded were forms documenting compliance with the Fair Housing Act, which outlaws racial discrimination in the housing market. The act monitors lending practices to prevent banks from redlining—redlining being the phenomenon whereby banks circle certain neighborhoods on the map and refuse to lend in those areas. It is a practice for which the bank with which I was dealing, unbeknownst to me, had been cited previously—as well as since. In any event, the act tracks the race of all banking customers to prevent such discrimination. Unfortunately, and with the creative variability of all illegality, some banks also use the racial information disclosed on the fair housing forms to engage in precisely the discrimination the law seeks to prevent.

I should repeat that to this point my entire mortgage transaction had been conducted by telephone. I should also note that I speak a Received Standard English, regionally marked as Northeastern perhaps, but not easily identifiable as black. With my credit history, my job as a law professor and, no doubt, with my accent, I am not only middle class but apparently match the cultural stereotype of a good white person. It is thus, perhaps, that the loan officer of the bank, whom I had never met, had checked off the box on the fair housing form indicating that I was white.

Race shouldn't matter, I suppose, but it seemed to in this case, so I took a deep breath, crossed out "white" and sent the contract back. That will teach them to presume too much, I thought. A done deal, I assumed. But suddenly the transaction came to a screeching halt. The bank wanted more money, more points, a higher rate of interest. Suddenly I found myself facing great resistance and much more debt. To make a long story short, I threatened to sue under the act in question, the bank quickly backed down and I procured the loan on the original terms.

What was interesting about all this was that the reason the bank gave for its new-found recalcitrance was not race, heaven forbid. No, it was all about economics and increased risk: The reason they gave was that property values in that neighborhood were suddenly falling. They wanted more money to buffer themselves against the snappy winds of projected misfortune.

Initially, I was surprised, confused. The house was in a neighborhood that was extremely stable. I am an extremely careful shopper; I had uncovered absolutely nothing to indicate that prices were falling. It took my realtor to make me see the light. "Don't you get it," he sighed. "This is what always happens." And even though I suppose it was a little thick of me, I really hadn't gotten it: For of course, I was the reason the prices were in peril. . . .

In retrospect, what has remained so fascinating to me about this experience was the way it so exemplified the problems of the new rhetoric of racism. For starters, the new rhetoric of race never mentions race. It wasn't race but risk with which the bank was so concerned. . . .

By this measure of mortgage-worthiness, the ingredient of blackness is cast not just as a social toll but as an actual tax. A fee, an extra contribution at the door, an admission charge for the high costs of handling my dangerous propensities, my inherently unsavory properties. I was not judged based on my independent attributes or financial worth; not even was I judged by statistical profiles of what my group actually does. (For in fact, anxiety-stricken, middle-class black people make grovelingly good cake-baking neighbors when not made to feel defensive by the unfortunate historical strategies of bombs, burnings or abandonment.) Rather, I was being evaluated based on what an abstraction of White Society writ large thinks we—or I—do, and that imagined "doing" was treated and thus established as a self-fulfilling prophecy. It is a dispiriting message: that some in society apparently not only devalue black people but devalue themselves and their homes just for having us as part of their landscape.

"I bet you'll keep your mouth shut the next time they plug you into the computer as white," laughed a friend when he heard my story. It took me aback, this postmodern pressure to "pass," even as it highlighted the intolerable logic of it all. For by these "rational" economic measures, an investment in my property suggests the selling of myself.

Source: Patricia J. Williams., "Of Race and Risk." Reprinted from the December 29, 1997, issue of *The Nation.*

2. IQ testing favors middle-class children, especially the White middle class, because of the types of questions included.
3. The entire criminal justice system, from the patrol officer to the judge and jury, is dominated by Whites who find it difficult to understand life in poverty areas.
4. Hiring practices often require several years of experience at jobs that are only recently opened to members of subordinate groups.

In some cases, even apparently neutral institutional standards can turn out to have discriminatory effects. In 1992, African American students at a Midwestern state university protested a policy under which fraternities and sororities that wished to use campus facilities for a dance were required to post a $150 security deposit to cover possible damage. The Black students complained that this policy had a discriminatory impact on minority student organizations. Campus police countered that the university's policy applied to *all* student groups interested in using these facilities. However, since overwhelmingly White fraternities and sororities at the school had their own houses, which they used for dances, the policy indeed affected only African American and other subordinate groups' organizations.

The U.S. population is becoming more diversified, and examples of institutional discrimination are confronting more different groups. Many Asian peoples have distinctive customs honoring their deceased family members. Among these traditions is the burning of incense at the grave site, placing food on the grave markers, and leaving fake money. These practices stem from ancestor worship but are often followed by Christian Chinese Americans who try to hold on to some of the "old ways." Cemetery proprietors maintain standards of what they regard as proper grave decoration in order to maintain a tidy appearance. Consequently, people of Asian descent find they are unable to bury their loved ones in the cemeteries most convenient to them and must travel to cemeteries that are more open to different ways of memorializing the dead. Cemeteries do not consciously seek to keep people out because they are Asian, but they develop policies, often with little thought, that fail to recognize the pluralistic nature of society (M. Eng 1998). Institutional discrimination continuously imposes more hindrances on, and awards fewer benefits to, certain racial and ethnic groups than it does to others. This is the underlying and painful context of American intergroup relations.

The Informal Economy

The secondary labor market affecting many members of racial and ethnic minorities has come to be called the informal economy. The **informal economy** refers to transfers of money, goods, or services that are not reported to the government. This label describes much of the work in inner-city neighborhoods and poverty-stricken rural areas, in sharp contrast to the rest of the marketplace. Workers are employed in the informal economy seasonally or infrequently. The work they do may resemble the work of traditional occupations, such as mechanic, cook, or electrician, but these workers lack the formal credentials to enter such employment. Indeed, workers in the informal economy may work sporadically or may moonlight in the regular economy. The informal economy also includes unregulated child-care services, garage sales, and the unreported income of crafts people and street vendors.

The informal economy, sometimes referred to as the **irregular** or **underground economy**, exists worldwide. In 1996, wide publicity was given to the presence of sweatshops throughout the world and in urban America that supplied clothing for major retailers such as Kmart. Most of these employees were immigrants or non-Whites. Conflict sociologists in particular note that a significant level of commerce occurs outside traditional economies. Individu-

Many people work in the informal economy with little prospect of moving into the primary, better-paying economy. Pictured is a street vendor in New York City.

ally, the transactions are small, but they can be significant when taken together. Within the apparel industry, it has been estimated that perhaps half of all U.S.-produced garments in small shops are made in businesses where two or more of the following laws are routinely violated: child labor, health and safety, minimum wage, and overtime. The informal economy taken in total makes up 10 to 20 percent of all economic activity in the United States (R. Ross 1998; D. Sontag 1993).

According to the **dual labor market model,** minorities have been relegated to the informal economy. Although the informal economy may offer employment to the jobless, it provides few safeguards against fraud or malpractice that victimizes the workers. There are also few of the fringe benefits of health insurance and pension that are much more likely to be present in the conventional marketplace. Therefore, informal economies are criticized for promoting highly unfair and dangerous working conditions. To be consigned to the informal economy is thus yet another example of social inequality. Sociologist Edna Bonacich (1972, 1976) outlined the dual or split labor market that divides the economy into two realms of employment, the secondary one being populated primarily by minorities working at menial jobs. Labor, even when not manual, is still rewarded less when performed by minorities. In keeping with the conflict model, this dual-market model emphasizes that minorities fare unfavorably in the competition between dominant and subordinate groups.

The workers in the informal economy are ill prepared to enter the regular economy permanently or to take its better-paying jobs. Frequent changes in employment or lack of a specific supervisor leaves them without the kind of job résumé that employers in the regular economy expect before they hire. Some of the sources of employment in the informal economy are illegal, such as fencing stolen goods, narcotics peddling, pimping, and prostitution. More likely, the work is legal but not transferable to a more traditional job. An example is an "information broker," who receives cash in exchange for such information as where to find good buys or how to receive maximum benefits from public assistance programs (S. Pedder 1991).

Workers in the informal economy have not necessarily experienced direct discrimination. Because of past discrimination, they are unable to secure traditional employment. Working in the informal economy provides income but does not lead them into the primary labor market. A self-fulfilling cycle continues that allows past discrimination to create a separate work environment.

The Underclass

Many members of the informal economy, along with some employed in traditional jobs, compose what is called the underclass of American society. The **underclass** consists of the long-term poor who lack training and skills. Conflict theorists, among others, have expressed alarm at the proportion of the nation's society living at this social stratum. Sociologist William Wilson (1987, 1988:15, 1996) drew attention to the growth of this varied grouping of families and individuals who are outside the mainstream of the occupational structure. Although estimates vary depending on the definition, in 1990, the underclass included more than 3 million adults of working age, not counting children or the elderly. In the central city, about 49 percent of the underclass in 1990 comprised African Americans; 29 percent, Hispanics (or Latinos); 17 percent, Whites; and 5 percent, other (W. O'Hare and B. Curry-White 1992).

The discussion of the underclass has focused attention on society's inability to address the problems facing the truly disadvantaged—many of whom are Black or Hispanic. Some scholars have expressed concern that the portrait of the underclass seems to blame the victim, making the poor responsible. Wilson and others have stressed that it is not bad behavior but structural factors, such as the loss of manufacturing jobs, that have hit ghetto residents so hard. As the labor market has become tighter, the subordinate groups within the underclass are at a significant disadvantage. Associated with this structural problem is isolation from social services. The disadvantaged lack contact or sustained interaction with the individuals or institutions that represent the regular economy. It is the economy, not the poor, that needs reforming (J. DeParle 1991; W. Kornblum 1991; S. Wright 1993).

Even though the concept of underclass has been useful, its use reflects the division over issues involving race and poverty. Proponents of intervention use the underclass to show the need for a basic restructuring of the economy. Others use the term to describe a lifestyle whose practitioners refuse to try to move out of poverty and conclude that the poor reject responsibility for their plight. There is little evidence to support this pessimistic conclusion. Wilson (1996), in a 1978–1988 survey of African Americans living in poor neighborhoods, found that they believed in the work ethic and felt that plain hard work was important to getting ahead. The underclass, therefore, describes a segment of the population whose job prospects, as well as educational opportunities, are severely limited.

It is a commonly held notion that there are jobs available for the inner-city poor but that they just do not seek them out. A study looked at jobs that were advertised in a help-wanted section of *The Washington Post*. The analysis showed that most of the jobs were beyond the reach of the underclass—perhaps 5 percent of all openings could even remotely be considered reasonable job prospects for people without skills or experience. During interviews with the employers, researchers found that an average of twenty-one people applied for each position, which typically was filled within three days of the time when the advertisement appeared. The mean hourly wage was $6.12, and 42 percent offered no fringe benefits, and the remaining positions offered "meager" fringe benefits after six months or one year of employment. The researchers concluded that this study, like others before it, counter the folk wisdom that there are plenty of jobs around for the underclass (J. Pease and L. Martin 1997).

Poverty is not new, yet the concept of an underclass describes a very chilling development: workers, whether employed in the informal economy or not, are beyond the reach of any safety net provided by existing social programs. Concern in the late 1990s about government spending and federal deficits have led to cutbacks of many public assistance programs and of close scrutiny of those remaining. In addition, membership in the underclass is not an intermittent condition but a long-term attribute. The underclass is understandably alienated and engages sporadically in illegal behavior. This alienation and the illegal acts gain the underclass little support from the larger society to address the problem realistically.

The term *underclass* is often invoked to establish the superiority of the dominant group. Even if it is not stated explicitly, there is a notion that society and institutions have not failed the underclass but that somehow they are beyond hope. All too frequently, the underclass is treated as a homogeneous group, the object of scorn, fear, and embarrassment.

Discrimination Today

Dateline NBC in August 1998 sent two young men—one African American and the other White—to shopping malls. They looked at merchandise in Eddie Bauer, Timberland, and other stores. Consistently, the Black shopper was tailed by in-store security. Often the guards, many of whom were themselves Black, left their assigned posts at the front of the store to follow the Black shopper. Confronted with the differential treatment of their customers, store executives indicated that they gave no instructions to follow Black customers closely. White viewers were surprised by what they saw, whereas Black viewers generally saw little new to them in the report. Discrimination may take many forms and may surface because of specific procedures or feelings of distrust (NBC News 1998).

Discrimination is widespread in the United States. It sometimes results from prejudices held by individuals. More significantly, it is found in institutional discrimination and the presence of the informal economy. The presence of an underclass is symptomatic of many social forces, and total discrimination—past and present discrimination taken together—is one of them.

Not so subtly, discrimination shows itself even when people are prepared to be customers. A 1990 study had Black and White men and women follow a script to buy new cars in the Chicago area. After 164 visits, the results showed that a White woman could be expected to pay $142 more for a car than a White man, a Black man $421 more, and a Black woman $875 more. African Americans and women were perceived as less knowledgeable and therefore were the victims of a higher markup in prices. A similar study in housing, nationwide in twenty-five metropolitan areas, showed that African Americans and Hispanics faced discrimination in a majority of their responses to advertisements. Housing agents showed fewer housing units to Blacks and Hispanics, steered them to minority neighborhoods, and gave them far less assistance in finding housing that met their needs. Other recent studies reveal that lenders are 60 percent more likely to turn down a mortgage request from a minority applicant than from an equally qualified White and that lenders give minority applicants far less assistance in filling out their forms (I. Ayres 1991; J. Yinger 1995).

Discrimination also emerges when we look at data for groups other than Blacks and Hispanics. National studies have documented that White ethnics, such as Irish Catholics and Jewish Americans, are less likely to be in certain positions of power than White Protestants, despite equal educational levels (R. Alba and G. Moore 1982). The victims of discrimination are not limited to people of color.

Measuring Discrimination

How much discrimination is there? As in measuring prejudice, problems arise in quantifying discrimination. Measuring prejudice is hampered by the difficulties in assessing attitudes and by the need to take many factors into account. It is further restrained by the initial challenge of identifying different treatment. A second difficulty of measuring discrimination is assigning a cost to the discrimination. Some tentative conclusions about discrimination can be made, however. Figure 3.2 uses income data to show vividly the disparity in income between African Americans and Whites, and between men and women. The first comparison is of all workers. White men, with a median income of $37,196, earn 35 percent more than Black men and 89 percent more than Hispanic women, who earn only $19,817 in wages.

Clearly, White males earn most, followed by Black males, White females, Black females, Hispanic men, and Hispanic females. The sharpest drop is between White and Black males. Even worse, relatively speaking, is the plight of women. **Double jeopardy** refers to subordinate status twice, defined as experienced by women of color. This disparity between Black women and White men has remained unchanged over the more than fifty years during which such data have been tabulated. The disparity illustrates yet another instance of the double jeopardy experienced by minority women. Also, Figure 3.2 includes only data for full-time, year-round workers, and therefore the figure excludes housewives and the unemployed. Even in this comparison, the deprivation of Blacks, Hispanics, and women is confirmed again.

Are these differences entirely the result of discrimination in employment? No, individuals within the four groups are not equally prepared to compete for high-paying jobs. Past discrimination is a significant factor in a person's

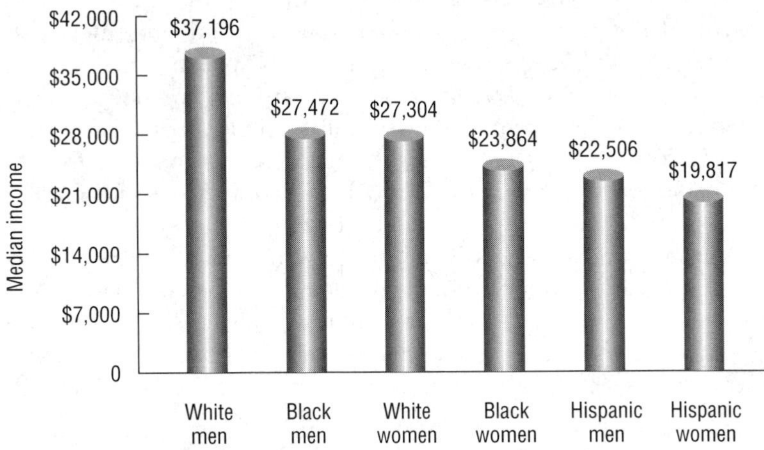

Figure 3.2 Median Income by Race, Ethnicity, and Gender, 1998
Even a brief analysis reveals striking differences in earning power in the United States between White men and other groups. Furthermore, the double jeopardy is apparent for African American and Hispanic women.

Note: Median income is from all sources and is limited to year-round, full-time workers over 15 years old.

Source: U.S. Bureau of the Census 1999i:32–33.

present social position. As discussed previously and illustrated in Figure 3.1, past discrimination continues to take its toll on modern victims. Taxpayers, predominantly White, were unwilling to subsidize the public education of African Americans and Hispanics at the same levels as White pupils. Even as these actions have changed, today's schools show the continuing results of this uneven spending pattern from the past. Education is clearly an appropriate variable to control. In Table 3.1, median income is compared, holding education constant, which means that we can compare Blacks and Whites and men and women with approximately the same amount of formal schooling. More education means more money, but the disparity remains. The gap between races does narrow somewhat as education increases. However, both African Americans and women lag behind their more affluent counterparts. The contrast remains dramatic: women with a degree or graduate work ($30,692) earn less than men who fail to finish college ($31,627).

What do these individual differences look like if we consider them on a national level? Economist Andrew Brimmer (1995), citing numerous government studies, estimates that about 3 or 4 percent of the gross domestic product (GDP, or the value of goods and services) is lost annually by the failure to use African Americans' existing education. There had been little change in this economic cost from the mid-1960s to the mid-1990s. This estimate would

Table 3.1 Median Income by Race and Sex, Holding Education Constant

Even at the very highest levels of schooling, the income gap remains between Whites and Blacks. Education also has little apparent effect on the income gap between male and female workers.

	Race, 1996		*Ratio*	*Sex, 1998*		*Ratio*
	White	*Black*	*Black to White*	*Male Workers*	*Female Workers*	*Women to Men*
Total	$25,876	$20,262	.78	$30,654	$16,258	.53
High School						
1–3 Years	15,135	13,054	.86	17,462	9,582	.55
4 years	21,307	17,285	.81	26,542	13,766	.52
College						
Some college	25,587	22,283	.87	31,627	18,445	.55
Bachelor's degree or more	36,941	31,639	.86	50,272	30,692	.61

Notes: Figures are median income from all sources except capital gain. Included are public assistance payments, dividends, pensions, unemployment compensation, and so on. Incomes are for all workers over 25 years of age. Data for Whites are for White non-Hispanics. "Some college" includes Associate Degree-holders for race, excludes them for data by gender.

Source: U.S. Bureau of the Census 1998b: 26,27; 1999i.

be even higher, of course, if we took into account economic losses due to the underutilization of the academic talents of women and other minorities. Now that education has been held constant, is the remaining gap caused by discrimination? No, not necessarily. Table 3.1 uses only the amount of schooling, not its quality. Racial minorities are more likely to attend inadequately financed schools. Some efforts have been made to eliminate disparities among school districts in the amount of wealth available to tax for school support, but with little success. In a 1973 case, *San Antonio Independent School District* v. *Rodriguez,* the U.S. Supreme Court ruled that attendance at an underfinanced school in a poor district does not constitute a violation of equal protection. The inequality of educational opportunity may seem less important in explaining sex discrimination. Even though women are usually not segregated from men, educational institutions encourage talented women to enter fields that pay less (nursing or elementary education) than occupations requiring similar amounts of training.

Eliminating Discrimination

Two main agents of social change work to reduce discrimination: voluntary associations organized to solve racial and ethnic problems and the federal government including the courts. The two are closely related: most efforts initiated by the government were urged by associations or organizations representing minority groups, following vigorous protests against racism by African Americans. Resistance to social inequality by subordinate groups has been the key to change. Rarely has any government of its own initiative sought to end discrimination based on such criteria as race, ethnicity, and gender.

All racial and ethnic groups of any size are represented by private organizations that are to some degree trying to end discrimination. Some of these organizations originated in the first half of the twentieth century, but most either have been founded since World War II or have become significant forces in bringing about change only since then. These include church organizations, fraternal social groups, minor political parties, and legal defense funds, as well as more militant organizations operating under the scrutiny of law-enforcement agencies. The purposes, membership, successes, and failures of these resistance organizations dedicated to eliminating discrimination are discussed throughout the balance of this book.

Government action toward eliminating discrimination is also relatively recent. Antidiscrimination actions have been taken by each branch of the government: the executive, the judicial, and the legislative.

The first antidiscrimination action at the executive level was President Franklin D. Roosevelt's 1943 creation of the Fair Employment Practices Commission (FEPC), which handled thousands of complaints of discrimination, mostly from African Americans, despite strong opposition by powerful economic and political leaders and many Southern Whites. The FEPC had little actual power. It had no authority to compel employers to stop discriminating but could only ask for voluntary compliance. Its jurisdiction was limited to federal government employees, federal contractors, and labor unions. State and local governments and any business without a federal contract were not covered. Furthermore, the FEPC never enjoyed vigorous support from the White House, was denied adequate funds, and was part of larger agencies that were hostile to the commission's existence. This weak antidiscrimination agency was finally dropped in 1946, to be succeeded by an even weaker one in 1948. The judiciary, charged with interpreting laws and the U.S. Constitution, has a much longer history of involvement in the rights of racial, ethnic, and religious minorities. Its early decisions, however, protected the rights of the dominant group, as in the 1857 U.S. Supreme Court's *Dred Scott* decision, which ruled that slaves remained slaves even when living or traveling in states where slavery was illegal. Not until the 1940s did the Supreme Court revise earlier decisions and begin to grant African Americans the same rights as those held by Whites. The 1954 *Brown* v. *Board of Education* decision, which stated that "separate but equal" facilities, including education, was unconstitutional, heralded a new series of rulings, arguing, in effect, that to distinguish among races in order to segregate was inherently unconstitutional.

It was assumed incorrectly by many that *Brown* and other judicial actions would lead quickly to massive change. In fact, little change occurred initially, and resistance to racism continued. The immediate effect of many court rulings was minimal because the Executive branch and the Congress did not wish to violate the principle of **states' rights,** which holds that each state is sovereign in most of its affairs and has the right to order them without interference from the federal government. In other words, supporters of states' rights felt that the federal government had to allow state governments to determine how soon the rights of African Americans would be protected. Gradually, U.S. society became more committed to the rights of individuals. Legislation in the 1960s committed the federal government to protecting civil rights actively, rather than merely leaving action up to state and local officials.

The most important legislative effort to eradicate discrimination was the Civil Rights Act of 1964. This act led to the establishment of the Equal Employment Opportunity Commission (EEOC), which had the power to investigate complaints against employers and to recommend action to the Department of Justice. If the Justice Department sued and discrimination was found, the court could order appropriate compensation. The act covered employment practices of all businesses with more than twenty-five employees, as well as nearly all employment agencies and labor unions. A 1972 amendment broadened the coverage to employers with as few as fifteen employees.

The act also prohibited the application of different voting registration standards to White and Black voting applicants. It prohibited as well discrimination in public accommodations, that is, hotels, motels, restaurants, gasoline stations, and amusement parks. Publicly owned facilities, such as parks, stadiums, and swimming pools, were also prohibited from discriminating. Another important provision forbade discrimination in all federally supported programs and institutions, such as hospitals, colleges, and road construction projects.

The Civil Rights Act of 1964 covered discrimination based on race, color, creed, national origin, and sex. Although the inclusion of gender in employment criteria had been forbidden in the federal civil service since 1949, most laws and most groups pushing for change showed little concern about sex discrimination. There was little precedent for attention to sex discrimination even at the state level. Only Hawaii and Wisconsin had enacted laws against sex discrimination before 1964. As first proposed, the Civil Rights Act did not include mention of gender. One day before the final vote, opponents of the measure offered an amendment on gender bias in an effort to defeat the entire act. The act did pass with prohibition against sex bias included—an event that can only be regarded as a milestone for women seeking equal employment rights with men (Commission on Civil Rights 1975; E. Roth 1993).

The Civil Rights Act of 1964 was not perfect. Since 1964, several acts and amendments to the original act have been added to cover the many areas of discrimination it left untouched, such as criminal justice and housing. Even in those areas singled out for enforcement in the Civil Rights Act of 1964, discrimination still occurs. Federal agencies charged with its enforcement complain that they are underfunded or are denied wholehearted support by the White House. Also, regardless of how much the EEOC may want to act in a case, the individual who alleges discrimination has to pursue the complaint over a long time, marked by long periods of inaction.

Although civil rights laws have often established rights for other minorities, the Supreme Court made these rights explicit in two 1987 decisions involving groups other than African Americans. In the first of the two cases, an Iraqi American professor asserted that he had been denied tenure because of his Arab origins; in the second, a Jewish congregation brought suit for damages in response to the defacing of its synagogue with derogatory symbols. The Supreme Court ruled unanimously that, in effect, any member of an ethnic minority may sue under federal prohibitions against discrimination. These decisions paved the way for virtually all racial and ethnic groups to invoke the Civil Rights Act of 1964 (S. Taylor 1987a).

A particularly insulting form of discrimination seemed finally to be on its way out in the late 1980s. Many social clubs had limitations forbidding membership to minorities, Jews, and women. For years, exclusive clubs argued that they were merely selecting friends, but in fact, a principal function of these clubs has been providing a forum to transact business. Denial of membership meant more than the inability to attend a luncheon; it also seemed to exclude one from part of the marketplace, as Lawrence Otis Graham observed at the beginning of this chapter. The Supreme Court ruled unanimously in the 1988 case *New York State Clubs Association* v. *City of New York* that states and cities may ban sex discrimination by large private clubs where business lunches and similar activities take place. Although the ruling does not apply to all clubs and leaves the issue of racial and ethnic barriers unresolved, it did serve to chip away at the arbitrary exclusiveness of private groups (S. Taylor 1988).

Memberships and restrictive organizations remain perfectly legal. The rise to national attention in 1996 of the amateur champion and professional golfer Tiger Woods, of mixed Native American, African, and Asian ancestry, brought to public view that there were at least twenty-three golf courses he would be prohibited from playing by virtue of race (J. McCormick and S. Begley 1996; H. Yu 1996).

The inability of the Civil Rights Act, similar legislation, and court decisions to end discrimination is not due entirely to poor financial and political support, although they played a role. The number of federal employees assigned to investigate and prosecute bias cases declined in the 1990s. By 1996, the EEOC was looking at 121,230 unresolved complaints. Thus, even if the EEOC had been given top priority, discrimination would remain. The civil rights legislation attacked the most obvious forms of discrimination. Many discriminatory practices, such as those described as institutional discrimination, are seldom obvious (D. Price 1996).

Environmental Justice

Discrimination takes many forms and is not necessarily apparent even when its impact can be far-reaching. Take the example of Kennedy Heights, a well-kept working-class neighborhood nestled in the southeastern part of Houston. This community faces a real threat, and it is not from crime or drugs. The threat that they fear is under their feet, in the form of three oil pits abandoned by Gulf Oil back in 1927. The residents, most of whom are African American, argue that they have suffered high rates of cancer, lupus, and other illnesses because the chemicals from the oil fields poison their water supply. The residents first sued Chevron USA in 1985, and the case is still making its way through the courtrooms of no less than six states and the federal judiciary.

Lawyers and other representatives for the residents say that the oil company is guilty of *environmental racism* because it knowingly allowed a predominantly Black housing development to be built on the contaminated land. They are able to support this charge on the basis of documents, including a 1954 memorandum from an appraiser who suggested that the oil pits be drained of any toxic substances and the land filled for "low-cost houses for White occupancy." When the land did not sell right away, an oil company official in a 1967 memorandum suggested a tax-free land exchange with a de-

The location of health hazards near minority and low-income neighborhoods is regarded as a concern of environmental justice. Pictured is an old refinery adjacent to homes in Richmond, California.

veloper who intended to use the land for "Negro residents and commercial development." For this latter intended use by African Americans, there was no mention of environmental cleanup of the land. The oil company counters that it just assumed the developer would do the necessary cleanup of the pits (A. Manning 1997; S. Verhovek 1997).

The conflict perspective sees the case of the Houston suburb as one where pollution harms minority groups disproportionately. **Environmental justice** refers to the efforts to ensure that hazardous substances are controlled so that all communities receive protection regardless of race or socioeconomic circumstance. Following Environmental Protection Agency and other organization reports documenting discrimination in the locating of hazardous waste sites, an Executive Order was issued in 1994 that requires all federal agencies to ensure that low-income and minority communities have access to better information about their environment and have an opportunity to participate in shaping government policies that affect their community's health. Initial efforts to implement the policy have met widespread opposition, including criticism from some proponents of economic development who argue that to conform to guidelines unnecessarily delays or blocks altogether locating new industrial sites. Effort by the EPA further to clarify environmental justice guidelines in 1998 created more problems when the agency proceeded without sufficient consultation with states, cities, and industry (J. Cushman 1998).

Sociologist Robert Bullard (1990) has shown that low-income communities and areas with significant minority populations are more likely to be adjacent to waste sites than are affluent White communities. Similarly, undergraduate student researchers at Occidental College in California found in 1995 that the poor, African Americans, Hispanics, Asian Americans, and Native Americans were especially likely to be living near Los Angeles County's 82 potential environmental hazards (Moffat 1995). Issues of environmental justice are not restricted to metropolitan areas. Another continuing problem is abuse of Native American reservation land. Many American Indian leaders are concerned that tribal lands are too often regarded as "dumping grounds" for toxic waste that go to the highest bidder.

As with other aspects of discrimination, experts disagree. There is controversy within the scientific community over the potential hazards of some of the problems, and there is even some opposition within the subordinate communities being affected. This complexity of the issues in terms of social class and race is apparent, as some observers question the wisdom of an Executive Order that slows economic development's coming to areas in dire need of employment opportunities. On the other hand, some counter that such businesses typically employ few less-skilled workers and make the environment less livable only for those left behind. Despite such varying viewpoints, environmental justice offers an excellent example of resistance and change in the 1990s that could not have been foreseen by the civil rights workers of the 1950s.

Affirmative Action

Affirmative action is the positive effort to recruit subordinate-group members, including women, for jobs, promotions, and educational opportunities. The phrase *affirmative action* first appeared in an Executive Order issued by President Kennedy in 1961. The order called for contractors to "take affirmative action to ensure that applicants are employed, and that employees are treated during employment, without regard to their race, creed, color, or national origin." However, at this early time no enforcement procedures were specified. Six years later, the order was amended to prohibit discrimination on the basis of sex, but affirmative action was still defined vaguely.

Today, *affirmative action* has become a catchall term for racial-preference programs and goals. It has also become a lightning rod for opposition to any programs that suggest special consideration of women or racial minorities.

Affirmative Action Explained

Affirmative action has been viewed as an important tool for reducing institutional discrimination. Whereas previous efforts had been aimed at eliminating individual acts of discrimination, federal measures under the heading of affirmative action have been aimed at procedures that deny equal opportunities even if they are not intended to be overtly discriminatory. This policy has been implemented to deal with both the current discrimination and the past discrimination outlined earlier in this chapter. The Commission on Civil Rights (1981:9–10) gave some examples of areas where affirmative action had been aimed at institutional discrimination:

- Height and weight requirements that are unnecessarily geared to the physical proportions of White males without regard to the actual requirements needed to perform the job and that therefore exclude females and some minorities.
- Seniority rules, when applied to jobs historically held only by White males, that make more recently hired minorities and females more subject to layoff—the "last hired, first fired" employee—and less eligible for advancement.
- Nepotism-based membership policies of some unions that exclude those who are not relatives of members, who, because of past employment practices, are usually White.
- Restrictive employment-leave policies, coupled with prohibitions on part-time work or denials of fringe benefits to part-time workers, which make it difficult for the heads of single-parent families, most of whom are women, to get and keep jobs and also to meet the needs of their families.
- Rules requiring that only English be spoken at the workplace, even when not a business necessity, a practice that results in discriminatory employment practices toward individuals whose primary language is not English.
- Standardized academic tests or criteria, geared to the cultural and educational norms of middle-class or White males, when these are not relevant predictors of successful job performance.
- Preferences shown by law and medical schools in the admission of children of wealthy and influential alumni, nearly all of whom are White.
- Credit policies of banks and lending institutions that prevent the granting of mortgages and loans in minority neighborhoods or that prevent the granting of credit to married women and others who have previously been denied the opportunity to build good credit histories in their own names.

Employers have also been cautioned against asking leading questions in interviews, such as "Did you know you would be the first Black to supervise all Whites in that factory?" or "Does your husband mind your working on weekends?" Furthermore, the lack of minority-group (Blacks, Asians, Native Americans, and Hispanics) or female employees may in itself represent evidence for a case of unlawful exclusion (Commission on Civil Rights 1981).

The Debate

How far can an employer go in encouraging women and minorities to apply for a job before it becomes unlawful discrimination against White males? Since the late 1970s, a number of bitterly debated cases on this difficult aspect of affirmative action have reached the U.S. Supreme Court. The most significant cases are summarized in Table 3.2. Furthermore, as we will see, the debate has moved into party politics.

Table 3.2 Key Decisions on Affirmative Action

In a series of split and often very close decisions, the Supreme Court has expressed a variety of reservations in specific situations.

Year	*Favorable/ Unfavorable to Policy*	*Case*	*Vote*	*Ruling*
1971	+	*Griggs* v. *Duke Power Co.*	9–0	Private employers must provide a remedy where minorities were denied opportunities even if unintentional
1978	–	*Regents of the University of California* v. *Bakke*	5–4	Prohibited specific number of places for minorities in college admissions
1979	+	*United Steelworkers of America* v. *Weber*	5–2	OK for union to favor minorities in special training programs
1984	–	*Firefighters Local Union No. 1784 (Memphis, TN)* v. *Stotts*	6–1	Seniority means recently hired minorities may be laid off first in staff reductions
1986	+	*International Association of Firefighters* v. *City of Cleveland*	6–3	May promote minorities over more senior Whites
1986	+	*New York City* v. *Sheet Metal*	5–4	Approved specific quota of minority workers for union
1987	+	*United States* v. *Paradise*	5–4	Endorsed quotas for promotions of state troopers
1987	+	*Johnson* v. *Transportation Agency, Santa Clara, CA*	6–3	Approved preference in hiring for minorities and women over qualified men and Whites

(continued)

Table 3.2 (continued)

Year	*Favorable/ Unfavorable to Policy*	*Case*	*Vote*	*Ruling*
1989	–	*Richmond* v. *Croson Company*	6–3	Ruled a 30 percent set-aside program for minority contractors unconstitutional
1989	–	*Martin* v. *Wilks*	5–4	Ruled Whites may bring reverse discrimination claims against court-approved affirmative action plans
1990	+	*Metro Broadcasting* v. *FCC*	5–4	Supported federal programs aimed at increasing minority ownership of broadcast licenses
1995	–	*Adarand Constructors Inc.* v. *Peña*	5–4	Benefits based on race are constitutional only if narrowly defined to accomplish a compelling interest
1996	–	*Texas* v. *Hopwood*	*	Let stand a lower court decision covering Louisiana, Mississippi, and Texas, that race could not be used in college admissions

* 5th U.S. Circuit Court of Appeals decision.

In the 1978 *Bakke* case (*Regents of the University of California* v. *Bakke*), by a narrow 5–4 vote, the Court ordered the medical school of the University of California at Davis to admit Allan Bakke, a qualified White engineer who had originally been denied admission solely on the basis of his race. The justices ruled that the school had violated Bakke's constitutional rights by establishing a fixed quota system for minority students. The Court added, however, that it was constitutional for universities to adopt flexible admissions programs that use race as one factor in making decisions.

Colleges and universities responded with new policies designed to meet the *Bakke* ruling while broadening opportunities for traditionally underrepresented minority students. However, in 1996, the Supreme Court allowed a lower court decision to stand that affirmative action programs for African American and Mexican American students at the University of Texas law school were unconstitutional. The ruling effectively prohibited schools in the lower court's jurisdiction of Louisiana, Mississippi, and Texas from taking race into account in admissions. Given this action, further challenges to affirmative action can be expected in higher education (D. Lederman and S. Burd 1996).

Even if the public in the United States acknowledges the disparity in earnings between White males and others, growing numbers of people doubt that everything done in the name of affirmative action is desirable. In 1991, national surveys showed that 24 percent of respondents agreed that "affirmative action programs designed to help minorities get better jobs and education go too far these days." Further analysis of the survey data reveals sharp racial division. In 1995, 46 percent of Whites and only 8 percent of African Americans indicated that affirmative action had gone too far (D. Lauter 1995). Beginning in the 1980s, the Supreme Court, increasingly influenced by conservative justices, has issued many critical rulings concerning affirmative action programs. In a key case in 1989, the Court invalidated, by a 6–3 vote, a Richmond, Virginia, law that had guaranteed 30 percent of public works funds to construction companies owned by minorities. In ruling that the Richmond statute violated the constitutional right of White contractors to equal protection under the law, the Court held that affirmative action programs are constitutional only when they serve the "compelling state interest" of redressing "identified discrimination" by the government or private parties. More recently, in 1994, a divided Supreme Court, by a 5–4 vote in *Adarand* v. *Peña,* held that federal programs that award benefits on the basis of race are constitutional only if they are "narrowly tailored" to accomplish a "compelling governmental interest." The Court's ruling was expected to encourage further

The national debate over affirmative action provoked vocal demonstrations, including this rally at the state capitol in Olympia, Washington.

legal challenges to federal affirmative action programs (Commission on Civil Rights 1995; L. Greenhouse 1989).

Has affirmative action actually helped to alleviate employment inequality on the basis of race and gender? This is a difficult question to answer given the complexity of the labor market and the fact that there are other antidiscrimination measures, but it does appear that affirmative action has had significant impact in the sectors where it has been applied. Sociologist Barbara Reskin (1998) studied available studies looking at workforce composition in terms of race and gender in light of affirmative action policies. She found that gains in minority employment can be attributed to affirmative action policies. This finding includes both firms mandated to follow affirmative action guidelines and those that took them on voluntarily. There is also evidence that some earnings gains can be attributed to affirmative action. Economists M. V. Lee Badgett and Heidi Hartmann (1995), reviewing twenty-six other research studies, came to similar conclusions: affirmative action and other federal compliance programs have had modest impact, but it is difficult to assess, given larger economic changes such as recessions or the massive increase in women in the paid labor force.

Sometimes the impact of affirmative action is clear, such as during the 1970s and 1980s—a period during which courts ordered about 40 percent of the nation's police departments to engage in affirmative action because they had systematically discriminated against minorities and women. Another 42 percent of police departments adopted voluntary plans, leaving over 80 percent of the nation's law enforcement departments working ambitiously to improve representation. The result is dramatic in that minority representation among police officers increased from 7 percent to 22.5 percent, and women's presence rose from 2 percent to 9 percent (Martin 1991).

Reverse Discrimination

While researchers debated the merit of affirmative action, the general public—particularly Whites but also some affluent African Americans and Hispanics—questioned the wisdom of the program. Particularly vocal were the charges of **reverse discrimination:** that government actions cause better-qualified White males to be bypassed in favor of women and minority men. Reverse discrimination is an emotional term because it conjures up the notion that somehow women and minorities will subject White males in the United States to the same treatment received by minorities during the last three centuries. Increasingly, critics of affirmative action called for color-blind policies, which would end affirmative action and, they argue, allow all people to be judged fairly. Of major significance—and often overlooked in public debates—is that a color-blind policy implies a very limited role for the state in addressing social inequality between racial and ethnic groups (A. Kahng 1978; D. Skrentny 1996; H. Winant 1994). Is it possible to have color-blind policies in the United States as we move into the twenty-first century? Supporters of affirmative action contend that as long as businesses rely on informal social networks, personal recommendations, and family ties, White men will have a distinct advantage built on generations of being in positions of power. Furthermore, an end to affirmative action should also mean an end to the many programs that give advantages to certain businesses, homeowners, veterans, farmers, and others. The vast majority of these preference-holders are White (M. Kilson 1995; R. Mack 1996).

Consequently, by the 1990s, affirmative action had emerged as an increasingly important issue in state and national political campaigns. Generally, discussion focused on the use of quotas in hiring practices. Supporters of affirmative action argue that hiring goals establish "floors" for minority inclusion but do not exclude truly qualified candidates from any group. Opponents insist that these "targets" are, in fact, quotas that lead to reverse discrimination. However, according to the U.S. Department of Labor, affirmative action has caused very few claims of reverse discrimination by White people. Fewer than one hundred of the more than three thousand discrimination opinions in federal courts from 1990 to 1994 even raised the issue of reverse discrimination, and reverse discrimination was actually established in only six cases (Joint Center for Political and Economic Studies 1996).

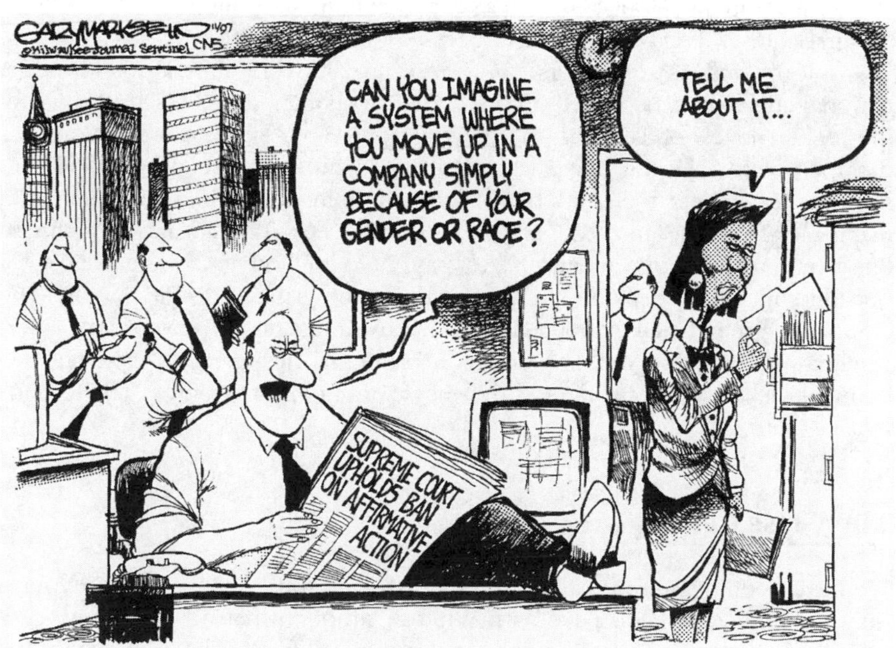

Gary Markstein: ©Milwaukee Journal Sentinel/Copley News Service

The state of California, in particular, was a battleground over this controversial issue. The California Civil Rights Initiative was placed on the ballot in 1996 as a referendum to amend the state constitution and to prohibit any programs that give preference to women and minorities for college admission, employment, promotion, or government contracts. Overall, 54 percent of the voters backed the state proposition, with 61 percent of men in favor compared with only 48 percent of women. Whites, who represented 74 percent of the voters, voted in favor of the measure overwhelmingly, with 63 percent backing Proposition 209. This outcome compares with 26 percent of African Americans, 24 percent of Hispanics, and 39 percent of Asian Americans favoring the end of affirmative action in state-operated institutions. Obviously, those voters—Whites and men—who perceived themselves as least likely to benefit from affirmative action overwhelmingly favored Proposition 209.

Legal challenges continue concerning Proposition 209, which is being implemented unevenly throughout the state. Much of the attention has focused on the impact that reducing racial preference programs will have in law and medical schools, where competition for admission is very high. Initial evidence is that there has been a significant decline at elite institutions, particularly at UCLA and the University of California at Berkeley but that less impact is being experienced at most institutions. These charges come just as a study in the prestigious *Journal of the American Medical Association* showed that whereas giving preference to ethnicity yields "powerful effects on the diversity of the student population," there is "no evidence of diluting the quality of the graduates" (R. Davidson and E. Lewis 1997:1153).

Ironically, just as supporters of Proposition 209 were cheering its passage, national attention was riveted on a scandal involving alleged discrimination at the highest levels of Texaco—the nation's fourteenth largest corporation. Audiotapes were released that showed senior company executives plotting to destroy documents that had been demanded in a discrimination suit and using racial epithets in discussing Black employees. Texaco, facing a threatened nationwide boycott, agreed to pay $176 million in compensation for outstanding grievances and complaints concerning racial discrimination. The company agreed to give about 11,000 African American employees an 11 percent pay hike, spend millions more on programs designed to wipe out discrimination, and let outsiders come inside to monitor progress (B. Roberts and J. White 1998).

The Glass Ceiling

We have been talking primarily about racial and ethnic groups as if they have uniformly failed to keep pace with Whites. Although that perception is accurate, there are tens of thousands of people of color who have matched and even exceeded Whites in terms of income. For example, in 1991, there were more than 133,000 Black households and over 134,000 Hispanic households that earned over $100,000. What can we say about affluent members of subordinate groups in the United States?

Prejudice does not necessarily end with wealth. Black newspaper columnist De Wayne Wickham (1993) wrote of the subtle racism he had experienced. He had witnessed a White clerk in a supermarket ask a White customer whether she knew the price of an item that the computer would not scan; when the problem occurred while the clerk was ringing up Wickham's groceries, she called for a price check. Affluent subordinate-group members routinely report being blocked as they move toward the first-class section aboard airplanes or seek service in upscale stores. Another journalist, Ellis Cose (1993), has termed these insults the soul-destroying slights to affluent minorities that lead to the "rage of a privileged class."

Discrimination persists for even the educated and qualified from the best family backgrounds. As subordinate-group members are able to compete successfully, they sometimes encounter attitudinal or organizational bias that prevents them from reaching their full potential. They have confronted what has come to be called the **glass ceiling.** This refers to the barrier that blocks the promotion of a qualified worker because of gender or minority membership (see Figure 3.3 on p. 102). Often people entering nontraditional areas of employment become *marginalized* and are made to feel uncomfortable, much like the situation of immigrants who feel a part of two cultures, as we discussed in Chapter 1.

The reasons for glass ceilings are as many as the occurrences. It may be that one Black or one woman vice-president is regarded as enough, so that the second potential candidate faces a block to movement up through management. Decision makers may be concerned that their clientele will not trust them if they have too many people of color or may worry that a talented woman could become overwhelmed with her duties as a mother and wife and thus perform poorly in the workplace.

Concern about women and minorities climbing a broken ladder led to the formation in 1991 of the Glass Ceiling Commission, with the U.S. Secretary of Labor chairing the twenty-one-member group. Initially, the commission regarded some of the glass ceiling barriers as the following:

- Lack of management commitment to establishing systems, policies, and practices for achieving workplace diversity and upward mobility
- Pay inequities for work of equal or comparable value
- Sex-, race-, and ethnic-based stereotyping and harassment
- Unfair recruitment practices
- Lack of family-friendly workplace policies

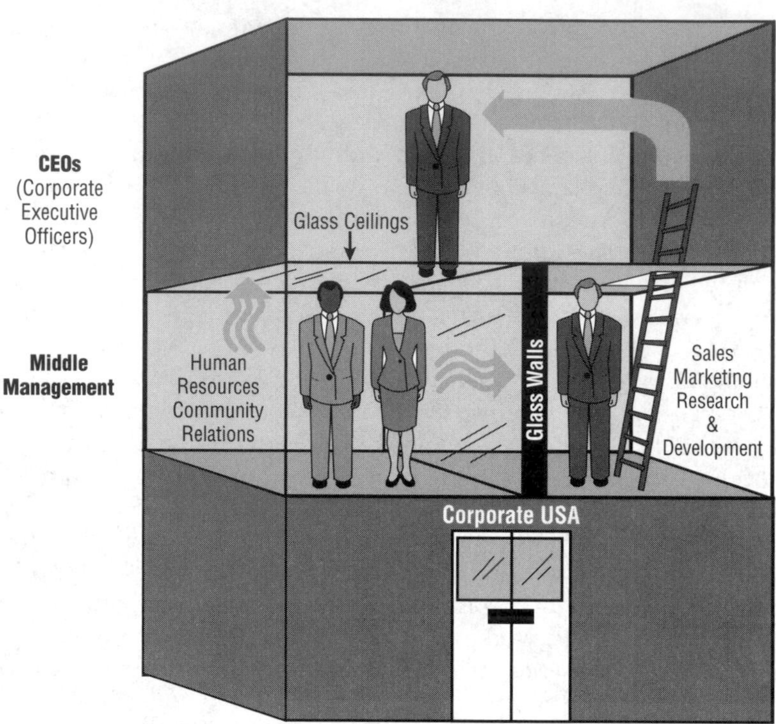

Figure 3.3 Glass Ceilings and Glass Walls
Women and minority men are moving up in corporations but encounter glass ceilings that block entry to top positions. In addition, they face glass walls that block lateral moves to areas from which executives are promoted.

- "Parent-track" policies
- Limited opportunities for advancement to decision-making positions

The commission report documented that the underrepresentation of women in managerial positions is due in large part to the presence of glass ceilings. As the commission noted, 97 percent of the senior managers of Fortune 1000 industrial and Fortune 500 service companies are White, and about 96 percent are male. A follow-up study in 1996 found little change, with only 2 percent or 50 of the top 2,500 executives to be women in the Fortune 500 companies (U.S. Department of Labor 1993, 1995a, 1995b; S. Silverstein 1996).

Although glass ceilings have been widely described and condemned in business during the 1990s, this tendency does not necessarily mean that there has been a dramatic move to eliminate them. A 1998 survey of Chicago's top 100 companies found only modest representation by women (7.5 percent) and minorities (5.8) among boards of directors. Yet 53 percent of the Chicago-area CEOs declared that they were satisfied with the makeup of their board of directors (S. Chandler 1998).

Glass ceilings are not the only barrier. Catalyst, a nonprofit research organization, conducted interviews in 1992 with senior and middle managers from larger corporations. The study found that, even before glass ceilings are encountered, women and racial and ethnic minorities face **glass walls** that keep them from moving laterally. Specifically, the study found that women tend to be placed in staff or support positions in areas such as public relations and human resources and are often directed away from jobs in core areas such as marketing, production, and sales. Women are assigned, and therefore trapped, in jobs that reflect their stereotypical helping nature, and thus they encounter glass walls that cut off access to jobs that might lead to broader experience and advancement (J. Lopez 1992).

How do members of subordinate groups respond to glass walls and glass ceilings? Some endure them, but others take their potential and begin their own businesses. Susan Crowe Chamberlain, past president of Women in Management, summarized the situation succinctly by saying that for many women and minority men, the real way to get to the top is to get out. Instead of fighting the ceiling, they form their own companies (R. Richman 1992: sec. 6, 11).

Focusing on the employed and even the relatively affluent should not lead us to ignore the underclass people employed in the informal economy or the Native Americans without economic opportunities on isolated reservations.

Court decisions, steps by government, and public opinion against affirmative action accompanied by charges of "reverse discrimination" have made it unclear what future actions, if any, may be taken to end racism.

Surveying the past ten years, Urban League President John Jacob said in 1994 that Blacks can do only so much themselves; self-development cannot succeed without an "opportunity environment." He called on President Clinton to endorse a "Marshall Plan for America" that would focus on job creation and job training (*USA Today* 1994). Yet even the affluent subordinate-group person is reminded of her or his second-class status through subtle racism or a glass ceiling.

Conclusion

Discrimination takes its toll, whether or not a person who is discriminated against is part of the informal economy. Even members of minority groups who are not today being overtly discriminated against continue to fall victim to past discrimination. We have also identified the costs of discrimination to members of the privileged group. The attitudes of Whites and even members of minority groups themselves are influenced by the images they have of racial and ethnic groups. These images come from what has been termed *statistical discrimination,* which causes people to act on the basis of stereotypes they hold and of the actions of a few subordinate-group members.

From the conflict perspective, it is not surprising to find the widespread presence of the informal economy proposed by the dual labor-market model. Derrick Bell (1994), an African American law professor, has made the sobering assertion that "racism is permanent." He contends that the attitudes of dominant Whites prevail and that society is willing to advance programs on behalf of subordinate groups only when they coincide with needs as perceived by those Whites. Bell observes that the criticism of the affirmative action program in the 1990s exceeded any concern over corporate downsizing, which led to a loss of 1.6 million manufacturing jobs from 1989 to 1993 alone.

Women are a particularly vulnerable group, for whether the comparisons are within or across racial and ethnic groupings, they face significant social disparities. This inequality will be a recurring theme throughout this book, but we can observe that it is present even in developing fields such as computer science. In 1990, women accounted for 35 percent of computer systems analysts and programmers, but data for 1997 show the proportion to be down to 29 percent. Is computer science openly discriminating against women? There is little evidence of blatant discrimination, but increasing numbers of women drop out of the field, claiming that they are not taken seriously, have few role models, and face a family-unfriendly environment. So, is the industry taking steps to address this need? Actually, the major initiative has been for the computer industry to lobby the federal government to increase the number of legal immigrants with the desired computer skills who are allowed to enter the country (Piller 1998).

The surveys presented in this chapter show gradual acceptance of the earliest efforts to eliminate discrimination but also show that support is failing, especially as it relates to affirmative action. Indeed, concerns about doing something about alleged reverse discrimination are as likely to be voiced as racial or gender discrimination or penetrating glass ceilings and glass walls.

Institutional discrimination remains a formidable challenge in the United States.

Attempts to reduce discrimination by attacking institutional discrimination have met with staunch resistance. Partly as a result of this outcry from some of the public, especially White Americans, the federal government gradually deemphasized its efforts in affirmative action during the 1980s and 1990s. Yet resistance continues. States and the federal government have not been as quick to jump on the antiaffirmative action bandwagon as many had predicted in the wake of the passage of Proposition 209. Indeed, even in California the resistance has been clear (Bobo 1998).

As we turn to examine the various groups that make up the American people, through generations of immigration and religious diversity, look for the types of programs designed to reduce prejudice and discrimination that were discussed here. Most of the material in this chapter has been about racial groups, especially Black and White Americans. It would be easy to see intergroup hostility as a racial phenomenon, but that would be incorrect. Throughout the history of the United States, relations among some White groups have been characterized by resentment and violence. The next two chapters examine the nature and relations of White ethnic groups.

Key Terms

absolute deprivation 76
affirmative action 93
discrimination 76
double jeopardy 86
dual labor market 82
environmental justice 92
glass ceiling 101
glass wall 103
informal economy 81
institutional discrimination 78
irregular or underground economy 81
relative deprivation 76
reverse discrimination 98
states' rights 89
total discrimination 77
underclass 83

Review Questions

1. Why might people still feel disadvantaged even though their incomes are rising and their housing circumstances have improved?
2. Why does institutional discrimination sometimes seem less objectionable than individual discrimination?
3. In what way does an industrial society operate on several economic levels?
4. Why are questions raised about affirmative action while inequality persists?
5. Distinguish between glass ceilings and glass walls. How do they differ from more obvious forms of discrimination in employment?

Critical Thinking

1. Discrimination can take many forms. Consider the college you attend. Select a case of discrimination that you think just about everyone would

agree is wrong. Then describe another incident in which the alleged discrimination was of a more subtle form. Who is likely to condemn, and who is likely to overlook such situations?

2. Resistance is a continuing theme of intergroup race relations. Discrimination implies the oppression of a group, but how may discrimination also serve to unify the oppressed group to resist such unequal treatment? How can acceptance, or integration, for example, weaken the sense of solidarity within a group?
3. Voluntary associations like the NAACP and government units such as the courts have been important vehicles for bringing about a measure of social justice. In what ways can the private sector, corporations and businesses, also work to bring about an end to discrimination?

Internet Exercises

1. The statistical data of the modern workforce are chronicled on the United States Department of Labor Women's Bureau homepage (http://www.dol.gov/dol/wb/). Log on to the site, paying special attention to the "Black Women in the Labor Force," "Facts About Asian American and Pacific Islander Women," and "20 Facts on Women Workers" subsections inside the "Pubs" link on this web site. Each month the site also features examples of women working in traditionally male-dominated fields. Which occupation is featured this month? Why did the women interviewed decide to pursue this specific career? What challenges and rewards have resulted from that choice? Which racial or ethnic group of women has had the highest level of participation in the U.S. labor force? Which has had the lowest? What sociological reasons could be proffered to explain these findings? What gains have black women made in the labor force in past decades? What challenges still exist? How much do black women earn in contrast to white women in similar occupations? What percentage of the U.S. work labor force comprises Asian American and Pacific Islander women? How does the income for these women compare with that of women from other racial and ethnic groups? How many women are there in the United States? How many are in the labor force? What percentage of the military is made up of women? Women earn how much in comparison with men? Why does this disparity exist? What are the leading occupations for employed women? Considering all you have learned from this site, how do these data reflect issues from this chapter, such as the glass ceiling, glass wall, and double jeopardy?

2. The Environmental Protection Agency maintains information and an FAQ on this issue at (http://es.epa.gov/oeca/ main/ej/index.html). How does the EPA define environmental justice? How does this definition compare with your understanding from the reading? What prompted the need for the environmental justice movements? What strategies and policies are in place to help bring about this justice by the EPA? What is Executive Order 12898, and when was it enacted? What is Title VI of the Civil Rights Act of 1964, and how does it relate to environmental justice? Search through the "Coal-

fired Power Plant Enforcement" subsection inside the Enforcement/Clean-up link. Which power plants recently were issued Notices of Violations? Where are these plants located? Are any near your home or school? What is the nature of the violations? What challenges might be faced by poor or minority communities trying to draw attention to ecological and environment dangers in their neighborhoods? Using a search engine (such as http://www. yahoo.com or http://www.lycos.com), can you find current examples of environmental justice movements? Where is the location of the community affected? Which groups live there? What was the environmental danger impacting the community? What was the response of the government, corporations, and the media? How does environmental justice reflect the conflict perspective of sociology?

3. Proposition 209 continues to attract attention and controversy. Visit the following site: (http://dir.yahoo.com/Regional/U_S__States/California/Government/Politics/Elections/Past_Elections/1996/Ballot_Measures/Proposition_209___California_Civil_Rights_Initiative/) and link to web sites on various sides of the debate. Be sure to click on the "Proposition 209—from the California Ballot Pamphlet" section, and read the actual text of the proposition. What are the specific provisions of the proposition? What arguments are offered by those for and against Proposition 209? What statistics and evidence are included to support each view? What is CADAP? How does the organization "Californians for Justice" define and view Affirmative Action? What is your opinion of their definitions and views? What was Proposition 187? What happened to that proposition? What steps and actions are being taken/recommended by pro-209 and con-209 organizations to achieve their goals? What has been the aftermath of Proposition 209's enactment? What is your opinion on 209? Would you want your state to adopt a similar proposition? Why, or why not?

Immigration and the United States

CHAPTER OUTLINE

HIGHLIGHTS

The diversity of the American people is unmistakable evidence of the variety of places from which immigrants have come. The different new arrivals did not necessarily welcome one another. Instead, they brought their European rivalries to the Americas. The Chinese were the first to be singled out for restriction, with the passage of the 1882 Exclusion Act. The initial Chinese immigrants became, in effect, scapegoats for America's sagging economy in the last half of the nineteenth century. Growing fears that too many non-American types were immigrating motivated the creation of the national origins system and the quota acts of the 1920s. These acts gave preference to certain nationalities, until the passage of the Immigration and Naturalization Act in 1965 ended that practice. Concern about illegal immigration—legal, too—has continued through the 1990s, leading to the 1994 passage of the controversial Proposition 187 in California. Restrictionist sentiment has grown, and debates rage over whether immigrants, even legal ones, should receive services such as education, government-subsidized health care, and welfare. Controversy also continues to surround the policy of the United States toward refugees.

Eduardo Román García, age 29, works for $260 a week in a car body shop in southern California. His situation is both similar to and different from that of many new arrivals in the United States. The similarities lie in his desire for a better life. He works to send as much money as possible back to his wife and two children in Veracruz, Mexico. He hopes he can remain in the United States because he knows there is little chance to find employment back home. Even if he found a job, Mexican factory wages start at $2.90 a day. He found his job and a place to live through a network of Mexican Americans. Indeed, his place of employment is owned by a man who entered the United States illegally twenty years ago but later became a citizen and now operates a business with ten employees. Román expected to work hard when he came. "Others told me it would be difficult in this country," he said, "but they said it was worth it [to come here] because you could live a little better" (E. Boyer 1996:B8; S. Dillon 1996).

Román's situation is different because his face was seen on national television in 1996. In April of that year, Román, along with eighteen others, was being transported illegally by truck into the United States when it was stopped by police. News crews covered the long chase and videotaped the beating of two unarmed suspects. If it had not been for the national attention, Román and the others would soon have been deported, but instead they were granted temporary work permits while they waited to testify at the trials of the police deputies. Meanwhile, the Mexican government expressed outrage at their citizens' treatment here, just as the United States many times has condemned treatment of Americans abroad (B. Shuster 1996).

This drama being played out in both an auto body shop and on a California freeway illustrates the themes in immigration today. Immigrants come to the United States trying to get ahead. In doing so, many come legally, applying for immigrant visas, whereas others enter illegally. In the United States, we do not like lawbreakers, but often we seek the services and low-priced products made by people who come here illegally. How do we control this immigration without violating the principles that we uphold of relatively free movement within the nation? How do we decide who enters? And how do we treat those who come here illegally?

The diversity of ethnic and racial backgrounds of Americans today is the living legacy of immigration. Except for descendants of Native Americans or of Africans brought here enslaved, today's population is entirely the product of individuals who chose to leave familiar places to come to a new country.

The social forces that cause people to emigrate are complex. The most important have been economic: financial failure in the old country and expectations of higher incomes and standards of living in the new land. Other factors include dislike of new regimes in their native lands, racial or religious bigotry, and a desire to reunite families. All these factors push individuals from their homelands and pull them to other nations such as the United States. Immigration into the United States in particular has at times been facilitated by cheap ocean transportation and by other countries' removal of restrictions on emigration.

The reception given to immigrants in this country, however, has not always been friendly. Open bloodshed, restrictive laws, and the eventual return of close to one-third of the immigrants and their children to their home countries attest to the uneasy feeling toward strangers who wish to settle here. Nevertheless, vast numbers of immigrants have still come. Figure 4.1 indicates the high but fluctuating number of immigrants that have arrived during every decade from the 1820s through the 1990s.

We can anticipate the largest number of legal immigrants during the 1990s, but, of course, in the period from 1900 through 1910, the country was much smaller, so the numerical impact was even greater. According to a 1999 U.S. Census Bureau estimate, approximately 9 percent of the population is foreign-born. This figure compares with a peak of 14.7 percent in 1990 and a low of 4.7 percent in 1970 (U.S. Bureau of the Census 1999b).

Opinion polls in the United States from 1946 through the present never show more than 13 percent of the public in favor of more immigration, and usually about 50 percent want less. Even a special 1995 survey of immigrants themselves found that only 15 percent wanted immigration increased, 44 percent wanted it left as is, and a sizable 30 percent advocated having immigration levels decreased. We want the door open until we get through, and then we want to close it (L. Saad 1995).

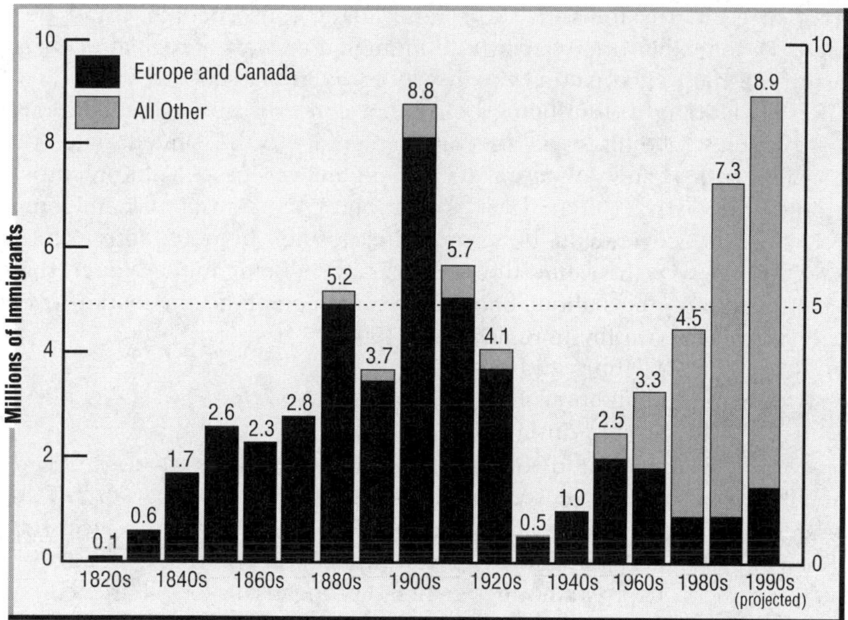

Figure 4.1 Immigration in the United States, 1820s through 1990s
Source: U.S. Immigration and Naturalization Service, 1999a, 1999b. Projection for the 1990s by the author based on immigration data.

Early Immigration

European explorers of North America were soon followed by settlers, the first immigrants to the Western Hemisphere. The Spanish founded St. Augustine in Florida in 1565, and the English, Jamestown, Virginia, in 1607. Protestants from England emerged from the colonial period as the dominant force numerically, politically, and socially. The English accounted for 60 percent of the 3 million White Americans in 1790. Although exact statistics are lacking for the early years of the United States, the English were soon outnumbered by other nationalities, as the numbers of Scottish-Irish and Germans, in particular, swelled. The English colonists, however, maintained their dominant position, as Chapter 5 will examine.

Throughout American history, immigration policy has been politically controversial. The policies of the English king, George III, were criticized in the U.S. Declaration of Independence for obstructing immigration to the colonies. Toward the end of the nineteenth century, the American republic itself was criticized for enacting immigration restrictions. In the beginning, however, the country encouraged immigration. At first, legislation fixed the residence requirement for naturalization at five years, although briefly, under the Alien

Act of 1798, it was fourteen years, and "dangerous" people could be expelled. Despite this brief harshness, immigration was unregulated through most of the 1800s, and naturalization was easily available.

Besides holding the mistaken belief that concerns about immigration are something new, we also assume that immigrants to the United States rarely reconsider their change of country. Detailed analysis of available records beginning in the early 1900s suggests that about 35 percent of all immigrants to the United States eventually emigrated back to their home country. The proportion varies, with the figures for some countries being much higher, but the overall pattern is clear: about one in three immigrants to this nation eventually chooses to return home (M. Wyman 1990).

The Anti-Catholic Crusade

The relative absence of federal legislation from 1790 to 1881 does not mean that all new arrivals were welcomed. **Xenophobia** (the fear or hatred of strangers or foreigners) led naturally to **nativism** (beliefs and policies favoring native-born citizens over immigrants). Roman Catholics in general and the Irish in particular were among the first Europeans to be ill treated. Anti-Catholic feeling, which originated in Europe, was brought by the early Protestant immigrants. The Catholics of colonial America, although few, were subject to limits on their civil and religious rights.

From independence until around 1820, little evidence appeared of the anti-Catholic sentiment of colonial days, but the cry against "popery" grew as Irish immigration increased. Prominent Americans encouraged hatred of these new arrivals. Samuel F. B. Morse, the inventor of the telegraph and an accomplished painter, wrote a strongly worded anti-Catholic work in 1834 entitled *A Foreign Conspiracy Against the Liberties of the United States*. Morse felt that the Irish were "shamefully illiterate and without opinions of their own" (1835:61). In the mind of the prejudiced American, the Irish were particularly unwelcome because they were Roman Catholics. Many Americans readily believed Morse's warning that the Pope planned to move the Vatican to the Mississippi River Valley (J. Duff 1971:34). Even poet and philosopher Ralph Waldo Emerson wrote of "the wild Irish . . . who sympathized, of course, with despotism" (J. Kennedy 1964:70). This antagonism was not limited to harsh words. From 1834 to 1854, mob violence against Catholics across the country led to death, the burning of a Boston convent, the destruction of a Catholic church and the homes of Catholics, and the use of U.S. Marines and state militia to bring peace to American cities as far west as St. Louis.

A frequent pattern saw minorities striking out against each other rather than at the dominant class. Irish Americans opposed the Emancipation Proclamation and the freeing of the slaves because they feared Blacks would compete for the unskilled work open to them. This fear was confirmed when free Blacks were used to break a longshoremen's strike in New York. Hence, much of the Irish violence during the 1863 riot was directed against Blacks, not against the Whites who were most responsible for the conditions in which the immigrants found themselves (J. Duff 1971; S. Warner 1968).

In retrospect, the reception given to the Irish is not difficult to understand. Many immigrated following the 1845–1848 potato crop failure and famine in Ireland. They fled not so much to a better life as from almost certain death. The Irish Catholics brought with them a celibate clergy, who struck the New England aristocracy as strange and reawakened old religious hatreds. The Irish were worse than Blacks, according to the dominant Whites, because unlike the slaves and even the freed Blacks, who "knew their place," the Irish did not suffer their maltreatment in silence. Employers balanced minorities by judiciously mixing immigrant groups to prevent unified action by the laborers. For the most part, nativist efforts only led the foreign-born to emphasize their ties to Europe.

By the 1850s, nativism became an open political movement pledged to vote only for "native" Americans, to fight Roman Catholicism, and to demand a twenty-one-year naturalization period. Party members were instructed to divulge nothing about their program and to say that they knew nothing about it. As a result, they came to be called the Know-Nothings. Although the Know-Nothings soon vanished, the antialien mentality survived and occasionally became formally organized into such societies as the Ku Klux Klan in the 1860s and the anti-Catholic American Protective Association in the 1890s. Revivals of anti-Catholicism continued well into the twentieth century. The most dramatic outbreak of nativism in the nineteenth century, however, was aimed at the Chinese. If there had been any doubt by the mid-1800s that the United States could harmoniously accommodate all, debate on the Chinese Exclusion Act would negatively settle the question once and for all (D. Gerber 1993; R. Wernick 1996).

The Anti-Chinese Movement

Before 1851, official records show that only forty-six Chinese had immigrated to the United States. Over the next thirty years, more than 200,000 came to this country, lured by the discovery of gold and the opening of job opportunities in the West. Overcrowding, drought, and warfare in China also encouraged them to take a chance in the United States. Another important factor was improved oceanic transportation: it was actually cheaper to travel from Hong Kong to San Francisco than from Chicago to San Francisco. The frontier communities of the West, particularly in California, looked on the Chinese as a valuable resource to fill manual jobs. As early as 1854, so many Chinese desired to emigrate that ships had difficulty handling the volume.

During the 1860s, railroad work provided the greatest demand for Chinese labor, until the Union Pacific and Central Pacific railroads were joined at Promontory, Utah, in 1869. The Union Pacific relied primarily on Irish labor-

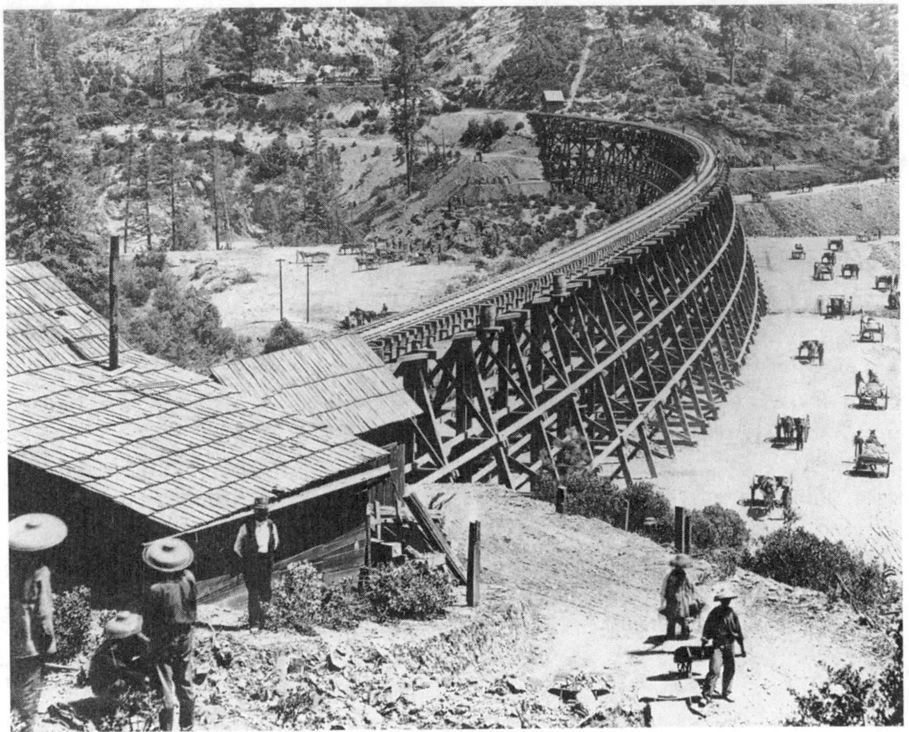

Chinese workers, such as these pictured in 1844, played a major role in building the railroads in the West.

ers, but 90 percent of the Central Pacific labor force was Chinese because Whites generally refused the backbreaking work over the Western terrain. Despite the contribution of the Chinese, White workers physically prevented even their presence when the golden spike was driven to mark the joining of the two railroads.

With the dangerous railroad work largely completed, people began to rethink the wisdom of encouraging Chinese to immigrate to do the work that no one else would do. Reflecting their xenophobia, White settlers found the Chinese immigrants and their customs and religion difficult to understand. Indeed, relatively few people actually tried to understand these immigrants from Asia. Easterners and legislators, although they had had no firsthand contact with Chinese Americans, were soon on the anti-Chinese bandwagon as they read sensationalized accounts of the lifestyle of the new arrivals.

Even before the Chinese immigrated, stereotypes of them and their customs were prevalent. American traders returning from China, European diplomats, and Protestant missionaries consistently emphasized the exotic and sinister aspects of life in China. The **sinophobes,** people with a fear of anything associated with China, appealed to the racist theory developed during the slavery controversy that non-Europeans were subhuman. Similarly, Americans were beginning to be more conscious of biological inheritance and disease, and so it was not hard to conjure up fears of alien genes and germs. The only real challenge the anti-Chinese movement had was to convince people that the negative consequences of unrestricted Chinese immigration outweighed any possible economic gain. Perhaps briefly, racial prejudice had earlier been subordinated to industrial dependence on Chinese labor for the work that Whites shunned, but acceptance of Chinese was short-lived. The fear of the "yellow peril" overwhelmed any desire to know more about Asian people and their customs (R. Takaki 1989).

Another nativist fear of Chinese immigrants was based on the threat they posed as laborers. Californians, whose labor force first felt the effects of the Chinese immigratation, found support throughout the nation as organized labor feared that the Chinese would be used as strikebreakers. By 1870, Chinese workers had been used for that purpose as far east as Massachusetts. When Chinese workers did unionize, they were not recognized by major labor organizations. Samuel Gompers, founder of the American Federation of Labor (AFL), consistently opposed any effort to assist Chinese workers and refused to consider having a union of Chinese restaurant employees admitted into the AFL (H. Hill 1967). Gompers worked effectively to see future Chinese immigration ended and produced a pamphlet entitled "Chinese Exclusion: Meat vs. Rice, American Manhood Against Asiatic Coolieism—Which Shall Survive?" (S. Gompers and H. Gustadt 1908). Although employers were glad to pay the Chinese low wages, laborers came to direct their resentment against the Chinese rather than against their compatriots' willingness to exploit the Chinese. Only a generation earlier, the same concerns had been felt about the Irish, but with the Chinese, the hostility was to reach new heights because of another factor.

Although many arguments were voiced, racial fears motivated the anti-Chinese movement: it was race that was the critical issue. The labor-market fears were largely unfounded, and most advocates of restrictions at the time knew that fact. There was no possibility at the time that Chinese would immigrate in numbers that would match those of Europeans, so it is difficult to find an explanation other than racism for the pervading fears (H. Winant 1994). From the sociological perspective of conflict theory, we can explain how the Chinese immigrants were welcomed only when their labor was necessary to fuel growth in the United States. When that labor was no longer necessary, the welcome mat for the immigrants was withdrawn. Furthermore, as conflict theorists would point out, restrictions were not applied evenly; Americans focused on a specific nationality group—the Chinese—in order to reduce the overall number of foreign workers in the nation. Because decision making at that time rested in the hands of the descendants of European immigrants, the steps to be taken were most likely to be directed against those who were least powerful: immigrants from China who, unlike Europeans seeking entry, had few allies among legislators and other policy makers.

In 1882, Congress enacted the Chinese Exclusion Act, which outlawed Chinese immigration for ten years. It also explicitly denied naturalization rights to those Chinese in the United States; that is, they were not allowed to become citizens. There was little debate in Congress, and discussion concentrated on how suspension of Chinese immigration could best be handled. No allowance was made for wives and children to be reunited with their husbands and fathers in the United States. Only brief visits of Chinese government officials, teachers, tourists, and merchants were exempted.

The balance of the nineteenth century saw the remaining loopholes allowing Chinese immigration closed. Beginning in 1884, Chinese laborers were not allowed to enter the United States from any foreign place, a ban that lasted ten years. Two years later, the Statue of Liberty was dedicated, with the poem by Emma Lazarus inscribed on its base. To the Chinese, the poem welcoming the tired, the poor, the huddled masses must have seemed a hollow mockery.

In 1892, Congress extended the Exclusion Act for another ten years and added that Chinese laborers had to obtain certificates of residence within a year or face deportation. After the turn of the century, the Exclusion Act was extended again. Two decades later, the Chinese were not alone; the list of people restricted by immigration policy expanded many times.

Italian Americans aboard a ship arrive at Ellis Island.

Restrictionist Sentiment Increases

As Congress closed the door to Chinese immigration, the debate on restricting immigration turned in new directions. Prodded by growing anti-Japanese feelings, the United States entered into the so-called Gentlemen's Agreement, completed in 1908. Japan agreed to halt further immigration to the United States, and the United States agreed to end discrimination against those Japanese who had already arrived. The immigration ended, but anti-Japanese feelings continued. Americans were growing uneasy that the "new immigrants" would overwhelm the culture established by the "old immigrants." The earlier immigrants, if not Anglo-Saxon, were from similar groups such as the Scandinavians, the Swiss, and the French Huguenots. These groups were more experienced in democratic political practices and had a greater affinity with the dominant Anglo-Saxon culture. By the end of the nineteenth century, however, more and more immigrants were neither English-speaking nor Protestant and came from dramatically different cultures.

For four years, the United States Immigration Commission, known popularly as the Dillingham Commission, exhaustively studied the effects of immigration. The findings, presented in 1911, were determined by the commission's assumption that there were types of immigrants. The two types were the old immigrants, mostly Anglo-Saxons, who were characterized as hard-working pioneers, and the new immigrants from southern Europe, who were branded as opportunists. It was not surprising that pressure for a more restrictive immigration policy became insurmountable. A literacy test was one of the results of hostility against the new immigrants (L. Fermi 1971; O. Handlin 1957).

In 1917, Congress finally overrode President Wilson's veto and enacted an immigration bill that included the controversial literacy test. Critics of the bill, including Wilson, argued that illiteracy does not signify inherent incompetence but reflects lack of opportunity for instruction (*New York Times* 1917a). Such arguments were not heeded, however. The act seemed innocent at first glance—it merely required immigrants to read thirty words in any language—but it was the first attempt to restrict immigration from western Europe. The act also prohibited immigration from the South Sea islands and other parts of Asia not already excluded. Curiously, this law that closed the door on non-Anglo-Saxons permitted waiver of the test if the immigrants came because of their home government's discrimination against their race (*New York Times* 1917b).

The National Origins System

Beginning in 1921, a series of measures was enacted that marked a new era in American immigration policy. Whatever the legal language, the measures were drawn up to block the growing immigration from southern Europe, such as from Italy and Greece. Anti-immigration sentiment, combined with the isolationism that followed World War I, caused Congress to restrict severely entry privileges not only to the Chinese and Japanese but to Europeans as well. The national origins system was begun in 1921 and remained the basis of immigration policy until 1965. This system used the country of birth to determine whether an individual could enter as a legal alien, and the number of previous immigrants and their descendants was used to set the quota of how many from a country could enter annually.

To understand the effect that the national origins had on immigration, it is necessary to clarify the quota system. The quotas were deliberately weighted in favor of immigration from northern Europe. Because of the ethnic composition of the country in 1920, the quotas placed severe restrictions on immigration from the rest of Europe and from other parts of the world. Immigration from the Western Hemisphere (that is, Canada, Mexico, Central and South America, and the Caribbean) continued unrestricted. The quota for each nation was set at 3 percent of the number of people descended from each nationality recorded in the 1920 census. Once the statistical manipulations were completed, almost 70 percent of the quota for the Eastern Hemisphere went to just three countries: Great Britain, Ireland, and Germany.

The absurdities of the system soon became obvious, but it was nevertheless continued. Because British immigration had fallen sharply, most of its quota of 65,000 went unfilled. The openings, however, could not be transferred, even though countries such as Italy, with a quota of only 6,000, had 200,000 people who wished to enter (F. Belair 1970). However one rationalizes the purpose behind the act, the result was obvious: any English person, regardless of skill and of any relationship to anyone already here, could enter the country more easily than, say, a Greek doctor whose children were American citizens. The quota for Greece was 305, with the backlog of people wishing to come reaching 100,000.

By the end of the 1920s, annual immigration had dropped to one-fourth of its pre–World War I level. The worldwide economic depression of the 1930s decreased immigration still further. A brief upsurge in immigration just before World War II reflected the flight of Europeans from the oppression of expanding Nazi Germany. The war virtually ended transatlantic immigration. The era of the great European migration to the United States had been legislated out of existence.

It is important to recall the living legacy of the great immigration. Millions of people in the Untied States are descended from these immigrants, and many maintain close ties to the old traditions. In "Listen to Their Voices," Raffi Ishkanian, now a high school social studies teacher, describes what it is like to be not only a college student but also an Armenian American. His father's parents immigrated from Armenia during the first years of the National Origins System—a nation between Turkey and Iran that became part of the Soviet Union and since has become politically independent of Russia. While a college student, he has had a summer internship with an Armenian community service organization.

LISTEN TO THEIR VOICES

Roots

Raffi Ishkanian

Ethnicity has had a definite impact on my life. My mother, although an "odar" (Armenian for non-Armenian), has adopted the culture entirely, with a great deal of enthusiasm. She is active in the church choir (which sings only in Armenian), is part of an Armenian Dance group, and has learned to cook most of the dishes. As a result, although I am genetically only half Armenian, I feel 100 percent Armenian. I attended the Armenian church and Armenian language school throughout my childhood. I live in the suburbs and did not have the benefit of having a lot of Armenians in my neighborhood. So like my father, I ended up with mostly non-Armenian friends. I always resented that I had to go to Armenian school on Fridays. My complaints found a deaf ear everywhere except amongst my Korean friends who had to go to Korean school and Korean church. I wanted to go to Catholic church. I hated that every time a substitute teacher would read off attendance and botch up my name, everyone was on the floor. I hated that whenever I got a trophy, my name was spelled wrong. I hated that whenever my name was in the paper for soccer, even when I got all-county honors, they spelled it wrong.

Yet, at the same time, I relished the tightness of my Armenian family. I loved how on holidays, and particularly Thanksgiving, we all got together. And as much as I hated that my church was different, I loved it. I loved the church picnics, the bazaars, the fact that almost all my parents' friends were there. I loved how it seemed like anywhere we went, if we found an Armenian, an instant friend was found. That ethnic bond was so strong. If we were in Canada, and ran into an Armenian, chances are we would find out that they were either a relative of a friend in church, or a good friend of so-and-so's in our church, or even from the same village back in Armenia. All I needed was people around me, in my immediate area, to appreciate it with me, to let me know it was okay to like these things that were so culturally different.

Like my father, in college I find myself liking more and more about my ethnicity and disliking less and less. I think that this is more than mere coincidence. The more education a person receives, the easier it becomes to see the value of one's ethnic identity. Children are uneducated as to the values of individuality. Childhood is one nonstop battle to fit in. Whether a kid is too smart, too slow, too unathletic, or too different, the kid is teased. In turn, the kid winds up hating that difference and perhaps education, combined with time, allows him or her to view that difference—that which makes him or her an individual—as an asset, rather than a handicap. I have become very proud of who I am. There are very few Armenians on this campus, yet rather than view that fact as a negative, I thrive on it. I jump at every chance I can get to talk about being Armenian, Armenia, or the genocide. It seems that today whenever an ethnic group gets together, the majority jumps on it as an excuse to say the group does not want to assimilate. These groups are needed because ethnicity is a vital part of a person's identity. For Armenians in particular, this struggle for recognition and distinction is vital. The genocide shattered the Armenian community into fragmented populations worldwide. The remembrance of these events, as for the victims of the Nazi Holocaust, is critical to the survival of the Armenian people. As long as my name is Raffi Ara Ishkanian, whether I want to be part of the Armenian ethnic community or not, my name will associate me with it, be it good or bad. And I am proud.

Source: Excerpted and reprinted from "Roots Paper" by Raffi Ishkanian, included in *Becoming American, Becoming Ethnic: College Students Explore Their Roots* edited by Thomas Dublin, 1996. Reprinted by permission of Raffi Ishkanian.

The 1965 Immigration and Naturalization Act

The national origins system was abandoned with the passage of the 1965 Immigration and Naturalization Act, signed into law by President Lyndon B. Johnson at the foot of the Statue of Liberty. The primary goals of the act were reuniting families and protecting the American labor market. The act also initiated restrictions on immigration from Latin America. After the act, immigration increased by one-third, but the act's influence was primarily on the composition rather than the size of immigration. The sources of immigrants now included Italy, Greece, Portugal, Mexico, the Philippines, the West Indies, and South America. The effect is apparent when we compare the changing sources of immigration over the last hundred years, as in Figure 4.2. The most recent period shows that Asian and Latin American immigrants combined to account for 57 percent of the people who were permitted entry. This pattern contrasts sharply with that of early immigration, which was dominated by arrivals from Europe.

The nature of immigration laws is exceedingly complex and is subjected to frequent, although often minor, adjustments. Generally, in the latter 1990s, approximately 660,000 people were legally admitted annually, who were seeking the following:

Family unification:
- Relatives of citizens 59%
- Relatives of legal residents 13%

Employment-based opportunities 11%
Political asylum (refugees and others) 9%
Other 8%

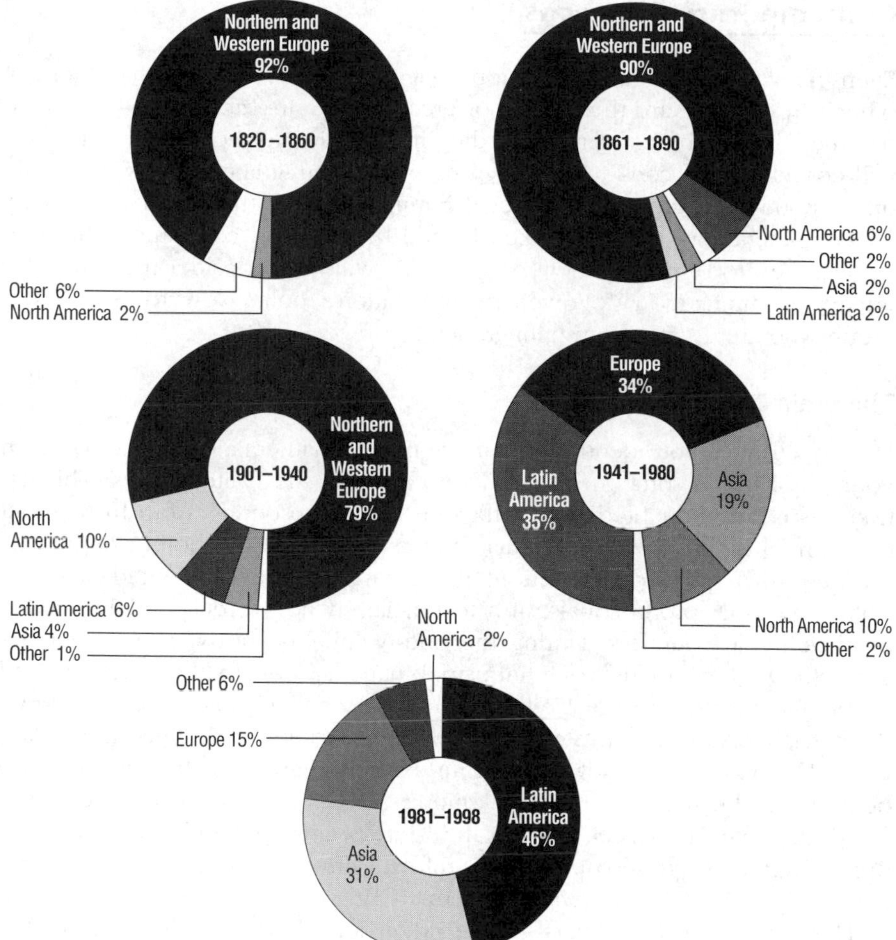

Figure 4.2 Legal Immigrants Admitted to the United States by Region of Last Residence, 1820–1998

Source: U.S. Immigration and Naturalization Service 1997:26–29; 1999a:8; 1999b:2; and author's estimates.

The liberalization of eligibility rules also brought a backlog of applications from relatives of American citizens who had earlier failed to qualify under the more restrictive national origins scheme. Backlogs of applicants still existed throughout the world, but the equal treatment for all underlying the 1965 legislation gave them greater hope of eventually entering the United States.

Overall, three-quarters of the immigrants come to join their relatives, a tenth are admitted for their special skills, and another tenth enter because of special refugees status (U.S. Immigration and Naturalization Service 1999a:7).

Contemporary Concerns

Even though our current immigration policies are less restrictive than those of other nations, they are the subject of great debate. In Table 4.1, we summarize the benefits and concerns regarding immigration to the United States. We will consider three continuing criticisms of our immigration policy: the brain drain, population growth, and illegal immigration. All three, but particularly illegal immigration, have provoked heated debates and continuing efforts to resolve the problems with new policies. We will then consider the economic impact of immigration, followed by the nation's policy toward refugees, a group who are distinct from immigrants.

The Brain Drain

How often have you identified your science or mathematics teacher or even your physician as someone who was not born in the United States? This nation has clearly benefited from attracting human resources from throughout the world, but this phenomenon has had its price for the nation of origin.

The term **brain drain** refers to the immigration to the United States of skilled workers, professionals, and technicians who are desperately needed by their home countries. During the mid-twentieth-century, many scientists and other professionals from industrial nations, principally Germany and Great Britain, came to the United States. More recently, however, the brain drain has pulled emigrants from developing nations, including India, Pakistan, Philippines, and several African nations. Earlier in the chapter, we heard Raffi Ishkanian speak of his Armenian roots. Thousands of skilled, educated Armenians now seek to enter the United States, pulled by the economic opportunity here but also pushed by difficult times in a country where earnings rarely exceed $50 a month (V. Bennett 1998).

The brain drain controversy was evident long before the passage of the 1965 Immigration Act. The 1965 act seemed, though, to encourage such im-

Table 4.1 Immigration Benefits and Concerns

Potential Benefits	*Areas of Concern*
Provide needed skills	Draining of needed resources from home country
Contribute to taxes	Sending remittances (or migradollars) home
May come with substantial capital to start business	Less skilled immigrants' competing with those already disadvantaged
Diversify the population—intangible gain	Population growth
Serve to maintain ties with countries throughout the world	Possibly complicating foreign policy through lobbying the government

migration by placing the professions in one of the categories of preference. Various corporations, including Motorola and Intel, now find that one-third of their high-tech jobs are held by people born abroad, although many received their advanced education in the United States. Furthermore, these immigrants have links to their old countries and are boosting U.S. exports to the fast-growing economic regions of Asia and Latin America (H. Bloch 1996).

Conflict theorists see the current brain drain as yet another symptom of the unequal distribution of world resources. In their view, it is ironic that the United States gives foreign aid to improve the technical resources of African and Asian countries while simultaneously maintaining an immigration policy that encourages professionals in such nations to migrate to our shores. These are the very countries that have unacceptable public health conditions and that need native scientists, educators, technicians, and other professionals. In addition, by relying on foreign talent, the United States does not need to take the steps necessary to encourage native members of subordinate groups to enter these desirable fields of employment.

Some of the effects of the brain drain have been lessened since 1982, when the entry of foreign-born and foreign-educated physicians was greatly

While many people in the United States express concern with immigration, in actuality, many immigrants bring skills needed here, which contributes to the brain drain in their home country. By Sharpnack/Washington Post National Weekly Edition.

restricted. Yet the United States continues to beckon to foreign professionals and to retain highly motivated foreign students, who remain in the United States after completing their education. A National Science Foundation study of Asian doctoral recipients found that 60 percent of the engineers and 85 percent of the scientists planned to stay in the United States (*Journal of Blacks in Higher Education* 1994).

One proposed solution to continuing international concern over the brain drain is to limit the number of professionals from a nation who may enter the United States in a year as students. Such legislation has not received widespread support from Congress. Furthermore, many industries wish to recruit from a global talent pool and voice their opposition to limits on skilled workers. Thus, the brain drain from developing countries continues.

Population Growth

The United States, like a few other industrial nations, continues to accept large numbers of permanent immigrants and refugees. Although such immigration has increased since the passage of the 1965 Immigration and Naturalization Act, the nation's birthrate has decreased. Consequently, the contribution of immigration to population growth has become more significant. Legal immigration accounted for one-fourth of the nation's growth in the 1990s. The respected environmentalist group Sierra Club debated for over a year, taking an official position favoring restricting immigration, recognizing that having more people puts greater strain on the nation's natural resources. Finally, in 1998, 60 percent of the members voted to keep a neutral position rather than enter the politically charged immigration debate (M. Cone 1998).

It is projected that immigrants who come to the United States in the period 1990–2080 and their descendants will add 72 million more people, or 25 percent of today's total, to the population. Assuming that native-born Americans maintain a low birthrate and that the immigrant contribution to the population of the United States is just 50 percent higher than at present, the contribution could run as high as 37 percent. By contrast, however, many other countries are currently receiving a much higher proportion of immigrants. Over the last ten years, more than 80 percent of population growth in Greece and Austria and more than 40 percent in Canada and Australia have come from immigration (Bouvier and Grant 1994; P. Martin and J. Widgren 1996:7).

The patterns of uneven settlement in the United States are expected to continue, so that future immigrants' impact on population growth will be felt much more in certain areas—California and New York rather than Iowa or Massachusetts. For example, California, which is the most extreme case, is expected to grow from 32 million people in 1995 to over 49 million people by the year 2025. Of this increase of 17 million people, nearly half will be new immigrants to the United States, and a sizable proportion of the remaining will be the children of recent immigrants. Although immigration and population growth may be viewed as a national concern, its impact is localized in certain areas, such as southern California and large urban centers nationwide (H. El Nasser 1996).

Illegal Immigration

The most bitterly debated aspect of U.S. immigration policy has been the control of illegal or undocumented immigrants. These immigrants and their families come to the United States in search of higher-paying jobs than their home countries can provide. As we noted at the beginning of the chapter, people like Eduardo Román García, who left his home in Veracruz, Mexico, seek employment in the United States even if they are not able to enter legally.

Immigrants are pulled here by the lure of prosperity and better lives for their children, whereas they are pushed out of their native lands by unemployment and poverty. Despite fears to the contrary, immigrants—whether legal or illegal—have had only a slight impact on the employment prospects of longtime U.S. citizens. Although some immigrants enter professional jobs, in general, immigrants are employed in jobs that employers find difficult to fill and that many residents do not want (G. Borjas 1990).

Illegal immigrants, and even legal immigrants, have become tied by the public to virtually every social problem in the nation. They become the scapegoats for unemployment; they are labeled as "drug runners" and even "terrorists." Yet their vital economic and cultural contribution to the United States is generally overlooked, as it has been for over a hundred years.

There were over 5 million illegal immigrants in the United States in 1998, and that number is increasing by about 275,000 annually. Although Mexican nationals make up about 54 percent of this total, undocumented aliens are here from throughout the world (P. Martin and E. Midgley 1999).

The cost of the federal government's attempt to police the nation's borders and locate illegal immigrants is sizable. There are significant costs for aliens, that is, foreign-born noncitizens, and for other citizens as well. Civil rights advocates have expressed concern that the procedures used to apprehend and deport people are discriminatory and deprive many aliens of their legal rights. American citizens of Hispanic or Asian origin, some of whom were born in the United States, may be greeted with prejudice and distrust, as if their names automatically imply that they are illegal immigrants. Furthermore, these citizens and legal residents of the United States may be unable to find work because employers wrongly believe that their documents are forged (Domestic Council Committee on Illegal Aliens 1976; M. Farber 1975).

In the context of this illegal immigration, Congress approved the Immigration Reform and Control Act of 1986, after nearly a decade of debate. The act marked a historic change in immigration policy compared with earlier laws, as summarized in Table 4.2. For the first time, hiring illegal aliens became illegal, so that employers are subject to fines and even prison sentences. It appears that the act has had mixed results in terms of illegal immigration. According to data compiled by the U.S. Border Patrol, arrests along the border declined substantially in the first three years after the law took effect. However, illegal immigration eventually returned to the levels of the early 1980s.

Although the Immigration Reform and Control Act prohibited employers from discriminating against legal aliens because they were not United States citizens, a 1990 report by the General Accounting Office revealed that the law had produced a "widespread pattern of discrimination" against people who looked or sounded like foreigners. The report estimated that some 890,000 employers had initiated one or more discriminatory practices in response to the 1986 immigration law. Although these firms employed nearly 7 million workers, fewer than 1,000 complaints of discrimination had been filed with government agencies—in good part because most employees were unaware of the protections included in the Immigration Reform and Control Act. A 1996 law weakened the ability of the government to sue employers who use immigration laws to discriminate against individuals (C. Brown 1990; D. Carney 1996).

Many illegal immigrants continue to live in fear and hiding, subject to even more severe harassment and discrimination than before. From a conflict perspective, these immigrants—primarily poor and Hispanic or Asian—are being firmly lodged at the bottom of the nation's social and economic hierarchies. However, from a functionalist perspective, employers, by paying low wages, are able to produce goods and services that are profitable for industry and more affordable to consumers. Despite the poor working conditions often experienced by illegal immigrants here, they continue to come because it is still in their best economic interest to work here in disadvantaged positions rather than to seek wage labor unsuccessfully in their home country.

Table 4.2 Major Immigration Policies

Policy	*Target Group*	*Impact*
Chinese Exclusion Act, 1882	Chinese	Effectively ended all Chinese immigration for over 60 years
National Origins System, 1921	Southern Europeans	Reduced overall immigration and significantly reduced likely immigration from Greece and Italy
Immigration and Naturalization Act, 1965	Western Hemisphere and the less skilled	Facilitated entry of skilled workers and relatives of U.S. residents
Immigration Reform and Control Act of 1986	Illegal immigration	Brought about modest reduction of illegal immigration

The public in the United States does occasionally notice that the pattern of taking advantage of immigrant workers has gone too far. In the 1960s, there were significant protests over the working conditions of migrant farm workers, many of whom came from Latin America and the Philippines. More recently, in 1996, national attention was drawn to several urban sweatshops, where illegal immigrants were discovered working under slavelike conditions. The garments they produced were sold in a number of national retail outlets such as Wal-Mart. Even though laws exist to prevent such situations, enforcement rarely occurs (W. Branigin 1995; C. Dugger 1996).

In the 1996 presidential campaign, immigration became an issue both in terms of the number of immigrants to be allowed to enter and the benefits they should receive. Congress proposed measures that would have restricted benefits such as schooling or public assistance to immigrants, even legal arrivals. Eventually a compromise passed, called the Illegal Immigration Reform and Immigrant Responsibility Act of 1996, which emphasized more effort to keep immigrants from entering the country illegally. Illegal immigrants will not have access to such benefit programs as Social Security and welfare, although enforcement of this measure appears to be weak. Legal immigrants, for now, will be entitled to such benefits, although welfare reform measures enacted at about the same time would likely restrict these benefits (D. Carney 1996).

Rex Rabin/Times Union

One unintended consequence of all this debate about restricting government benefits to new arrivals has been a surge in the number of immigrants seeking to become citizens. In 1997, over 1.5 million people successfully sought citizenship, compared with 300,000 annually in the early 1990s. These new citizens will have an impact on the political scene if they choose to exercise their right to vote. However, it remains unclear whether these newest citizens will necessarily be much different politically from the voting electorate they are now joining (M. Ojito 1998).

Policy makers continue to avoid the only real way to stop illegal immigration, and that is to discourage employment opportunities. The public often thinks in terms of greater surveillance at the border. A 1995 Gallup poll showed that 35 percent of the public favored erecting a Berlin-like wall along the border with Mexico. Actually, about half of the illegal immigrants come into the United States legally as students or as workers on visas but then overstay. Therefore, the solution lies in preventing illegal immigrants from obtaining employment. This solution would involve employee verification procedures, tougher penalties on employers, and perhaps national identity cards. Numerous government commissions have continued to support such measures in recent years. Conservatives, while favoring a crackdown on illegal immigration, oppose interfering further with employers' autonomy, and liberals are concerned about infringing on people's civil rights through greater workplace surveillance (D. Carney 1996; W. Cornelius 1996; M. Puente 1996b).

The Economic Impact of Immigration

There is considerable public and scholarly debate about the economic effects of immigration, both legal and illegal. Varied, conflicting conclusions have resulted from research ranging from case studies of Korean immigrants' dominance among New York City greengrocers to mobility studies charting the progress of all immigrants and their children. The confusion is due in part to the different methods of analysis. For example, the studies do not always include political refugees, who generally are less prepared than other refugees to become assimilated. Sometimes the research focuses only on economic effects, such as whether people are employed or on welfare; in other cases, it also considers cultural factors such as knowledge of English.

Perhaps the most significant factor is whether a study examines the national impact of immigration or only its effects on a local area. Overall, we can conclude from the research that immigrants adapt rather well and are an asset to the local economy. In some areas, heavy immigration may drain a community's resources. However, it can also revitalize a local economy.

According to survey data, many people in the United States hold the stereotypical belief that immigrants often end up on welfare and thereby cause increases in taxes. Economist David Card studied the 1980 "Mariel" boatlift that brought 125,000 Cubans into Miami and found that even this substantial addition of mainly low-skilled workers had no measurable impact on the wages or unemployment rates of low-skilled White and African American workers in the Miami area (D. Card et al. 1998; R. Wright 1995). Social science studies generally contradict many of the negative stereotypes about the economic impact of immigration. Both a 1997 National Research Council report and a 1998 Cato Institute and National Immigration Reform report found that immigrants are a net economic gain for the population. During the extended economic boom of the 1990s stretching into 2000, immigrants were pointed to as keeping inflation in check by reducing worker shortages in many parts of the country. However, as stated before, national gains do not preclude that in some areas and for some groups, immigration may be an economic burden or may create unwanted competition for jobs. Overall, however, at this time, no evidence suggests that the most recent wave of immigrants to the United States will join the nation's permanent underclass (G. Borjas and R. Freeman 1997; M. Goozner 1999; S. Moore 1998; R. Rumbaut 1998, J. Smith and B. Edmonston 1997).

Even more intense is the controversy over illegal immigrants' receipt of welfare and health benefits. Immigrants generally pay more in taxes than they

These recent immigrants near Calexico, California, are harvesting broccoli. Such immigrants working at low wages help keep produce prices low.

receive in benefits, even if they live in major cities such as Los Angeles that have a large population of immigrants. However, because most of the taxes go to the federal government and do not generally relieve local burdens, some states and municipalities are paying these costs themselves. For example, the state of California spends about $2.35 billion on illegal immigrants' education, health care, and other services. These workers generate $2.4 billion a year in taxes, or more than the costs. However, $1.3 billion of this revenue goes to the federal government, leaving California with a large bill while benefiting the nation overall. Studies in other states have shown a similar pattern (*Harvard Law Review* 1995; Martin and Midgley 1994; R. Paral 1996; J. Passel and R. Clark 1996).

In terms of public assistance, if we focus on the individual immigrants rather than on the impact on a region, the evidence is even clearer. Studies confirm that immigrants who do go on public assistance or live in subsidized public housing are likely to receive such assistance for a shorter period than their citizen counterparts (M. Fix and J. Passel 1999).

One economic aspect of immigration that has received increasing attention is the effort to measure remittances. **Remittances** (or **migradollars**) are the monies that immigrants return to their country of origin. The amounts, which are significant, measure in the tens of millions of dollars flowing from the United States to a number of countries, where they are a very substantial source of support for families and even venture capital for new businesses. Although some observers express concern over this outflow of money, others counter that it probably represents a small price to pay for the human capital that the United States is able to utilize in the form of the immigrants themselves.

States have sought legal redress because the federal government has not seriously considered granting impact aid to heavily burdened states. In 1994, Florida joined California in suing the U.S. government to secure strict enforcement of immigration laws and reimbursement for services rendered to illegal immigrants. As frustration mounted, California voters considered a 1994 referendum banning illegal immigrants from public schools, public assistance programs, and all but emergency medical care. Although the constitutionality of the proposal was doubtful, voters heavily favored the referendum. Surveys show that such a measure would pass nationwide (D. Carney 1996).

This California referendum, Proposition 187, symbolized the revolt against immigration, especially illegal immigration. Although 59 percent of California voters approved the measure in 1994, the vote showed significant ethnic differences: 65 percent of Whites, 47 percent of African and Asian Americans, and 33 percent of Hispanics favored this proposition. The so-called "Save Our State" (SOS) proposition denied illegal immigrants education, welfare, and nonemergency health care. Public employees, including teachers, were to report illegal immigrants to authorities.

Immediately after its approval, opponents of Proposition 187 filed lawsuits posing constitutional challenges to implementation. A federal appeals court

Tens of thousands of Hispanics gathered in Washington, D.C., in October 1996 to march for full participation in U.S. society, demanding expansion of health services, affirmative action, and streamlined citizenship programs.

struck down the anti-immigrant measure as unconstitutional, but appeals are expected. Supporters hoped the success of the proposition would lead to similar movements in other states, but none have materialized so far (D. Anderson 1998).

The concern about immigration in the 1990s is both understandable and perplexing. The nation has always been uneasy about new arrivals, especially those who are different from the more affluent and the policy makers. Yet the 1990s have been marked by relatively low unemployment, low inflation, and much-diminished anxiety about our economic future. This paradoxical situation—a strong economy and concerns about immigration framed in economic arguments—suggests that other concerns, such as ethnic and racial tension, are more important in explaining current attitudes toward immigration in the United States (W. Cornelius 1996).

Refugees

Refugees are people living outside their country of citizenship for fear of political or religious persecution. Enough refugees exist to populate an entire nation. There are approximately 15 million refugees worldwide. That figure makes the nation of refugees larger than Belgium, Sweden, or Cuba. The United States has touted itself as a haven for political refugees. However, as we shall see, the welcome to political refugees has not always been unqualified.

The United States makes the largest financial contribution of any nation to worldwide assistance programs and serves as the host to over 150,000 refugees. Many nations much smaller than the United States have many more refugees than that, with Jordan, Iran, and Zaire hosting over a million refugees each (U.S. Committee for Refugees 1996a).

The United States, insulated by distance from wars and famines in Europe and Asia, has been able to be selective about which and how many refugees are welcomed. Since the arrival of refugees uprooted by World War II, the United States has allowed three groups of refugees to enter in numbers greater than regulations would ordinarily permit: Hungarians, Cubans, and Southeast Asians. Compared with the other two groups, the nearly 40,000 Hungarians who arrived following the unsuccessful revolt against the Soviet Union of November 1956 were few indeed. At the time, however, theirs was the fastest mass immigration to this country since before 1922. With little delay, the United States amended the laws so that the Hungarian refugees could enter. Because of their small numbers and their dispersion throughout this country, the Hungarians are little in evidence four decades later. The much larger and longer period of movement of Cuban and Southeast Asian refugees into the United States continues to have a profound social and economic impact.

Despite periodic public opposition, the U.S. government is officially committed to accepting refugees from other nations. According to the United Nations treaty on refugees, which our government ratified in 1968, countries are obliged to refrain from forcibly returning people to territories where their lives or liberty might be endangered. It is not always clear, though, whether an individual is fleeing for his or her personal safety or to escape poverty. Although people in the latter category may be of humanitarian interest, they do not meet the official definition of refugees and are subject to deportation.

It is the practice of deporting people fleeing poverty that has been the subject of criticism. There is a long tradition in the United States of facilitating the arrival of people leaving Communist nations. Mexicans who are refugees from poverty, Liberians who are fleeing civil war, and Haitians who are running from despotic rule are not similarly welcomed. The plight of Haitians has become of particular concern.

Haitians fled their country, often on small boats, from the time of the military coup in 1991 that overthrew the elected government of President Jean-Bertrand Aristide until he was restored to power in October 1994. The U.S. Coast Guard intercepted many Haitians at sea, saving some of these boat people from death in their rickety and overcrowded wooden vessels.

The Haitians said they feared detentions, torture, and execution if they remained in Haiti. However, the Bush administration viewed most of the Haitian exiles as economic migrants rather than political refugees and opposed granting them asylum and permission to enter the United States. During the 1992 presidential campaign, candidate Bill Clinton denounced the policy of interdiction as "cruel" and illegal; yet after assuming the Presidency in 1993, he kept in place the policy of keeping Haitians from entering. In 1993, the U.S. Supreme Court, by an 8–1 vote, upheld the government's right to intercept Haitian refugees at sea and to return them to their homeland without asylum hearings. Steven Forester, an attorney at the Haitian Refugee Center in Miami, wondered how the justices could uphold a policy of forcibly returning Haitian refugees to "their military persecutors, . . . who the State Department condemns for their horrendous human rights practices" (L. Greenhouse 1993b; L. Rohter 1993:18).

In 1997, 122,000 people overseas sought to enter the United States as refugees, with 77,600 granted refugee status (most from Bosnia, followed by the former Soviet Union). The Immigration and Naturalization Service attempts to deal with the huge backlog of more than 455,000 residents who are waiting for hearings regarding their petitions. A massive bureaucracy that includes 325 asylum officers and 179 immigration judges has been developed to deal with the refugees. Currently, most of the refugees seeking to enter the United States are from Central America, the former Soviet Union, Haiti, and China. Refugees are a worldwide challenge to all nations, and the United States is no exception (U.S. Committee for Refugees 1996a, 1996b).

Conclusion

For its first hundred years, the United States allowed all immigrants to enter and become permanent residents. The federal policy of welcome did not mean, however, that immigrants would not encounter discrimination and prejudice. With the passage of the Chinese Exclusion Act, discrimination against one group of potential immigrants became law. The Chinese were soon joined by the Japanese as peoples forbidden by law to enter and prohibited from becoming naturalized citizens. The development of the national origins system in the 1920s created a hierarchy of nationalities, with people from northern Europe encouraged to enter while other Europeans and Asians encountered long delays. The possibility of a melting pot, which had always been a fiction, was legislated out of existence.

In the 1960s and again in 1990, the policy was liberalized, so that the importance of nationality was minimized and a person's work skills and relationship to an American were emphasized. This liberalization came at a time when most Europeans no longer desired to immigrate into the United States. The legacy of the arrival of the over 64 million immigrants since 1820 is apparent today in their descendants, such as Raffi Ishkanian.

Throughout the history of the United States, as we have seen, there has been intense debate over the nation's immigration and refugee policies. In a sense, this debate reflects the deep value conflicts in the culture of the United States, and it parallels the "American dilemma" identified by Swedish social economist Gunnar Myrdal (1944). One strand of our culture—well epitomized by the words "Give us your tired, your poor, your huddled masses"—has emphasized egalitarian principles and a desire to help people in their time of need. At the same time, however, hostility to potential immigrants and refugees—whether the Chinese in the 1880s, European Jews in the 1930s and 1940s, or Mexicans, Haitians, and Arabs today—reflects not only racial, ethnic, and religious prejudice but also a desire to maintain the dominant culture of the in-group by keeping out those viewed as outsiders. The conflict between these cultural values is central to the American dilemma of the 1990s.

At present, the debate about immigration is highly charged and emotional. Some people see it in economic terms, whereas others see the new arrivals as a challenge to the very culture of our society. Clearly, the general perception is that immigration presents a problem rather than offers a promise for the future. A 1997 national survey found the majority of respondents convinced that immigration would overburden the welfare system, take jobs away from people already here, and even lead to increased conflict between racial and ethnic groups (Princeton Survey Research Associates 1997).

Today's concern about immigrants follows generations of people coming to settle in the United States. This immigration in the past produced a very diverse country in terms of both nationality and religion even before the immigration of the last fifty years. Therefore, the majority of Americans today are not descended from the English, and Protestants are little over half of all worshipers. This diversity of religious and ethnic groups will be examined in Chapter 5.

Key Terms

brain drain 122
nativism 112
refugees 131
remittances (or migradollars) 130
sinophobes 115
xenophobia 112

Review Questions

1. Why are nationality and religion used to oppose immigration?
2. What were the social and economic issues when public opinion mounted against Chinese immigration into the United States?
3. Ultimately, what do you think is the major concern people have about contemporary immigration to the United States—the numbers of immigrants or their nationality?
4. What are the principles that appear to guide the refugee policy?

Critical Thinking

1. What is the immigrant root story of your family? Consider how your ancestors arrived in the United States and also how your family's past has been shaped by other immigrant groups.
2. Can you find evidence of the brain drain in terms of the professionals with whom you come in contact? Do you regard this phenomenon as a benefit? What groups in the United States may not have been encouraged to fill such positions by the availability of such professionals?

Internet Exercises

1. Stories, primary source material, and photographs of Asian immigration history are available on the Ancestors in the Americas web site (http://www.cetel.org/). Explore both the site and this chapter in order to reflect on these issues: What specific parallels can be drawn between the experiences of African slaves in the Americas and those of Chinese coolies? What were some of the historical and social reasons for the influx of Asian immigrants to American shores beginning in the seventeenth and eighteenth centuries? What were the rulings in the *People* v. *Hall* and *U.S.* v. *Wong Kim Ark* court cases? Why are these cases important? What was the impact of the Chinese Exclusion Act of 1882? Where and what was Angel Island? (see the Historical Documents section). Read some of the poetry written on the walls of Angel Island and the stories of Asians who first came to the Americas. What experiences do these poems and stories convey? What hopes and fears did people have? Describe what daily life was like for those who lived these stories. What are some of the significant contributions made by Asian immigrants to the United States? After compiling information from the web site and your textbook, compare and contrast the immigration experiences of Korean, Japanese, Filipino, and Chinese peoples. What common challenges did they face? What unique obstacles did they overcome? What single fact that you learned surprised you the most, and why?

2. Every twenty-one seconds, the world gains a new refugee. This fact and others are found on Refuge!, Amnesty International's interactive web page detailing struggles and challenges of people living outside their country of citizenship for fear of political or religious persecution (http://www.refuge.amnesty.org/htm/home.htm/). Visit each of the links listed below to learn more about refugees. In the "How Is a Refugee Made?" section, read the brief true stories of Sallay Goba, Renata Mandic, Fauziya, and Assam. What social or political forces led to each one's becoming a refugee? In what ways are their stories similar? In what ways are they different? Examine the "10 Facts" and "10 Pictures" links. Which statistic surprised you the most? Why? Have the information and photographs from your book and this web site changed your perception or understanding of refugees? Why, or why not? Finally, engage your sociological imagination by reflecting on the following: The site asks visitors to think about what they would take with them if forced to flee from their homes in ten minutes. Before actually click-

ing on this section online, make a list of items you would take. You cannot take your car, nor can you ride any form of public transportation—you will be carrying everything with you and traveling on foot. What items would you take? Why would you take these items and not others? Once your list is compiled, click on the web page's "10 Minutes" section to see what items real refugees commonly take with them. How does your list compare with theirs? Would you change your list after seeing the online information? What items would you now add or delete?

3. The history of Italian, Irish, Swedish, and Jewish emigrants/immigrants are highlighted on ThinkQuest's multimedia site "from one life to another" (http://library.thinkquest.org/26786/). Take a cyber "tour" by clicking on the "Tour" button, and view the photographs of immigrants traveling by boat in the "Slideshow." What strikes you most about the photographs? How were the people dressed? What items did they carry with them? What were living conditions like on these ships and boats? Read the information in the "Articles" section. Compare and contrast the causes of emigration and the experiences in America for the Italian, Irish, Swedish, and Jewish populations. What are the similarities and the differences? How many of each group came to the United States over the last few centuries? What did the Statue of Liberty symbolize for those coming to America, according to the web site? When was it built, and by whom? Who wrote the poem on the statue, and what does the poem refer to? Finally, take the "Challenge: Life Quiz," and see how well you do remembering all that you learned.

Ethnicity and Religion

CHAPTER OUTLINE

HIGHLIGHTS

The United States includes a multitude of ethnic and religious groups. Do they coexist in harmony or in conflict? How significant are they as sources of identity for their members? There was a resurgence of interest in their ethnicity among Whites in the 1960s and well into the 1970s, partly in response to the renewed pride in the ethnicity of Blacks, Hispanics, and Native Americans. We have an ethnicity paradox in which White ethnics seem to enjoy their heritage while at the same time seeking to assimilate into larger society. White ethnics are the victims of humor (or respectable bigotry) that some still consider socially acceptable, and they find themselves with little power in big business. Religious minorities have also experienced intolerance in the present as well as the past. Constitutional issues such as school prayer, secessionist minorities, creationism, and public religious displays are regularly taken to the Supreme Court. Italian Americans and the Amish are presented as case studies of the experiences of specific ethnic and religious groups in the United States.

Betty O'Keefe is a 60-year-old Californian who is a fifth-generation Irish American—that being so, her grandmother's grandmother came to the United States from Ireland. Sociologist Mary Waters (1990:97) asked O'Keefe what it was like growing up in the United States.

> *When I was in high school my maiden name was Tynan. This was 1940. I was dating some boys from school, and two different times when the parents found out I was an Irish Catholic, they told him he couldn't go out with me. The Protestants were like that.... One of his brothers later married someone named O'Flannery and I was so thrilled. I said I hope your mother is turning in her grave. So I am happy that my children have the name O'Keefe. So that people know right away what their background is. I think it is better. They would never be put in the position I was in.*
>
> *Do you think something like that could happen now?*
>
> *I don't think so openly. But I think it is definitely still there. You are not as bad (being an Irish Catholic) as a Black, but you are not Protestant. You are not Jewish either, which would be worse, but still you are not of their church.*

Their names may be Badovich, Hoggarty, Jablonski, Reggio, or Williams. They may follow any one of thousands of faiths and gather at any of the 360,000 churches, mosques, synagogues, and temples. Our nation's motto is *E Pluribus Unum,* and although there may be doubt that we are truly united into one common culture following a single ideology, there is little doubt about our continuing diversity as a nation of peoples.

Indeed, the very complexity of relations between dominant and subordinate groups in the United States today is partly the result of its heterogeneous population. No one ethnic origin or religious faith encompasses all the inhabitants of the United States. Even though its largest period of sustained immigration is two generations past, an American today is surrounded by remnants of cultures and practitioners of religions whose origins are foreign to this country. Religion and ethnicity continue to be significant in defining an individual's identity.

Ethnic Diversity

The ethnic diversity of the United States in the 1990s is apparent to almost everyone. Passersby in New York City were undoubtedly surprised once when two street festivals met head to head. The procession of San Gennaro, the patron saint of Naples, marched through Little Italy, only to run directly into a Chinese festival originating in Chinatown. Teachers in many public schools frequently face students who speak only one language, and it is not English. Students in Chicago are taught in Spanish, Greek, Italian, Polish, German, Creole, Japanese, Cantonese, or the language of a Native American tribe. In the Detroit metropolitan area, classroom instruction is conveyed in twenty-one languages, including Arabic, Portuguese, Ukrainian, Latvian, Lithuanian, and Serbian. In many areas of the United States, you can refer to a special Yellow Pages in which you may find a driving instructor who speaks Portuguese or a psychotherapist who will talk to you in Hebrew.

Germans are the largest ancestral group; the 1990 U.S. Census showed almost one-fourth of Americans saying they had at least some German ancestry. Although most German Americans are assimilated, it is possible to see the ethnic tradition in some areas, particularly in Milwaukee, whose population has 48 percent German ancestry. There, three Saturday schools teach German, and it is possible to affiliate with thirty-four German-American clubs and visit a German library that operates within the public library system (D. Carvajal 1996; K. Johnson 1992; M. Usdansky 1992a).

As shown in Table 5.1, Germany is one of twenty-one European nations from which at least 1 million people claim to have ancestry. The numbers are striking when one considers the size of some of the sending countries. For example, there are almost 39 million Irish Americans, whereas the Republic of Ireland had a population of 3.7 million in 1998. Similarly, nearly 5 million people claim Swedish ancestry, whereas there are 8.9 million people living in Sweden today. Now, of course, many Irish and Swedish Americans are of mixed ancestry, but not everyone in Ireland is Irish, nor is everyone in Sweden Swedish.

Why Don't We Study Whiteness?

Race is socially constructed, as we learned in Chapter 1. Sometimes, we come to define race in a clear-cut manner—a descendant of a Pilgrim is White, for example. But sometimes race is more ambiguous—people who are the chil-

Table 5.1 Population by European Ancestry, 1990

The major sources of European ancestry in the present population in the United States are Germany, Ireland, England, Italy, and France.

Ancestry Group	*Total (1,000)*	*Ancestry Group*	*Total (1,000)*
Austrian	865	Lithuanian	812
British	1,119	Norwegian	3,869
Croatian	944	Polish	9,366
Czech	1,296	Portuguese	1,153
Danish	1,635	Russian	2,953
Dutch	6,227	Scandinavian	679
English	32,652	Scotch-Irish	5,618
European	467	Scottish	5,394
Finnish	659	Slovak	1,883
French	10,321	Swedish	4,681
German	57,947	Swiss	1,045
Greek	1,110	Ukrainian	741
Hungarian	1,582	Welsh	2,034
Irish	38,736	Yugoslavian	258
Italian	14,665		

Source: U.S. Bureau of the Census, 1996:53.

dren of an African American and Vietnamese American union are biracial or "mixed," or whatever they come to be seen by others. Our recognition that race is socially constructed has sparked a renewed interest in what it means to be White in the United States. Two aspects of White as a race are useful to consider: the historical creation of whiteness, and the way that contemporary White people reflect on their racial identity.

When the English immigrants established themselves as the political founders of the United States, they also came to define what it meant to be White. Other groups that today are regarded as White, such as Irish, German, Norwegian, or Swedish, were not always considered White in the eyes of the English. Differences in language and religious worship, as well as past allegiance to a king in Europe different from the English ruler—all caused these groups to be seen not as Whites in the Western Hemisphere but more as nationals of their home country who happened to be residing in North America. The old distrust in Europe, where, for example, the Irish were viewed by the English as socially and culturally inferior, continued on this side of the Atlantic Ocean. Karl Marx, writing from England, reported that the average English worker looked down on the Irish in the same way that poor Whites in the American South looked down on Black people (N. Ignatiev 1994, 1995; D. Roediger 1994).

LISTEN TO THEIR VOICES

When the Boats Arrived

Diane Glancy

Some of my ancestors came from Europe on boats. Others were already here when the boats arrived. I have done a lot of my writing examining the Indian part of my heritage, which came through my father. The white part didn't seem to need definition. It just was. Is. And shall be. But what does it mean to be part white? What does whiteness look like viewed from the other, especially when that other is also within oneself?

I can say whiteness is the dominant culture, for now anyway. Or I can say I was taught that whiteness gives definition instead of receiving it. It is the upright. The unblemished. The milk or new snow. It is the measure by which others are measured. There's nothing off center in it to make it aware of itself as outside or other. It doesn't need examination or explanation, but is the center around which others orbit. It is the plumb line. Other races/cultures/ethnicities are looked at in terms of their distance from whiteness. Whiteness is a heritage I can almost enter, but I have *unwhiteness* in me. There is something that is not milk or new snow. I am a person of part color. I can feel my distance from whiteness. There is a dividing line into it I cannot cross. But neither can I cross fully into the Indian, because I am of mixed heritage.

When I look at my white heritage, it is as fragmented and hard to pinpoint as the native side. My mother's family came from England and Germany. They settled in Pennsylvania, then Virginia, and finally on the Missouri-Kansas border. What do I know of them any more than of my father's family? The European part of the family were practical, middle-of-the-road people. They got their work done. They didn't say a lot about it. They were fair-minded and tenacious. They were churchgoers and voters who migrated from the farm to the city in my parents' generation. They educated their children and died without much ceremony.

As for the white culture I saw in my mother's family—every Christmas Eve, they served Canadian bacon, which my father brought from the stockyards where he worked. I received an Easter basket on Easter. I got a sparkler on the Fourth of July. But that hardly defines culture.

I can look at the whiteness in my mother's family and say there was a determination, a punctuality, a dependability. There was a sense of Manifest Destiny, which was another tool for dominance. There was a need for maintenance and responsibility. A sense of a Judeo-Christian God. A holding to one's own. There was a need to be goal-oriented. To make use of resources.

There also was opportunity to do all these things.

Who can say what will happen to whiteness as the people of color become the majority in the new century? Who can say what will happen as the cultures of the minorities deepen, as the white is mixed with others and gets harder to define? Can the white culture continue to be defined by its lack of ceremonies, its Elvises and White Castles, its harbor of ideas? Will it continue to invent its inventiveness? Will it continue to thrive?

I guess I would define white American culture as industriousness without overwhelming tradition. It doesn't seem to have anchors, but slides past others into port. Into the port it created, after all.

Source: Diane Glancy. "When the Boats Arrived." Reprinted by permission from *The Hungry Mind Review,* Spring 1998.

In "Listen to Their Voices," Diane Glancy, Macalester College professor of Native American literature and creative writing, draws on both "insider" and "outsider" perspectives on being White in the United States. As she describes, she is descended from Native Americans (American Indians) as well as from English and Germans. As this chapter continues, we will consider in a variety of ways what it meant to be White in the United Sates at the beginning of the twentieth century.

As European immigrants and their descendants assimilated to the English and distanced themselves from other oppressed groups, such American Indians and African Americans, they came to be viewed as White rather than as part of a particular culture. Writer Noel Ignatiev (1994:84), contrasting being White with being Polish, argues that "Whiteness is nothing but an expression of race privilege." This strong statement argues that being White, as opposed to being Black or Asian, is characterized by being a member of the dominant group.

Contemporary White Americans generally give little thought to "being White." Hence there is little interest in studying "whiteness" or considering "being White" except that it is "not being Black." White people are occasionally reminded when filling out a form that asks for race or when they hear White people in general accused of being racist. Unlike non-Whites, who are much more likely to interact with Whites, take orders from Whites, see Whites as the leading figures in the mass media, Whites enjoy the privilege of not being reminded of their Whiteness.

There is a new interest in the 1990s that seeks to look at whiteness but not from the vantage point of a White supremacist. Rather, focusing on White people as a race or on what it means today to be White goes beyond any definition that implies superiority over non-Whites. This is still a relatively new field of inquiry, even in academic fields, so the area is still in the process of being defined. However, as we will discuss later, as African Americans, Hispanics, and Native Americans celebrated their roots, many Whites felt left out. In response, although they did not celebrate being White, they sought out their ethnic roots, such as being Polish American or Irish American. As sociologist Mary Waters (1990) reports in her book *Ethnic Options*, this undertaking is not difficult because White people are well aware of their ancestry. They are more likely to know about their ancestors' birthplaces than they do about their religion, occupation, education, or year of birth.

Religious Pluralism

In popular speech, the term *pluralism* has often been used in the United States to refer explicitly to religion. Although certain faiths figure more prominently in the worship scene, there has been a history of religious tolerance in the United States, in contrast to most other nations. Today there are over 1,500 religious bodies in the United States, ranging from the more than 60 million members of the Roman Catholic Church to sects with fewer than 1,000 adherents.

There is an increasingly non-Christian presence in the United States. In 1900, an estimated 96 percent of the nation was Christian, just over 1 percent nonreligious, and about 3 percent all other faiths. Today, it is estimated that the nation is 85 percent Christian, nearly 8 percent nonreligious, and about 6 percent all other faiths. The United States has a long Jewish tradition, and Muslims number close to 5 million. A smaller but also growing number of people adhere to such Eastern faiths as Hinduism, Buddhism, Confucianism, and Taoism (D. B. Barret and T. Johnson 1998).

The diversity of religious life in the United States is apparent from Figure 5.1, which shows the Christian faiths that dominate various areas of the country numerically. For many nations of the world, a map of religions would hardly be useful, because one faith accounts for almost all religious followers in the country. The diversity of beliefs, rituals, and experiences that characterizes religious life in the United States reflects both the nation's immigrant heritage and the First Amendment prohibition against establishing a state religion (ACLU 1996a).

Sociologists use the word **denomination** for a large, organized religion that is not linked officially with the state or government. By far the largest denomination in the United States is Roman Catholicism, yet at least twenty-three other religious denominations have 1 million or more members (see Table 5.2). Protestants collectively accounted for about 58 percent of the nation's adult population in 1998, compared with 25 percent for Roman Catholics and about 2 percent for Jews (*Gallup Poll Monthly* 1998:40).

One notable characteristic of religious practice in the United States is the almost completely separate worship practices of Blacks and Whites. During the 1976 presidential campaign, an unusual amount of attention was directed to the segregation practiced by churches in the United States. The church attended by Jimmy Carter in Plains, Georgia, captured headlines when it closed its doors to a Black civil rights activist who was seeking membership. The Plains church later opened its membership to African Americans at Carter's

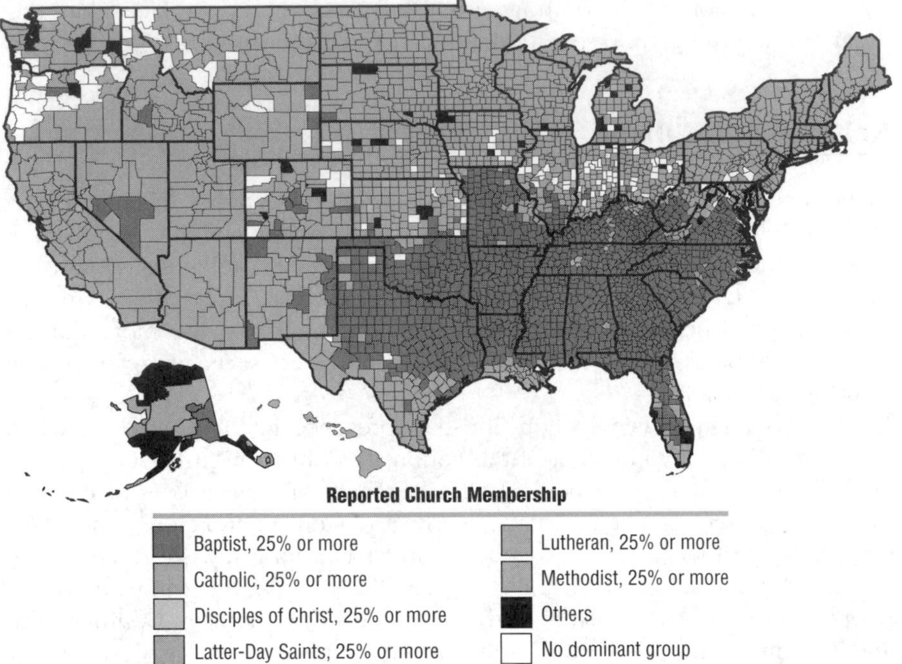

Figure 5.1 Predominant Christian Denominations by Counties, 1990
The diversity of Christian religious life in the United States is apparent in the figure. Many Christian denominations account for 25 percent or more of the church members in a county. Among non-Christian faiths, only Judaism may figure so significantly—in New York County (Manhattan) of New York City and in Dade County, Florida (which includes Miami Beach).
Source: M. Bradley et al. 1992.

urging. Such formal racial restrictions are unusual, but today the church hour on Sunday mornings still fits the description "the most segregated hour of the week." Of all major Protestant denominations, the United Methodist Church boasts the largest Black constituency, but that is only 3 percent. Overall, no more than 10 percent of Black Christians belong to predominantly White denominations, usually attending all-Black congregations. At the local or church level, it is estimated that only 1 percent of Black Christians belong to White churches (K. Briggs 1976; R. Stark 1987).

About seven in ten Americans (69 percent) are counted as church members, but it is difficult to assess the strength of their religious commitment. A persuasive case can be made that religious institutions continue to grow stronger through an influx of new members despite mounting secularism in society. Some observers think that, after reaching a low in the 1960s, religion

Table 5.2 Churches with More Than a Million Members, 2000

Denomination	*Membership*
The Roman Catholic Church	62,018,436
Southern Baptist Convention	15,729,356
The United Methodist Church	8,400,000
National Baptist Convention, USA, Inc.	8,200,000
The Church of God in Christ	5,499,875
Evangelical Lutheran Church in America	5,178,225
The Church of Jesus Christ of Latter-day Saints	4,923,100
Presbyterian Church (U.S.A.)	3,574,959
National Baptist Convention of America, Inc.	3,500,000
The Lutheran Church—Missouri Synod	2,594,404
Assemblies of God	2,525,812
African Methodist Episcopal Church	2,500,000
Progressive National Baptist Convention, Inc.	2,500,000
National Missionary Baptist Convention of America	2,500,000
Episcopal Church	2,364,559
Greek Orthodox Archdiocese of America	1,954,500
American Baptist Churches in the U.S.A.	1,507,400
Churches of Christ	1,500,000
Pentecostal Assemblies of the World, Inc.	1,500,000
Baptist Bible Fellowship International	1,200,000
United Church of Christ	1,421,088
African Methodist Episcopal Zion Church	1,252,369
Christian Churches and Churches of Christ	1,071,616
Jehovah's Witnesses	1,040,283
The Orthodox Church in America	1,000,000

Source: "Membership Statistics in the United States" *Yearbook of American and Canadian Churches 2000,* edited by Eileen W. Lindner, pp. 339–351. Data for National Baptist Convention is from the 1998 yearbook.

is becoming important to people again. The past upheavals in American religious life are reflected on the covers of *Time* magazine, which have cried out variously, "Is God Dead?" (April 8, 1966), "Is God Coming Back to Life?" (December 26, 1969), and "The Jesus Revolution" (June 21, 1971). Much more recently, *Newsweek* proclaimed that "Science Finds God" (July 20, 1998). At present, there is little statistical support for the view that the influence of religion on society is diminishing (*Gallup Poll Monthly* 1998:38).

In reviewing data on church attendance and feelings about organized religion, however, we surmise that religion is not uniformly on the upswing. There is a great deal of switching of denominations, and, as in the past, there is considerable interest in new ways of expressing spirituality. Some new groups encounter hostility from organized, established faiths that question the tactics used to attract new members and financial support. It would be incorrect to conclude either that religion is slowly being abandoned or that Americans are turning to religion with the zeal of new converts. The future may bring not only periods of religious revivalism but also times of decline in religious fervor.

It would also be incorrect to focus only on older religious organizations. Local churches that developed into national faiths during the 1990s, such as the Calvary Chapel, Vineyard, and Hope Chapel, have created a following among Pentecostal believers, who embrace a more charismatic form of worship devoid of many traditional ornaments, with pastors and congregations alike favoring informal attire. New faiths develop with increasing rapidity in what can only be termed a very competitive market for individual religious faith. In addition, people, with or without religious affiliation, become fascinated with spiritual concepts such as angels or become a part of loose-knit fellowships such as the Promise Keepers, an all-male movement of evangelical Christians founded in 1990. Religion in the United States is an ever-changing social phenomenon (D. Miller 1997; D. Miller and R. Schaefer 1998).

Throughout our discussion, we have considered how the media distort, if not stereotype, racial and ethnic groups. This distortion also appears to be true in media depiction of the role of religion in our daily lives. Although a 1998 national survey showed that 59 percent considered religion very important to them, one would not recognize that state of affairs by watching motion pictures or television, where religion rarely appears as a subject except at times of scandal or in offering an inside look at some satanic cult. An analysis of the top-grossing films shows religion and religious characters increasingly depicted in a negative light and as less likely to reach their goals than are nonreligious characters. Religion is relatively absent from television: it appears only once every 3.3 hours, and the appearance is not necessarily positive. For example, for every one positive depiction of the devout laity, there were ten negative ones. Furthermore positive portrayals of clergy barely outnumber negative ones. Historically, spirituality appeared routinely on such shows as *M*A*S*H* (Father Francis Mulcahy), *The Waltons, Little House on the Prairie,* and *Highway to Heaven*. However, since 1991, among hundreds of programs, only *Dr. Quinn: Medicine Woman, Northern Exposure, Picket Fences, Good News, Soul Man, Touched By an Angel, 7th Heaven*, and *Promised Land* have regularly had positive religion-oriented story lines. (*Gallup Poll Monthly* 1998:37; T. Johnson 1998).

The Rediscovery of Ethnicity

Robert Park (1950:205), a prominent early sociologist, wrote in 1913 that "a Pole, Lithuanian, or Norwegian cannot be distinguished, in the second generation, from an American, born of native parents." At one time, sociologists saw the end of ethnicity as nearly a foregone conclusion. W. Lloyd Warner and Leo Srole (1945) wrote in their often-cited Yankee City series that the future of ethnic groups seemed to be limited in the United States and that they would be quickly absorbed. Oscar Handlin's *Uprooted* (1951) told of the destruction of immigrant values and their replacement by American culture. Although Handlin was among the pioneers in investigating ethnicity, assimilation was the dominant theme in his work.

Many writers have shown almost a fervent hope that ethnicity would vanish. The persistence of ethnicity was for some time treated by sociologists as dysfunctional, because it meant a continuation of old values that interfered with the allegedly superior new values. For example, to hold on to one's language delayed entry into the larger labor market and the upward social mobility that it afforded. Ethnicity was expected to disappear not only because assimilation would eradicate language differences but also because aspirations to higher social class and status demanded that ethnicity vanish. Somehow, it was assumed that one could not be ethnic and middle class at the same time, much less affluent.

The Third-Generation Principle

Historian Marcus Hansen's (1952) **principle of third-generation interest** was an early exception to the assimilationist approach to White ethnic groups. Simply stated, Hansen maintained that in the third generation—the grandchildren of the original immigrants—ethnic interest and awareness would actually increase. According to Hansen, "What the son wishes to forget the grandson wishes to remember." Hansen's principle has been tested several times since it was first put forth. John Goering (1971), in interviewing Irish and Italian Catholics, found that ethnicity was more important to members of the third generation than it was to the immigrants themselves. Similarly, Mary Waters (1990), in her interviews of White ethnics living in suburban San Jose, California, and suburban Philadelphia, Pennsylvania, observed many grandchildren wishing to study their ancestors' language even though it would be a foreign language to them. They also expressed interest in learning more of their ethnic group's history and a desire to visit the homeland.

Social scientists in the past were quick to minimize the ethnic awareness of blue-collar workers. In fact, ethnicity was viewed as merely another aspect of White ethnics' alleged racist nature, an allegation that will be examined later in this chapter. Curiously, the very same intellectuals and journalists who bent over backward to understand the growing solidarity of Blacks, Hispanics, and Native Americans refused to give White ethnics the academic attention they deserved (D. Wrong 1972).

The new assertiveness of Blacks and other non-Whites of their rights in the 1960s unquestionably presented White ethnics with the opportunity to reexamine their own position. "If solidarity and unapologetic self-consciousness might hasten Blacks' upward mobility, why not ours?" asked the White ethnics, who were often only half a step above Blacks in social status. The African American movement pushed other groups to reflect on their past. The increased consciousness of Blacks and their positive attitude toward African culture and the contributions worldwide of African Americans are embraced in what we termed earlier (Chapter 1) the Afrocentric perspective. The mood, therefore, was set in the 1960s for the country to be receptive to ethnicity. By legitimizing Black cultural differences from White culture, along with those of Native Americans and Hispanics, the country's opinion leaders legitimized other types of cultural diversity.

Symbolic Ethnicity

Observers comment both on the evidence of assimilation and, at the same time, of the signs of ethnic identity that seem to support a pluralistic view of society. How can both be possible?

First, there is the very visible evidence of **symbolic ethnicity,** which may lead us to exaggerate the persistence of ethnic ties among White Americans. According to sociologist Herbert Gans (1979), ethnicity today increasingly involves the symbols of ethnicity, such as eating ethnic food, acknowledging ceremonial holidays such as St. Patrick's Day, and supporting specific political issues or the issues confronting the old country. A recent example was the push in 1998 by Irish Americans to convince state legislatures to make it compulsory in public schools to teach about the Irish potato famine, which was a significant factor in immigration to the United States. This symbolic ethnicity may be more visible, but this type of ethnic heritage does not interfere with what people do, read, or say, or even whom they befriend or marry. Richard Alba (1990) surveyed Whites in the Albany, New York, area in the mid-1980s and found that even though there had been a decline in distinctions among ethnic groups, ethnic identity was still acknowledged. Heritage may not have disappeared, and indeed, the past, however defined, may even be important in today's frantic world.

The ethnicity of the 1990s embraced by English-speaking Whites is typically symbolic. It does not include active involvement in ethnic activities or participation in ethnic-related organizations. In fact, sizable proportions of White ethnics have gained large-scale entry into almost all clubs, cliques, and fraternal groups. Such acceptance is a key indicator of assimilation. Ethnicity has become increasingly peripheral to the lives of the members of the ethnic group. Although they may not relinquish their ethnic identity, other identities become more important (M. Gordon 1964).

Second, the ethnicity that does exist may be more a result of living in the United States than actual importing of practices from the past or the old country. Many so-called ethnic foods or celebrations, for example, began in the United States. The persistence of ethnic consciousness, then, may not de-

Immigrants and their descendants often prosper by serving their ethnic community. In a Chicago deli, a clerk serves up a plate of olives.

pend on foreign birth, a distinctive language, and a unique way of life. Instead, it may reflect the experiences in the United States of a unique group that developed a cultural tradition distinct from that of the mainstream. For example, in Poland the *szlachta,* or landed gentry, rarely mixed socially with the peasant class. In the United States, however, even with those associations still fresh, they interacted together in social organizations as they settled in relatively concentrated communities that were segregated physically and socially from others (N. Glazer 1971; N. Glazer and P. Moynihan 1970; H. Lopata 1993).

Third, maintaining ethnicity can be a critical step toward successful assimilation. This **ethnicity paradox** facilitates full entry into the dominant culture. The ethnic community may give its members not only a useful financial boost but also the psychological strength and positive self-esteem that will allow them to compete effectively in larger society. Thus, we may witness people participating actively in their ethnic enclave while at the same time trying to cross the bridge into the wider community (B. Lal 1995). Ethnicity, therefore, gives continuity with the past, in the form of an affective or emotional tie. The significance of this sense of belonging cannot be emphasized enough. Whether reinforced by distinctive behavior or by what Milton Gordon (1964) called a sense of "peoplehood," ethnicity is an effective, functional source of cohesion. Proximity to fellow ethnics is not necessary for a person to maintain social cohesion and in-group identity. Fraternal organizations or sports-related groups can preserve associations among ethnics who are separated geographically. Members of ethnic groups may even maintain their feelings of in-group solidarity after leaving ethnic communities in the central cities for the suburban fringe.

The Price Paid by White Ethnics

Many White ethnics shed their past and wish only to be Americans, with no ancestral ties to another country. Boris Shlapak, who played forward on a professional soccer team, changed his name to Ian Stone because "American kids need to identify with soccer players as Americans" (C. Terry 1975). Stone, who by his own admission "never felt ethnic," was not concerned about being a figure to whom Slavic Americans would look as a hero. Some ethnics do not wish to abandon their heritage, but in order to retain their past as a part of their present, they must pay a price because of prejudice and discrimination.

Prejudice toward White Ethnic Groups

Our examination of immigration to the United States in Chapter 4 pointed out the mixed feelings that have greeted European immigrants. Apparently, they are still not well received. In 1944, well after most immigration from Poland had ended, the Polish-American Congress, an umbrella organization of forty Polish fraternities, was founded to defend the image of Polish Americans. Young Polish Americans are made to feel ashamed of their ethnic origin when teachers find their names unpronounceable and when they hear Polish jokes bandied about in a way that anti-Black or anti-Semitic humor is not. One survey found that half of second-generation Polish Americans encounter prejudice. Curiously, it was socially proper to condemn the White working class as racist but quite improper to question the negative attitude of middle-class people toward White ethnics. Michael Lerner (1969) called this hostility toward White ethnics **respectable bigotry.** Polish jokes are acceptable, whereas anti-Black humor is considered to be in poor taste.

An important component of Lerner's respectable bigotry is not ethnic prejudice but class prejudice. In 1973, researchers surveyed Whites living in areas of Florida that had undergone school desegregation. After identifying whether or not a respondent had protested against school desegregation, the researchers sought to determine whether the opposition had been caused by racial prejudice. The affluent and well educated, the researchers found, were more disturbed by the possibility of interacting more with working-class people, regardless of race. Although not conclusive, the study suggests that, even if affluent Whites are more tolerant of racial minorities, they may be less accepting of class differences (M. Giles et al. 1976).

White ethnics in the early 1970s felt that the mass media unfairly ridiculed them and their culture while celebrating Black Power and African culture. Italian Americans, for instance, remain concerned that their image is overwhelmed by stereotypes of organized crime, spaghetti, overweight mothers, and sexy women. Even television's Italian police seem to conform to the old stereotypes. In response to such stereotyping, the Columbian Coalition, founded in 1971, employs lawyers to handle cases of Italian Americans who claim they are victims of bigotry. Italian Americans are also not pleased by their conspicuous absence from the Roman Catholic Church hierarchy in the United States and from high political office. The Italians are well aware that another ethnic group, the Irish, dominates the American Catholic hierarchy, with 57 percent of the bishops in the country, although that group has only 17 percent of the Catholic population. Not all Italian Americans are convinced that such self-help organizations as the Columbian Coalition, the Italian American Civil Rights League, or the Americans of Italian Descent are the answer. Despite disagreement over methods, most would agree that attitudes need changing. Italian Americans are just one example, however. Across the country and among all ethnic groups, appreciation of ethnic heritage is increasing (R. Gambino 1974a, 1974b; N. Glazer and D. Moynihan 1970; M. Novak 1996; N. Pileggi 1971; R. Severo 1970).

The Prejudice of Ethnics

In the 1960s, as the civil rights movement moved to the North, White ethnics replaced the Southern White as the typical bigot portrayed in the mass media. The chanting of protesters resulted in ugly incidents that made White ethnics and bigots synonymous. This stereotype of the prejudiced White ethnic has rarely been questioned. The danger of this and any other stereotype is that it becomes indistinguishable from fact. David Matza (1964) referred to these mental pictures, which "tend to remain beyond the reach of such intellectual correctives as argument, criticism and scrutiny. . . . Left unattended, they return to haunt us by shaping or bending theories that purport to explain major social phenomena" (p. 1). This 1964 picture of ethnics and the degree of truth behind it needs to be examined.

The first issue to resolve is whether White ethnic groups are more prejudiced than other Whites. Sociologist Andrew Greeley (1974a, 1977; N. Nie et al. 1974) examined attitudes toward race, social welfare, and American involvement in Vietnam. The evidence pointed to minimal differences between ethnics and others. Some of the differences actually showed greater tolerance and liberalism among White ethnics. White ethnics, for example, were more in favor of welfare programs and more opposed to this country's participation in the Vietnam war.

Even when more sophisticated statistical analysis is introduced, the overall finding remains unchanged. No evidence supports the image of White ethnics as bigots. Greeley (1974a) concludes, "Our argument is not that ethnics are the last bastion of liberalism in America today, but rather that it is a misrepresentation of the facts to picture them as a vanguard of conservatism" (p. 202). Working-class ethnic neighborhoods, however, have undeniably been the scene of ugly racial confrontations. If ethnics are no more bigoted than others, how have such incidents come to occur, and how has this reputation developed? For that answer, the unique relationship between White ethnic groups and African Americans must be understood.

In retrospect, it should be no surprise that one group that has been antagonistic to African Americans is the White ethnics. For many citizens, including White ethnics, the United States they remembered from the 1950s seemed to change. When politicians told people in the 1960s, "We must fight poverty and discrimination," this statement translated to White ethnics as, "Share your job, share your neighborhood, but pay more taxes." Whites recalled how in several generations, they had moved from membership in a poor immigrant group to becoming a prosperous part of the working class. Government assistance to the poor was virtually nonexistent then, public education was more restricted, and subsidized training programs were absent. Why was it different now? Many White ethnics found it difficult to understand why African Americans seemed to be singled out as a cause for concern in the 1960s when White ethnics perceived that they too had real needs (N. Glazer and P. Moynihan 1970; M. Novak 1996; I. Sanders and E. Morawska 1975; G. Tyler 1972).

White ethnics went so far as to turn their backs on federal aid offered them, because they did not wish to have their neighborhoods marked as "poverty pockets," nor did they wish to be associated with Black-oriented programs. In Newark, New Jersey, Italians successfully prevented an antipoverty office from being established and thereby cut off the jobs that its programs would have created (F. Barbaro 1974). This ethnic opposition to publicly sponsored programs was not new. James Wilson and Edward Banfield (1964) studied elections in seven major cities between 1956 and 1963 for referenda to build new hospitals, parks, and schools. The results indicated that the least support came from White ethnics, who would have paid the least and benefited the most.

The prevailing conception of urban America has been that the city is Black and the suburbs are White. Although the latter was almost true, the former was definitely not. Along with poor African Americans and Hispanics in the big city were many White ethnics who were "economically unmonied and geographically immobile." White ethnics thought they were being made to pay for past injustices to Black Americans and others, even though they were not in key decision-making roles. White ethnics found it difficult to be happy with minority-group gains (J. Conforti 1974; G. Tyler 1972).

White ethnics not only have separated themselves from African Americans but also have chosen to distinguish themselves from WASPs (White Anglo-

Saxon Protestants) as well, as the next section indicates. White ethnics have learned that they are not considered part of the dominant group and that in order to achieve a larger slice of government benefits, they must now function as a self-interest group, just as racially subordinate groups have done.

Case Example: The Italian Americans

Although each European country's immigration to the United States has created its own social history, the case of Italians, though not typical of every nationality, offers insight into the White ethnic experience. Italians immigrated even during the colonial period, and they played prominent roles dur-

Italian Americans gather in Massachusetts to celebrate a cultural festival.

ing the American Revolution and the early days of the republic. Mass immigration, however, began in the 1880s, peaking in the first twenty years of the twentieth century, when Italians accounted for one-fourth of European immigration.

Italian immigration was concentrated not only in time but also by geography. The majority of the immigrants were landless peasants from rural southern Italy, the Mezzogiorno. This is not just a trivial bit of information. Although many people in the United States may assume that Italians are a nationality with a single culture, that is not true either culturally or economically. The Italian people recognize multiple geographic divisions reflecting sharp cultural distinctions. Indeed, today there is an observable movement in Padania, the region of northern Italians, to establish its own parliament and to secede from Italy.

Many Italians, especially in the early years of mass immigration in the nineteenth century, received their jobs through an ethnic labor contractor, the *padrone*. Similar arrangements have been used by Asian, Hispanic, and Greek immigrants, whose labor contractors, most often immigrants, have mastered sufficient English to mediate for their compatriots. Exploitation was common within the *padrone* system through kickbacks, provision of inadequate housing, and withholding of wages. By World War I, 90 percent of Italian girls and 99 percent of Italian boys in New York City were leaving school at the age of fourteen to work, but by that time, Italian Americans were sufficiently fluent in English to seek out work on their own, and the *padrone* system had disappeared. Along with manual labor, the Roman Catholic Church was a very important part of the Italian Americans' life at this time. Yet they found little comfort in a Catholic church dominated by an earlier immigrant group: the Irish. The traditions were different; weekly attendance for Italian Americans was overshadowed by the religious aspects of the *feste* (or festivals) held throughout the year in honor of saints (the Irish viewed the *feste* as practically a form of paganism). These initial adjustment problems were overcome with the establishment of ethnic parishes—a pattern repeated by other non-Irish immigrant groups. Thus, parishes would be staffed by Italian priests, sometimes imported for that purpose. Although the hierarchy of the church would adjust more slowly, Italian Americans were increasingly able to feel at home in their local parish church. Today, over 70 percent of Italian Americans identify themselves as Roman Catholics (R. Alba 1985; B. Kosmin and S. Lachman 1993; A. Rolle 1972).

A controversial aspect of the Italian American experience involves organized crime, as typified by Al Capone (1899–1947). Arriving in U.S. society in the bottom layers, Italians lived in decaying, crime-ridden neighborhoods that became known as Little Italies. For a small segment of these immigrants, crime did serve as a significant means of upward social mobility. In effect, entering and leading criminal activity were one aspect of assimilation—admittedly not a positive one. Complaints linking ethnicity and crime actually began in colonial times with talk about the criminally inclined Irish and Germans, and the process continues with contemporary stereotyping about such groups as Colombian drug dealers and Vietnamese street gangs. Yet the image of Italians as criminals has persisted from Prohibition-era gangsters to the view of mob families today. As noted earlier, it is not at all surprising that groups such as the Columbian Coalition have been organized to counter such negative images.

The fact that Italians are often characterized as criminal, even in the mass media, is another example of what we have termed respectable bigotry toward White ethnics. The persistence of linking Italians, or any other minority group, with crime is probably attributable to attempts to explain a problem by citing a single, naive cause: the presence of perceived undesirables. As recently as 1999, for example, a major recording company was marketing a CD collection of songs performed by Italian American artists such as Dean Martin and Jerry Vale under the title of "Mob Hits" (R. Alba 1985; D. Bell 1953; R. Daniels 1990; R. Gambino 1974a; P. Lupsha 1981; J. O'Kane 1992).

The immigration of Italians was slowed by the national origins system, described in the previous chapter. As Italian Americans settled permanently, the mutual-aid societies that had grown up in the 1920s to provide basic social services began to dissolve. More slowly, education came to be valued by Italian Americans as a means of upward mobility. Even becoming more educated, however, did not ward off prejudice. In 1930, for example, President Herbert Hoover rebuked Fiorello La Guardia, then an Italian American member of Congress from New York City, stating that "the Italians are predominantly our murderers and bootleggers" and recommending that La Guardia "go back to where you belong" because, "like a lot of other foreign spawn, you do not appreciate this country which supports you and tolerates you" (E. Baltzell 1964:30). Even though U.S. troops, including 500,000 Italian Americans, battled Italy during World War II, some hatred and sporadic violence emerged against Italian Americans and their property. However, the actions were not limited to individual actions. They were even confined by the federal government in specific areas of California by virtue of their ethnicity alone, while 10,000 were relocated from coastal areas. In addition, 1,800 Italian Americans who were citizens of Italy were actually placed in an internment camp in Montana. The internees were eventually freed on Columbus Day 1942 as President Roosevelt lobbied the Italian American community to gain full support for the impending land invasion of Italy (B. Beyette 1995; J. Brooke 1997; S. Fox 1990).

In politics, Italian Americans have been quite a bit more successful, at least at the local level, where family and community ties can be translated into votes. However, political success did not come easily, because many Italian immigrants anticipated returning to their homeland and did not always take neighborhood politics seriously. It was even more difficult for Italian Americans to break into national politics: not until 1962 was an Italian American named to a cabinet-level position. Geraldine Ferraro's being named the Democratic vice-presidential candidate in 1984 was every bit as much an achievement for Italian Americans as it was for women (E. Cornacchia and D. Nelson 1992).

In 1990, people of Italian ancestry accounted for about 6 percent of the population, although less than 1 percent of them had actually been born in Italy. Italian Americans still remain the seventh-largest immigrant group. Just how ethnically conscious is the Italian American community? Although the number is declining, 1.3 million Americans speak Italian at home; only Spanish, French, and German are spoken more within the family. For another 10 million Italian Americans, however, the language tie to their culture is absent, and depending on their degree of assimilation, only traces of symbolic ethnicity may remain.

Ethnicity, Religion, and Social Class

Generally, several social factors influence a person's identity and life chances. Pioneer sociologist Max Weber described **life chances** as people's opportunities to provide themselves with material goods, positive living conditions, and favorable life experiences. Religion, ethnicity, or both may affect life chances.

Religion and ethnicity do not necessarily operate together. Sometimes, they have been studied as if they were synonymous. Groups have been described as Irish Catholic, Swedish Lutheran, or Russian Jewish, as if religion and ethnicity had been merged into some type of national church. In the 1990s, the religion-ethnicity tie took on new meaning as Latin American immigration invigorated the Roman Catholic Church nationwide, and West Indian immigration, particularly to New York City, brought new life to the Episcopal Church.

In the 1960s, sociologists felt that religion was more important than ethnicity in explaining behavior (N. Glazer and D. Moynihan 1963; W. Herberg 1983). They based this conclusion not on data but on the apparently higher visibility of religion in society. Using survey data collected between 1963 and 1972, Andrew Greeley came to different conclusions (1974a, 1974b). He attempted to clarify the relative importance of religion and ethnicity by measuring four areas:

1. Personality characteristics, such as authoritarianism, anxiety, and conformity
2. Political participation, such as voting and civic activity
3. Civil liberties and civil rights, such as support for legislation
4. Family structure, such as the role of women, marital happiness, and sexual adjustment

Celebrating Eid al-Adha, a three-day feast of charity commemorating Abraham's willingness to sacrifice his son, worshipers at a neighborhood mosque in New York spill onto the sidewalk.

The sample consisted of German and Irish Americans, both Protestant and Catholic. If religion was more significant than ethnicity, Protestants, whether of German or Irish ancestry, and Catholics, regardless of ethnicity, would have been similar in outlook. Conversely, if ethnicity was the key, then the similarities would be among the Germans of either faith or among the Irish as a distinct group.

On seventeen of the twenty-four items that made up the four areas measured, the differences were greater between German Catholics and Irish Catholics than between German Catholics and Protestants or between Irish Catholics and Protestants. Ethnicity was a stronger predictor of attitudes and beliefs than religion. In one area, political party allegiance, religion was more important, but this finding was the exception rather than the rule. (The significance of religion will be examined later in this chapter.)

In sum, Greeley found ethnicity to be generally more important than religion in predicting behavior. In reality, it is very difficult to separate the influences of religion and ethnicity on any one individual, but Greeley's research cautions against discounting the influence of ethnicity in favor of religion.

In addition, as already noted several times, social class is yet another significant factor. Sociologist Milton Gordon (1978) developed the term **ethclass** (ethnicity and class) to denote the importance of both factors. All three factors—religion, ethnicity, and class—combine to form one's identity, determine one's social behavior, and limit one's life chances. For example, in certain ethnic communities, friendships are limited, to a degree, to people who share the same ethnic background and social class. In other words, neither race and ethnicity nor religion nor class alone places one socially. One must consider several elements together as reflected in ethclass.

Religion in the United States

Divisive conflicts along religious lines are relatively muted in the United States compared with those in, say, Northern Ireland or the Middle East. Although not entirely absent, conflicts about religion in the United States seem to be overshadowed by civil religion. **Civil religion** refers to the religious dimension in American life that merges the state with sacred beliefs.

Sociologist Robert Bellah (1967) borrowed the phrase "civil religion" from the eighteenth-century French philosopher Jean-Jacques Rousseau to describe a significant phenomenon in the contemporary United States. Civil religion exists alongside established religious faiths, and it embodies a belief system incorporating all religions but not associated specifically with any one religion. It is the type of faith to which presidents refer in inaugural speeches and to which American Legion posts and Girl Scout troops swear allegiance. In 1954, Congress added the phrase "under God" to the Pledge of Allegiance as a legislative recognition of religion's significance. Presidents of the United States beginning with Ronald Reagan and continuing through Bill Clinton typically conclude even their most straightforward speech with "God Bless the United States of America," which, in effect, evokes the civil religion of the nation.

Functionalists see civil religion as reinforcing central American values that may be more expressly patriotic than sacred in nature. Frequently, the mass media following major societal upheavals, from the 1995 Oklahoma City bombing to the 1998 issuance of the Starr Report listing impeachable offenses of President Clinton, show church services with clergy praying and asking for national healing. Bellah sees no sign that the importance of civil religion has diminished in promoting collective identity, but he does acknowledge that it is more conservative than during the 1970s (see also R. Bellah 1968, 1970, 1989; M. Marty 1976, 1985; J. Mathisen 1989).

In the following section, we will explore the diversity among the major Christian groups in the United States, such as Roman Catholics and Protestants. However, as already noted, significant numbers of people in the United States practice religions long established in other parts of the world, such as Islam, Hinduism, and Buddhism, to name the three major ones, in addition to Judaism, which is discussed in Chapter 13. The greater visibility of religious diversity in the United States is primarily the result of immigrants' bringing their religious faith with them and not assimilating to the dominant Christian rituals.

Diversity among Roman Catholics

Social scientists have persistently tended to ignore the diversity within the Roman Catholic Church in the United States. Recent research has not sustained the conclusions that Roman Catholics are melding into a single group, following the traditions of the American Irish Catholic model, or that they are all attending English-language churches. A recent finding of special interest is that religious behavior has been different for each ethnic group within the Roman Catholic Church. The Irish and the French Canadians left societies that were highly competitive both culturally and socially. Their religious involvement in the United States is more relaxed than it was in Ireland and Quebec. The influence of life in the United States, however, has increased German and Polish involvement in the Roman Catholic Church, whereas Italians have remained relatively inactive. Variations by ethnic background continue to emerge in studies of contemporary religious involvement in the Roman Catholic Church.

Since the mid-1970s, the Roman Catholic Church in America has received a significant number of new members from the Philippines, Southeast Asia, and particularly Latin America. Although these new members have been a stabilizing force offsetting the loss of White ethnics, they have also challenged a church that for generations was dominated by Irish, Italian, and Polish parishes. Perhaps the most prominent subgroup in the Roman Catholic

Church is the Hispanics, who now account for one-third of all Roman Catholic parishioners. Some Los Angeles churches in or near Hispanic neighborhoods must now schedule fourteen Masses each Sunday to accommodate the crowds of worshipers. According to one estimate, Latinos constitute one out of four or one out of five of Roman Catholics nationwide (J. Bonfante 1995; L. Stammer 1999).

The Roman Catholic Church, despite its ethnic diversity, has clearly been a powerful force in reducing the ethnic ties of its members, making it also a significant assimilating force. The irony in this role of Catholicism is that so many nineteenth-century Americans heaped abuse on Catholics in this country for allegedly being un-American and having a dual allegiance. The history of the Catholic church in the United States may be portrayed as a struggle within the membership between the Americanizers and the anti-Americanizers, with the former ultimately winning. Unlike the various Protestant churches that accommodated immigrants of a single nationality, such as the Swedish Lutherans or Korean Presbyterians, the Roman Catholic Church had to Americanize a variety of linguistic and ethnic groups. The Catholic Church may have been the most potent assimilating force after the public school system. Comparing the assimilationist goal of the Catholic Church and the present diversity in it leads us to the conclusion that ethnic diversity has continued in the Roman Catholic Church in spite of, and not because of, this religious institution (Fishman et al. 1966; A. Greeley 1977).

Diversity among Protestants

Protestantism, like Catholicism, is often portrayed as a monolithic entity. Little attention is given to the doctrinal and attitudinal differences that sharply divide the various denominations, in both laity and clergy. Several studies, however, document the diversity. Unfortunately, many opinion polls and surveys are content to learn if a respondent is a Catholic or a Protestant or a Jew. Rodney Stark and Charles Glock (1968), in their massive undertaking, found sharp differences in religious attitudes within Protestant churches. For example, 99 percent of Southern Baptists had no doubt that Jesus was the divine Son of God, as contrasted to only 40 percent of Congregationalists. On the basis of the data, Glock and Stark (1965) identified four "generic theological camps" among Protestants:

1. *Liberals:* Congregationalists, Methodists, and Episcopalians
2. *Moderates:* Disciples of Christ and Presbyterians
3. *Conservatives:* American Lutherans and American Baptists
4. *Fundamentalists:* Missouri Synod Lutherans, Southern Baptists, and various small sects

Roman Catholics generally hold religious beliefs similar to those of conservative Protestants, except on essentially Catholic issues such as papal infallibility (the authority of the spiritual role in all decisions regarding faith and morals). Whether or not there are four distinct camps is not important: the point is that the familiar practice of contrasting Roman Catholics and Protestants is clearly not productive. Some differences between Catholics and Protestants are inconsequential compared with the differences among Protestant sects.

Religious faiths may be distinguished by secular criteria as well as doctrinal issues. Research has consistently shown that denominations can be arranged in a hierarchy based on social class. As Figure 5.2 reveals, certain faiths, such as Episcopalianism, Judaism, and Presbyterianism, have a higher proportion of affluent members. Members of other faiths, including Baptists and Evangelicals, are comparatively poor. Of course, all Protestant groups draw members from each social stratum. Nonetheless, the social significance of these class differences is that religion becomes a mechanism for signaling social mobility. A person who is moving up in wealth and power may seek out a faith associated with a higher social ranking. Similar contrasts are shown in formal schooling in Figure 5.3.

Protestant faiths have been diversifying, and many of their members have been leaving them for churches that follow strict codes of behavior or fundamental interpretations of biblical teachings. This trend is reflected in the decline of the five "mainline" churches: Baptist, Episcopalian, Lutheran, Methodist, and Presbyterian. In 1998, these faiths accounted for about 20 percent of total church membership, compared with 51 percent twenty-five years

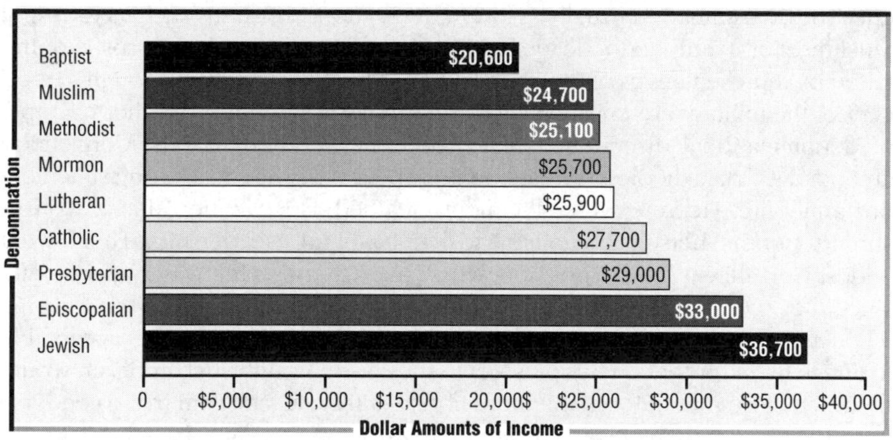

Figure 5.2 Income and Denominations

Denominations attract different income groups. All groups have both affluent and poor members, yet some have a higher proportion of members with high incomes, and others are comparatively poor.

Source: From *One Nation Under God* by Seymour P. Lachman and Barry A. Kosmin. Copyright © 1993 by Seymour P. Lachman and Barry A. Kosmin. Reprinted by permission of Harmony Books, a division of Random House, Inc.

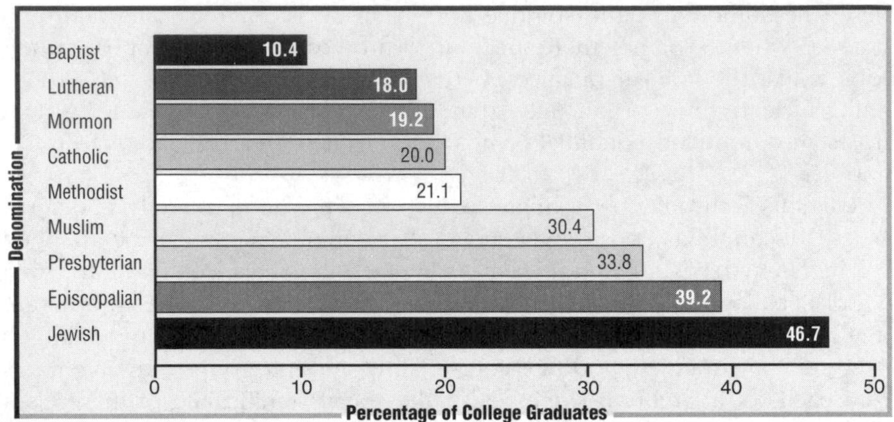

Figure 5.3 Education and Denominations

There are sharp differences in the proportion of college graduates by denomination.

Source: From *One Nation Under God* by Seymour P. Lachman and Barry A. Kosmin. Copyright © 1993 by Seymour P. Lachman and Barry A. Kosmin. Reprinted by permission of Harmony Books, a division of Random House, Inc.

earlier. With a broader acceptance of new faiths and continuing immigration, it is unlikely that these mainline churches will regain their dominance (*Gallup Poll Monthly* 1998:41).

Even though Protestants may seem to define the civil religion and the "accepted" dominant orientation, some Christian faiths feel that they too experience the discrimination usually associated with non-Christians such as Jews and Muslims. For example, the leadership of the military's chaplain corps is dominated by representatives of the liberal and moderate faiths, even though 41 percent of the military are conservatives and fundamentalists. As another example of denominational discrimination, in 1998, the Southern Baptist Convention amended its basic theological statements of beliefs to include a strong statement on family life. However, the statement included a declaration that a woman should "submit herself graciously" to her husband's leadership. There were widespread attacks on this position, which many Baptists felt was inappropriate since they were offering guidance for their denomination's members. In some respects, Baptists felt this was a form of respectable bigotry. It was acceptable to attack them for their views on social issues even though such criticism would be much more muted for many more liberal faiths, which seem free to endorse abortion (T. Bowman 1998; G. Niebuhr 1998).

Women and Religion

Religious beliefs have often placed women in an exalted, but protected, position. As religions are practiced, this position has often meant being "protected" from becoming leaders. Perhaps the only major exception in the United States is the Christian Science church, in which the majority of practitioners and readers are women. Women may be evangelists, prophets, and even saints, but they find it difficult to enter the clergy within their own congregations.

Even today, the largest denomination in the United States, Roman Catholicism, does not permit women to be priests. A 1996 Gallup survey found that 65 percent of Roman Catholics in this country favor the ordination of women, compared with only 29 percent in 1974, but the church hierarchy has continued to maintain its long-standing requirement that priests be male (D. Briggs 1996).

The largest Protestant denomination, the Southern Baptist Convention, has voted against ordaining women (although some of its autonomous churches have women ministers). Other religious faiths that do not allow women clergy include the Lutheran Church–Missouri Synod, the Greek Orthodox Archdiocese of North and South America, the Orthodox Church in America, the Church of God in Christ, the Church of Jesus Christ of Latter-day Saints, and Orthodox Judaism.

Despite these restrictions, there has been a notable rise in female clergy in the last twenty years. The U.S. Bureau of the Census (1996) shows that 6 percent of clergy were women in 1983, but that figure had increased to 11 percent in 1995. Increasingly, some branches of Protestantism and Judaism have been convinced that women have the right to become spiritual leaders. Yet a lingering question remains: once ordained, are these female ministers and rabbis necessarily accepted by congregations? Will they advance in their calling as easily as their male counterparts, or will they face blatant or subtle discrimination in their efforts to secure desirable posts within their faiths?

It is too early to offer any definitive answers to these questions, but thus far, women clearly continue to face lingering sexism after ordination. Evidence to date indicates that women find it more difficult than men to secure jobs in larger, more prestigious congregations. Although they may be accepted as junior clergy or as copastors, women may fail to receive senior clergy appointments. In both Reform and Conservative Judaism, women rabbis are rarely hired by the largest and best-known congregations. Consequently, women clergy in many denominations appear to be gathered at the low end of the pay scale and the hierarchy (*Religion Watch* 1995a).

Women clergy are aware that their struggle for equality is far from over. Reverend Joan Forsberg, an administrator at the Yale Divinity School, tells women graduates that they must view their efforts as part of a larger, long-term process of change. "Even if you don't see change overnight," she notes, "you must remind yourself that you are making a difference for future generations" (U. King 1995; E. Lehman 1993; W. Swatos 1994).

Religion and the U.S. Supreme Court

Religious pluralism owes its existence in the United States to the First Amendment declaration that "Congress shall make no law respecting an establishment of religion, or prohibiting the free exercise thereof." The U.S. Supreme

Court has consistently interpreted this wording to mean not that government should ignore religion but that it should follow a policy of neutrality to maximize religious freedom. For example, the government may not help religion by financing a new church building, but it also may not obstruct religion by denying a church adequate police and fire protection. We will examine four issues that continue to require clarification: school prayer, secessionist minorities, creationism, and the public display of religious symbols.

Among the most controversial and continuing disputes has been whether prayer has a role in the schools. Many people were disturbed by the 1962 Supreme Court decision in *Engel* v. *Vitale* that disallowed an allegedly non-denominational prayer drafted for use in the New York public schools. The prayer was: "Almighty God, we acknowledge our dependence upon Thee, and we beg Thy blessings upon us, our parents, our teachers, and our country." Subsequent decisions overturned state laws requiring Bible reading in public schools, laws requiring recitation of the Lord's Prayer, and laws permitting a daily one-minute period of silent meditation or prayer.

What about prayers at public gatherings? In 2000, the Supreme Court ruled 6–2 in *Santa Fe Independent School District* v. *Doe* that prayers led by students at high school football games are unconstitutional. The court felt that delivery of a pre-game prayer, even by a student, has the improper effect of

Although courts have consistently ruled against prayer in public schools, the practice continues in the United States.

coercing those present to participate in an act of religious worship. The Supreme Court has not agreed with school boards that prayers at a graduation or an athletic event were not coercive.

Despite such judicial pronouncements, children in many public schools in the United States are led in regular prayer recitation or Bible reading. Many communities believe that schools should transmit this aspect of the dominant culture of the United States by encouraging prayer. In a 1985 survey (the most recent available), 15 percent of public school administrators (including 42 percent of school administrators in the South) reported that prayers were said in at least one of their schools. Moreover, according to a 1995 survey, 71 percent of adults in the United States favored a constitutional amendment that would permit organized prayer in public schools (J. Bacon 1987; Gallup and Moore 1995).

Among religious groups are several that have been in legal and social conflict with the rest of society. Some can be called **secessionist minorities,** in that they reject both assimilation and coexistence in some form of cultural pluralism. The Amish are one such group that comes into conflict with outside society because of their beliefs and way of life. The Old Order Amish shun most modern conveniences, and later in this chapter, we will consider them as a case study of maintaining a lifestyle dramatically different from that of larger society.

Are there limits to the free exercise of religious rituals by secessionist minorities? Today, tens of thousands of members of Native American religions believe that the ingestion of the powerful drug peyote is a sacrament and that those who partake of peyote will enter into direct contact with God. In 1990, the Supreme Court ruled that prosecuting people who use illegal drugs as part of a religious ritual is not a violation of the First Amendment guarantee of religious freedom. The case arose because Native Americans were dismissed from their jobs for the religious use of peyote and were then refused unemployment benefits by the State of Oregon's employment division. In 1991, however, Oregon enacted a new law permitting the sacramental use of peyote by Native Americans (*New York Times* 1991).

In another ruling on religious rituals, in 1993, the Supreme Court unanimously overturned a local ordinance in Florida that banned ritual animal sacrifice. The high court held that this law violated the free-exercise rights of adherents of the Santeria religion, in which the sacrifice of animals (including goats, chickens, and other birds) plays a central role. In the same year, Congress passed the Religious Freedom Restoration Act that said that the government may not enforce laws that "substantially burden" the exercise of religion. Presumably this action will give religious groups more flexibility in practicing their faith. However, many local and state officials are concerned that the law has led to unintended consequences, such as forcing states to accommodate prisoners' requests for questionable religious activities or to permit a church to expand into a historic district in defiance of local laws. A Supreme Court clarification is expected to try to unravel these complex issues (L. Greenhouse 1993a, 1996b).

The third area of contention has been whether the biblical account of creation should be or must be present in school curricula and whether this account should receive the same emphasis as scientific theories. In the famous "monkey trial" of 1925, Tennessee schoolteacher John Scopes was found guilty of teaching the scientific theory of evolution in public schools. Since then, however, Darwin's evolutionary theories have been presented in public schools with little reference to the biblical account in Genesis. People who support the literal interpretation of the Bible, commonly known as **creationists,** have formed various organizations to crusade for creationist treatment in American public schools and universities.

In a 1987 Louisiana case, *Edwards* v. *Aguillard,* the Supreme Court ruled that states may not require the teaching of creationism alongside evolution in public schools if the primary purpose of such legislation is to promote a religious viewpoint. Nevertheless, the teaching of evolution and creationism has remained a controversial issue in many communities across the United States (P. Applebome 1996; H. Chalfant et al. 1994; S. Taylor 1987).

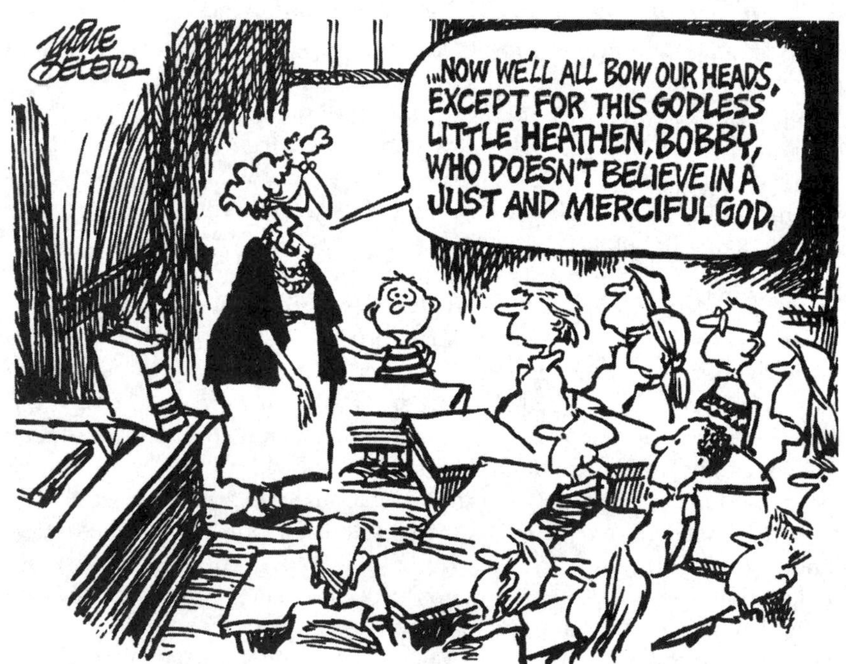

The fourth area of contention has been a battle over public displays that depict symbols or that seem associated with a religion. Can manger scenes be erected on public property? Do people have a right to be protected from large displays such as a cross or a star atop a water tower overlooking an entire town? In a series of decisions in the 1980s through to 1995, the Supreme Court ruled that tax-supported religious displays on public government property may be successfully challenged but are not permissible if they are made more secular. Displays that combine a crèche, the Christmas manger scene depicting the birth of Jesus, or the Hanukkah menorah, and that also include Frosty the Snowman or even Christmas trees have been ruled secular. These decisions have been dubbed "the plastic reindeer rules." In 1995, the Court clarified the issue by stating that privately sponsored religious displays may be allowed on public property if other forms of expression are permitted in the same location. The final judicial word has not been heard, and all these rulings should be viewed as tentative because the Court cases have been decided by close votes, and changes in the Supreme Court composition may alter the outcome of future cases (R. Bork 1995; M. Hirsley 1991; T. Mauro 1995).

Limits of Religious Freedom: The Amish

The Amish offer an interesting case study of a religious group that has endured despite challenges from both within and outside the close-knit community. They are members of a conservative Christian group in North America, primarily members of the Old Order Amish Mennonite Church. The group originated in Europe as followers of Jakob Ammann, a seventeenth-century Mennonite elder whose teachings caused controversy and internal splits during the years 1693–1697 among the Mennonites in Switzerland, Alsace, and south Germany.

The Amish began migrating to North America early in the eighteenth century and settled first in eastern Pennsylvania, where a large settlement is still found. Those who continued the characteristic lifestyle of the Amish are primarily members of the Old Order Amish Mennonite Church. In the late twentieth century, there were about fifty Old Order Amish settlements in the United States and Canada; the largest were located in Pennsylvania, Ohio, Indiana, Iowa, Illinois, and Kansas. Estimates place the membership at about 80,000, with approximately 75 percent living in three states—Ohio, Pennsylvania, and Indiana. Amish practice self-segregation, living in settlements divided into church districts that are autonomous congregations composed of about seventy-five baptized members. If the district becomes much larger, it is again divided, because the members meet in each other's homes. There are no church buildings. Amish homes are large, with the main floor often having removable walls so that a household can take their periodic turn hosting the Sunday service (Linder 1998).

Each Amish district has a bishop, two to four preachers, and an elder; but there are no general conferences, mission groups, or cooperative agencies. The Amish differ little from the Mennonites in formal religious doctrine. Holy Communion is celebrated twice each year, and both groups practice washing of feet. Adults are baptized when they are admitted to formal membership in the church at about age 17 to 20. Old Order Amish services are conducted in German with a mixture of English, commonly known as Pennsylvania Dutch (from *Deutsch,* the German word for "German").

The Amish are best known for their severely plain clothing and their nonconformist way of life. Sociologists sometimes use the term "secessionist minorities" to refer to groups like the Amish who reject assimilation and practice coexistence or pluralism with the rest of society primarily on their own terms. Although Jakob Amman is not a central figure among the Amish today, the practice of *Meidung*, or shunning, persists. Sociologists view it as central to the Amish system of social control. The social norms of this secessionist minority that have evolved over the years are known as the *Ordnung*. These "understandings" specify the color and style of clothing, the color and style of buggies, the use of horses for fieldwork, the use of the Pennsylvania Dutch dialect, worship services in the homes, unison singing without instruments, and marriage within the church, to name a few.

The Amish practice self-segregation, living in settlements divided into church districts.

Amish people are distinctive in their appearance. Clothing serves as an important source of group identity. The men wear broad-brimmed black hats, beards—but not mustaches—and homemade plain clothes fastened with hooks and eyes instead of buttons. The women wear bonnets, long full dresses with capes over the shoulders, shawls, and black shoes and stockings. No jewelry of any kind (except for wedding rings) is worn, and no cosmetics are used. Such personal items are viewed as being not functional and thus encouraging a needless focus on oneself rather than the larger Amish community and especially on God. This cultural nonconformity is thought by the Amish to be obedience to biblical strictures, but it is primarily the continuance of seventeenth-century European rural custom. The Amish also shun telephones and electric lights, and they drive horses and buggies rather than automobiles. The *Ordnung* also prohibits filing a lawsuit, entering military service, getting divorced, using air transportation, and even using wall-to-wall carpeting. The Amish are generally considered excellent farmers, but they often refuse to use modern farm machinery. Concessions have been made but do vary from one Amish settlement to another. Among common exceptions to the *Ordnung* is the use of chemical fertilizers, insecticides, and pesticides, as well as the use of indoor bathroom facilities, and modern medical and dental practice.

Conversely, larger society has made concessions to the Amish to facilitate their lifestyle. For example, the 1972 United States Supreme Court, in *Yoder* v. *Wisconsin,* allowed Wisconsin Amish to escape prosecution from laws that required parents to send their children to school to age 18. Amish education ends at about the age of 13, since the community feels their members have received all the schooling necessary to prosper as Amish people. Associated with this ruling, states waive for the Amish certification requirements for their teaching staff (who are other Amish people), minimum wage requirements for the teachers, and school building requirements.

The Amish do not totally reject social change. For example, until the late 1960s, church members could be excommunicated for being employed in other than agricultural pursuits. Although you will not find Amish computer programmers, there are Amish engaged as blacksmiths, harness makers, buggy repairers, and carpenters. Non-Amish often make use of these craftspeople as well.

The movement by the Amish into other occupations is sometimes a source of tension with larger society, or the "English," as the Amish refer to non-Amish people. Conflict theorists observe that as long as the Amish remained totally apart from dominant society in the United States, they experienced relatively little hostility. As they entered the larger economic sector, however, intergroup tensions developed in the form of growing prejudice. The Amish today may underbid their competitors. The Amish entry into the commercial marketplace has also strained the church's traditional teaching on litigation and insurance—both of which are to be avoided. Mutual assistance has been the historical path taken, but that does not always mesh well with the "modern" businessperson. Following legal action taken on their behalf, Amish businesses typically have been allowed to be exempt from paying Social Security and workers' compensation—another sore point with "English" competitors.

The Amish entrepreneur represents an interesting variation of the typical ethnic businessperson whom one might encounter in a Chinatown, for example. Research on ethnic businesses often cites discrimination against minorities and immigrants as a prime force prodding the development of minority enterprises. The Amish represent a very different case, because it is their own restrictions on education, factory work, and certain occupations that have propelled them into becoming small-business owners. However, stratification is virtually absent among the Old Order Amish. The notion of ethclass would have no meaning, as the Amish truly regard one another as equal.

Children are not sent to high schools. This practice had caused the Amish some difficulty because of compulsory school attendance laws, and some Amish parents have gone to jail rather than allow their children to go to high school. Eventually, as noted earlier, the Supreme Court, in *Yoder* v. *Wisconsin*, upheld a lower court's decision that a Wisconsin compulsory-education law violated the Amish right to religious freedom. Not all court rulings, however, have been friendly to Amish efforts to avoid the practices and customs of the English. In another court case, the effort by the Amish to avoid using the legally mandated orange triangles for marking slow-moving vehicles (such as their buggies) was rejected. If you travel through Amish areas, you can now see their horse-drawn buggies displaying this one symbol of modernity.

A growing area of Amish-English legal clashes is over the custom of young Amish children's working as laborers. Amish families in western and central Pennsylvania in 1998 protested the federal government's enforcement of labor laws that are intended to protect children from workplace hazards. The Amish are turning to new businesses, such as sawmills and wood shops, as their available farmland begins to disappear. That adjustment means more children's being on the shop floor. The Amish contend that their religious and cultural traditions hold that children should work, but the U.S. Department of Labor takes a different view. From 1996 to 1998, the government leveled tens of thousands of dollars in fines against Amish companies for using underage workers. The Department of Labor's view is that there is no basis in the law for different treatment of people based on race, gender, ethnic origin, religion, or cultural background. The Amish counter that letting children work alongside their fathers instills core values of hard work, diligence, cooperation, and responsibility, values that they say are central to their faith. English businesses see this underage employment as another form of unfair competition by the Amish. The Amish are hoping to work with the Department of Labor to hammer out a legislative compromise to the child labor issue, perhaps allowing some children on the shop floor doing limited work away from dangerous tools.

The Old Order Amish have developed a pluralistic position that has become increasingly difficult to maintain as their numbers grow and as they enter the economy in competition with the English or non-Amish (B. Dart 1998; D. Kraybill 1989; D. Kraybill and S. Nolt 1995; Public Broadcasting System 1998).

Conclusion

Considering ethnicity and religion reinforces our understanding of the patterns of intergroup relations that was first presented in Chapter 1. Figure 5.4 shows the rich variety of relationships as defined by people's ethnic and religious identity.

Any study of life in the United States, but especially one focusing on dominant and subordinate groups, cannot ignore religion and ethnicity. The two are closely related, as certain religious faiths predominate in certain nationalities. Both religious activity and interest in their past heritage by White ethnics continue to be prominent features of the contemporary scene. People have been and continue to be ridiculed or deprived of opportunities solely because of their ethnic or religious affiliation. To get a true picture of a person's place in society, we need to consider both ethnicity and social class (or what has been termed *ethclass*) in association with their religious identification.

The issue of the persistence of ethnicity is an intriguing one. Some people may only casually exhibit their ethnicity and practice what has been termed *symbolic ethnicity*. However, can people immerse themselves in their ethnic culture without having society punishing them

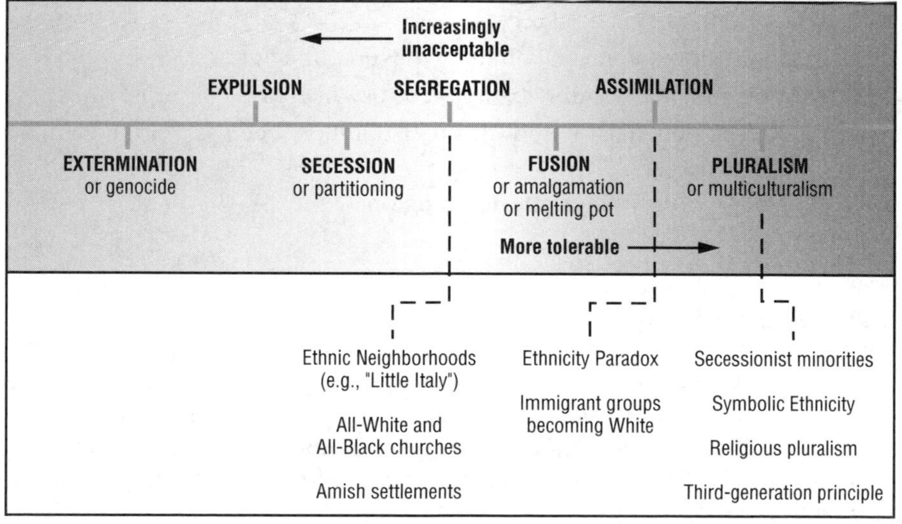

Figure 5.4 Intergroup Relations Continuum

for their will to be different? The tendency to put down White ethnics through respectable bigotry continues. Despite this intolerance, ethnicity remains a viable source of identity for many citizens today. There is also the ethnicity paradox, which finds that practicing one's ethnic heritage often strengthens people and allows them to move successfully into the larger society.

The issue of religious expression also raises a variety of intriguing questions. Women, in particular, are at a disadvantage in organized religion. How might this situation change in decades ahead? How will the courts and society resolve the issues of religious freedom? This is a particularly important issue in such areas as school prayer, secessionist minorities, creationism, and public religious displays. Some examination of religious ties is fundamental to completing an accurate picture of a person's social identity.

Ethnicity and religion are a basic part of today's social reality and of each individual's identity. The emotions, disputes, and debate over religion and ethnicity in the United States are powerful indeed.

Key Terms

civil religion 158
creationists 166
denomination 143
ethclass 157
ethnicity paradox 149
life chances 156
principle of third-generation interest 147
respectable bigotry 150
secessionist minority 165
symbolic ethnicity 148

Review Questions

1. In what respect are the ethnic and the religious diversity of the United States related to each other?
2. Is assimilation automatic within any given ethnic group?
3. Can "blaming the victims" be applied to White ethnic groups?
4. To what extent has a non-Christian tradition been developing in the United States?
5. How have court rulings affected religion?

Critical Thinking

1. When do you see ethnicity's becoming more apparent? When does it appear to occur only in response to other people's advancing their own ethnicity? From these situations, how can ethnic identity be both positive and perhaps counterproductive or even destructive?
2. Why do you think we are so often reluctant to show our religion to others?

3. How does religion reflect the conservative-liberal position on social issues? Consider how religious groups address services for the homeless, the need for child care, the acceptance or rejection of gays and lesbians, and a woman's right to terminate a pregnancy versus the fetus's right to survive?

Internet Exercises

1. Select two of the denominations listed in Table 5.2. Search for web sites dealing with your selections on Yahoo! (http://www.yahoo.com). Visit these sites, especially officially sanctioned homepages to learn more. Compare and contrast the two denominations by answering the following for each: How many members belong? What beliefs, rituals, and ceremonies are espoused and practiced? What are the origins of the group? When and why did the denomination form? Have members experienced prejudice and/or discrimination concerning their beliefs? If so, what form did the prejudice and/or discrimination take specifically? Who are the leaders? Compare demographic characteristics of believers: identify, if available on the web site, racial, ethnic, social class, age, and geographic compositions. Referring to the research and conclusion of Andrew Greeley on p. 156, does there appear to be a connection between ethnicity, religion, and social class for your two selections? Why, or why not? In what ways are the denominations similar? In what ways are they different?

2. Explore the history and culture of Italians in the United States through cyberspace by visiting the National Italian American Foundation homepage (http://www.niaf.org/). What current examples are offered on the NIAF homepage of positive and negative media images of Italians? What is your opinion on these examples? Which seven states have the largest Italian American population? Which city has the largest? Can you offer sociological and historical reasons why these geographic locations have larger Italian American populations than others? Utilize the links provided to reveal the widespread contributions that have been made by Italians to "The Arts," "Entertainment," "Sports," "Government," and "Education." What inventions and devices did Italian Americans create? Click on "Related Links" to connect to Festivals Throughout Italy. Choose a month and a region of Italy to read about celebrations from around the nation. On what day or days do the festivals occur? What or whom do the festivals honor or remember? What kinds of activities and rituals are performed? What role does religion play in these festivals? What fact that you learned regarding the history and culture of Italian Americans surprised you the most, and why?

3. The secessionist and plain-living Amish, ironically, are the subject of many web sites dedicated to studying their religion and lifestyle. Visit the following sites to reflect on the pictures, stories, and histories of the Amish: The Homepage of Joel Hartman (http://web.missouri.edu/~rsocjoel/rs150/tabocon.html) and Religious Movements Homepage: The Amish (http://cti.itc.virginia.edu/~jkh8x/soc257/nrms/amish.html). On The Homepage of Joel Hartman, be sure to solve the "Puzzles and Exercises" reproduced from the ones used in Amish classrooms. What are the objectives of these lessons? What religious and lifestyle values are being taught through such games? What topics and themes are found in the Amish poems on the homepage?

What current challenges do the Amish face as they continue to try and remain separate from the dominant American culture? How do the Amish religious and plain-living values produce problems in terms of health care (see the link Plain Prey). On the Religious Movements Homepage, be sure to review the case information on *Wisconsin* v. *Yoder*. Why is this case important? What events precipitated the arrest of Yoder and the other Amish parents? What wider impact, do you believe, did the case have on religious freedom in the United States? To get a taste of everyday Amish life, click on "The Plain People" section. How is an Amish wedding different from more mainstream celebrations? How is it similar? Why is dressing plainly important to the Amish? How have your views of the Amish changed after reading the chapter and visiting the web sites?

6 The Nation as a Kaleidoscope

CHAPTER OUTLINE

HIGHLIGHTS

The nation is likened to a kaleidoscope because the diverse population has not fused into a melting pot, nor is the future composition likely to be as static as a salad bowl. Racial and ethnic subordinate groups are making progress economically and educationally, but so are Whites. Even relatively successful Asian Americans are undeserving of their model-minority stereotype. We can consider the changing composition of society not only in terms of our face-to-face interaction every day but also in terms of the changing workforce.

What metaphor do we use to describe a nation whose racial, ethnic, and religious minorities are on the way to becoming numerical majorities in cities and soon in states? Although *E Pluribus Unum* may be reassuring, it does not describe what a visitor sees along the length of Fifth Avenue in New York City or in Monterey Park outside Los Angeles.

For several generations, the melting pot has been used as a convenient description of our culturally diverse nation. The analogy of an alchemist's cauldron was clever (even if a bit jingoistic): in the Middle Ages, the alchemist attempted to change less costly metals into gold and silver.

The term *melting pot* originated as the title of a 1908 play by Israel Zangwill. In this play, a young Russian Jewish immigrant to the United States composes a symphony that portrays a nation that serves as a crucible (or pot) where all ethnic and racial groups dissolve into a new, superior stock.

The belief in the United States as a melting pot became widespread in the first part of the twentieth century, particularly since it suggested that the United States had an almost divinely inspired mission to destroy artificial divisions and to create a single humankind. However, the dominant group had indicated its unwillingness to welcome Native Americans, African Americans, Hispanics, Jews, and Asians, among many others, into the melting pot.

Even though the metaphor of the melting pot is still used today, observers recognize that it hides as much about a multiethnic United States as it discloses. Therefore, the metaphor of a salad bowl emerged in the 1970s to portray a country ethnically diverse. Just as we can distinguish the lettuce from the tomatoes from the peppers in a tossed salad, we can see the ethnic restaurants and the persistence of "foreign" language newspapers. The dressing over the ingredients is akin to the shared value system and culture, covering but not hiding the different ingredients of the salad.

Yet even the notion of a salad bowl is wilting. Like its melting-pot predecessor, the picture of a salad is static—certainly not like the changes that we see in the United States. It also hardly calls to mind the myriad of cultural pieces that make up the fabric or the mosaic of our diverse nation.

The kaleidoscope offers another familiar, yet more useful, analogy. Patented in 1817 by Scottish scientist Sir David Brewster, the kaleidoscope is both a toy and increasingly a table artifact of upscale living rooms. Users of this optical device are aware that when they turn a set of mirrors, the colors and patterns reflected off pieces of glass, tinsel, or beads seem to be endless. The growing popularity of the phrase "people of color" seems made for the kaleidoscope that is the United States. The changing images correspond to the often bewildering array of groups found in our country.

How easy is it to describe the image to someone else as we gaze into the eyepiece of a kaleidoscope? It is a challenge similar to that faced by educators who toil with what constitutes the ethnic history of the United States. We can forgive the faux pas made by the *Washington Post* writer who described the lack of Hispanic-speaking (rather than Spanish-speaking) police as a factor contributing to the recent hostilities in the U.S. capital. Little wonder, given the bewildering ethnic patterns, that Chicago politicians striving to map for the first time a "safe" Hispanic congressional district find themselves scrutinized by Blacks fearful of losing their "safe" districts. We can forgive Marlon Brando for sending an American Indian woman to refuse his Oscar, thus protesting Hollywood's portrayal of Native Americans. Was he unaware of Italian Americans' disbelief when his performance in *The Godfather* won an award?

It is difficult to describe the image created by a kaleidoscope, since it changes dramatically and with little effort. Similarly, in the kaleidoscope of the United States, we find it a challenge to describe the multiracial nature of this republic. Perhaps in viewing the multiethnic, multiracial United States as a kaleidoscope, we may take comfort that the Greek word *kalos* means "beautiful" (R. Schaefer 1992).

In order to develop a better understanding of the changing image through the kaleidoscope, we will first try to learn what progress has taken place and why miscommunication among our diverse peoples seems to be the rule rather than the exception.

The Glass Half Empty

A common expression makes reference to a glass half full or half empty of water. If one is thirsty, it is half empty and in need of being replenished. If one is attempting to clear dirty dishes, it is half full. For many people, especially Whites, the progress of subordinate groups or minorities makes it difficult to understand calls for more programs and new reforms, and impossible to understand when minority neighborhoods erupt in violence.

In absolute terms, the glass of water has been filling up, but people at the beginning of the new century do not compare themselves with people in the 1960s. Hispanic Americans and African Americans regard the appropriate reference group to be Whites today; compared with them, the glass is half empty at best.

Figure 6.1 shows the present picture and recent changes, comparing African Americans and Hispanics with Whites. We see that the nation's largest

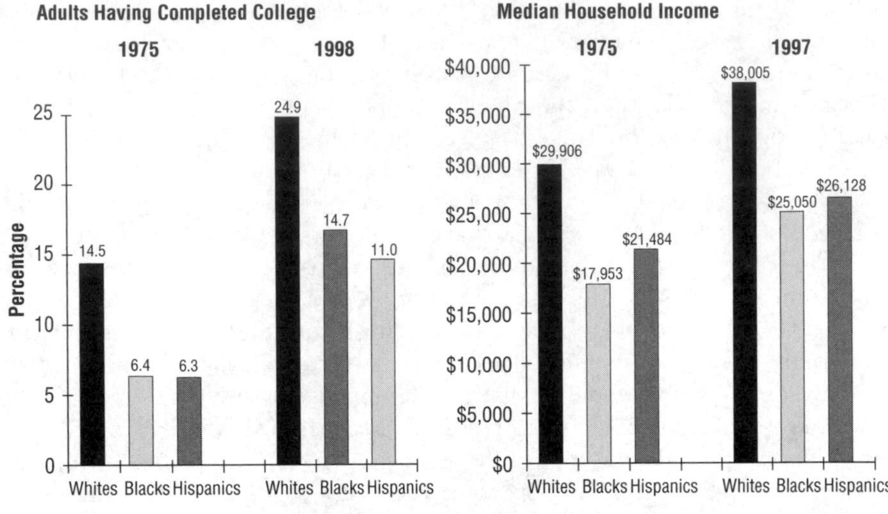

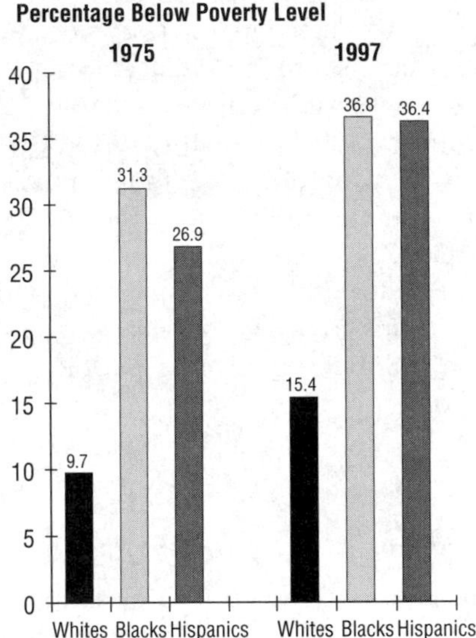

Figure 6.1 Recent Changes in Schooling and Income

Despite modest gains in income and significant advances in completing college, Blacks and Hispanics are far outdistanced by Whites. All three groups have shown gains in the proportion that live in poverty.

Note: Education data for persons 25 and over. Hispanic education data estimated by the author from data for 1970, 1980, and 1991.

Source: U.S. Bureau of the Census 1993a: 155, 461, 469; 1999a: 170, 477, 483.

minority groups—African Americans and Hispanics—have higher household income and have completed more schooling since 1975. But White Americans also have higher incomes and more schooling since then. The gap remains, and, if one analyzes it closely, has actually increased in some instances. Both Blacks and Hispanics in 1997 had yet to reach the income and educational levels that Whites had exceeded back in 1975.

Similarly, many minority Americans remain entrenched in poverty—one out of three Hispanics and African Americans. Little has changed since 1975. True, Whites have experienced a rise in poverty, but the proportions of African Americans and Latinos below the poverty threshold have also increased. We have chosen 1975 because that was a year for which we have comparable data for Hispanics (or Latinos) and Whites and African Americans. However, the patterns would be no different if we considered 1950, 1960, or 1970.

Is There a Model Minority?

The desperate situation of African Americans, Latinos, and Native Americans does not resemble the picture of Asian Americans as a group. Obviously, Asians in the United States are a diverse group, ranging from the descendants of Chinese who immigrated over 150 years ago, to Vietnamese, Laotians, and Cambodians who arrived in the United States as a result of the Vietnam War, to Indian and Pakistani physicians and teachers whose immigration is given preference by our current policy.

"Asian Americans are a success! They achieve! They succeed! There are no protests, no demands. They just do it!" This is the general image that people in the United States so often hold of Asian Americans as a group. They constitute a **model or ideal minority** because, although they have experienced prejudice and discrimination, they seem nevertheless to have succeeded economically, socially, and educationally without resorting to political or violent confrontations with Whites. Some observers point to the existence of a model minority as a reaffirmation that anyone can get ahead in the United States. Proponents of the model-minority view declare that because Asian Americans have achieved success, they have ceased to be subordinate and are no longer disadvantaged. This is only a variation of "blaming the victim"; with Asian Americans, it is "praising the victim." An examination of aspects of their socioeconomic status will allow a more thorough exploration of this view (W. Hurh and K. Kim 1989).

Asian Americans as a group do have impressive school enrollment rates in comparison with the total population. In 1997, half of Asian Americans twenty-five years or older held bachelor's degrees, compared with 29 percent of the White population. These rates vary among Asian American groups, with Asian Indians, Chinese Americans, and Japanese Americans having higher levels of educational achievement (U.S. Bureau of the Census 1998d).

This encouraging picture does have some qualifications, however, which call into question the optimistic model-minority view. According to a study of California's state university system that was released in 1991, although Asian Americans are often viewed as successful overachievers, they have unrecognized and overlooked needs, and they experience discomfort and harassment on campus. As a group, they also lack Asian faculty and staff members to whom they can turn for support. They confront many identity issues and have to do a sort of "cultural balancing act" along with all the usual pressures faced by college students. The report noted that an "alarming number" of Asian American students appear to be experiencing intense stress and alienation, problems that have often been "exacerbated by racial *harassment*" (K. Ohnuma 1991:5; D. Takagi 1992; J. Tamaki 1998).

Even the positive stereotype of Asian American students as "academic stars" can be dysfunctional or counterproductive to people so labeled. Asian Americans who do only modestly well in school may face criticism from their parents or teachers for their failure to conform to the "whiz kid" image. In fact, despite the model-minority label, the high school dropout rate for Asian Americans is increasing rapidly. California's special program for low-income, academically disadvantaged students has a 30 percent Asian American clientele, and the proportion of Asian students in the programs is on the rise (F. Lee 1991; J. Tachibana 1990).

Asian Americans are subject to stereotypes, one of which, "straight-A student," reflects the model-minority image.

That Asian Americans as a group work in the same occupations as Whites suggests that they have been successful, and many have. The pattern, however, shows some differences. Asian immigrants, like other minorities and immigrants before them, are found disproportionately in the low-paying service occupations. At the same time, they are also concentrated at the top in professional and managerial positions. Yet, as we will see, they rarely reach the very top. They hit the "glass ceiling" (as described in Chapter 3) or, as some others say, try to "climb a broken ladder," before they reach management. In 1998, there were only sixty-five Asian Americans on any of the boards of the nation's 1,000 largest corporations—that number amounts to less than 1 percent. In California, where the Asian American presence is very visible, the situation is a bit better. An analysis found that Asian Americans, who make up 10 percent of the state's workforce, hold about that share of administrative and managerial jobs, but they remain underrepresented in top levels of management (D. Lee 1998; E. Lee 1993).

Another sign of the apparent "success" of Asian Americans is their high incomes as a group. Like other elements of the image, however, this sign deserves closer inspection. Asian American family income approaches parity with that of Whites because of their greater achievement than Whites in formal schooling. If we look at specific educational levels, Whites earn more than their Asian counterparts of the same age. Asian Americans' average earnings increased by at least $2,300 for each additional year of schooling, whereas Whites gained almost $3,000 (W. O'Hare and J. Felt 1991; M. Zhou and Y. Kamo 1994).

There are striking contrasts among Asian Americans. They have the lowest divorce rate of any racial group in the United States (3 percent), the lowest unemployment rate (3.5 percent), the lowest rate of teen pregnancy (6 percent), and the highest household family income ($35,000). Nevertheless, for every Asian American family with an annual income of $75,000 or more, another earns less than $10,000 a year. In New York City's Chinatown neighborhood, about one-quarter of all families live below the poverty level. In San Diego, dropout rates were close to 60 percent among Southeast Asians in 1997. Even relatively successful Asian Americans continue to face obstacles because of their racial heritage. According to a study of three major public hospitals in Los Angeles, Asian Americans account for 34 percent of all physicians and nurses, but they fill only 11 percent of management positions at these hospitals (U.S. Bureau of the Census 1998e; A. Dunn 1994; S. Sengupta 1997).

At first glance, one might be puzzled to see criticism of a positive generalization such as "model minority." Why should the stereotype of adjusting without problems be a disservice to Asian Americans? The answer is that this incorrect view helps to exclude Asian Americans from social programs and conceals unemployment and other social ills. When representatives of Asian groups do seek assistance for those in need, they are resented by those who are convinced of the model-minority view. If a minority group is viewed as successful, it is unlikely that its members will be included in programs designed to alleviate the problems they encounter as minorities. The positive stereotype reaffirms the American system of mobility: new immigrants as well as established subordinate groups ought to achieve more merely by working within the system. At the same time, viewed from the conflict perspective outlined in Chapter 1, this becomes yet another instance of "blaming the victim"; if Asian Americans have succeeded, Blacks and Hispanics must be responsible for their own low status (W. Ryan 1976).

Talking Past One Another

African Americans, German Americans, Korean Americans, Puerto Ricans, Native Americans, Mexican Americans, and many others live in the United States and interact on a daily basis, sometimes directly face-to-face and constantly through the media. But communication does not mean that we listen to, much less understand, one another.

Sometimes we assume that as we become a nation that is educated, we will set aside our prejudices. Yet in recent years, our college campuses have been the scenes of tension, insults, and even violence. Fletcher Blanchard, Teri Lilly, and Leigh Ann Vaughn (1991) conducted an experiment at Smith College and found that even overheard statements can influence expressions of opinion on the issue of racism.

The researchers recruited a student, who was instructed to approach seventy-two White students as each was walking across the campus, and to say that she was conducting an opinion poll for a class. Each time she did so, she also stopped a second White student—actually a confederate who was working with the researchers—and asked the second student to participate in the survey as well. Both students were asked how Smith College should respond to anonymous racist notes that were actually sent to four African American students in 1989. However, the confederate was always instructed to answer first. In some cases, the confederate condemned the notes, and in others, justified them. Blanchard and his colleagues (1991) concluded that "hearing at least one other person express strongly antiracist opinions produced dramatically more strongly antiracist public reactions to racism than hearing others express equivocal opinions or opinions more accepting of racism" (pp. 102–103). However, a second experiment demonstrated that, when the confederate expressed sentiments justifying racism, the subjects were much less likely to express antiracist opinions than were those who heard no one else offer opinions. In this experiment, social control (through the process of conformity) influenced people's attitudes and the expression of those attitudes.

Why is there so much disagreement and tension? There is a growing realization that people do not mean the same thing when they are addressing problems of race, ethnicity, gender, or religion. A husband regularly does the dishes and so feels that he is an equal partner in doing the housework, not recognizing that the care of his infant daughter is left totally to his wife. A manager is delighted that he has been able to hire a Puerto Rican salesperson but makes no effort to see that the new employee will adjust to an all-White, non-Hispanic staff.

We talk, but do we talk past one another? Surveys, as noted in Chapter 2, regularly show that different racial groups have different perceptions, whether of the jury verdict on whether four Los Angeles police officers inappropriately beat motorist Rodney King or whether discrimination occurs in the labor force. Sociologist Robert Blauner (1989, 1992) contends that Blacks and Whites see racism differently. Minorities see racism as central to society, as ever-present, whereas Whites regard it as a peripheral concern and a national concern only when accompanied by violence or involving a celebrity. African Americans and other minorities consider racist acts in a broader context: "It is racist if my college fails to have Blacks significantly present as advisers, teachers, and administrators." Whites would generally accept a racism charge if there had been an explicit denial of a job to an appropriately qualified minority member. Furthermore, Whites would apply the label *racist* only to the person or the few people who were actually responsible for the act. Members of minority groups would be more willing to call most of the college's members

People of different races, religions, and ethnic backgrounds talk to each other, but do they talk past one another?

racist for allowing racist practices to persist. For many Whites, the word *racism* is a red flag, and they are reluctant to give it the wide use typically employed by minorities, that is, those who have been oppressed by racism (Lichtenberg 1992). Is just one view correct—either the broader minority perspective, or the more limited White outlook? No, but both are a part of the social reality in which we all live. We need to recognize both interpretations.

Indicative of these different interpretations is the sentiment expressed by Toni Morrison, who won the 1987 Pulitzer Prize for *Beloved*, the fictional story of a group of slaves struggling to survive before and after the Civil War, and who won the Nobel Prize for Literature in 1993. In "Listen to Their Voices," Morrison offers the insult she felt while being in our nation's capital—a city full of monuments—looking for evidence of her people. The need to confront racism, however perceived, is not to make Whites guilty and ab-

LISTEN TO THEIR VOICES

A Bench by the Side of the Road

Toni Morrison

There is no place you or I can go, to think about or not think about, to summon the presences of, or recollect the absences of slaves; nothing that reminds us of the ones who made the journey and of those who did not make it. There is no suitable memorial or plaque or wreath or wall or park or skyscraper lobby. There's no 300-foot tower. There's no small bench by the road. There is not even a tree scored, an initial that I can visit or you can visit in Charleston or Savannah or New York or Providence or, better still, on the banks of the Mississippi.

But somebody told me that there's a gentleman in Washington who makes his living by taking busloads of people around to see the monuments of the city. He has complained because there is never anything there about black people that he can show. And he's black. I can't explain to you why I think it's important but I really do. . . . I think it would refresh. Not only that, not only for black people. It could suggest the moral clarity among white people when they were at their best, when they risked something, when they didn't have to risk and could have chosen to be silent; there's no monument for that either.

I don't have any model in mind, or any person, or even any art form. I just have the hunger for a permanent place. It doesn't have to be a huge, monumental face cut into a mountain. It can be small, some place where you can put your feet up. It can be a tree. It doesn't have to be a statue of liberty.

Source: Morrison 1989. From "A Bench by the Side of the Road" by Toni Morrison. © 1989 by Toni Morrison. An interview in *The World: The Journal of the Unitarian Universalist Association*, January/February 1989, Vol. 3. Reprinted by permission of International Creative Management, Inc. Copyright © 1989 by Toni Morrison.

solve Blacks, Asians, Hispanics, and Native Americans of any responsibility for their present plight. Rather, to understand racism, past and present, is to understand how its impact has shaped both a single person's behavior and that of the entire society (L. Duke 1992).

The Changing Face of the Workforce

Talking past one another extends well beyond the college cafeteria. The workforce itself is undergoing massive change in the United States. Even though predictions are not always reliable, sociologists and labor specialists project a labor force that is increasingly composed of women and racial and ethnic minorities. In 1960, there were twice as many men in the labor force as women. During the period from 1998 to 2008, an equal number of men and women are expected to enter the labor force. It is possible that by 2015, the total numbers of male and female workers may be the same.

The dynamics of race and ethnicity are even more dramatic. The number of African American, Latino, and Asian American workers continues to increase at a rate faster than the number of White workers. It is projected that from 1998 to 2008, whereas 25 million Whites will enter the labor force, 17.4 million Blacks, Latinos, and Asian Americans will also enter. Figure 6.2 shows these patterns in 1986 and projected to 2008 (H. Fullerton 1997, 1999).

Immigration cannot be emphasized enough as a cause for the changing face of labor in the United States. There are significant variations regionally,

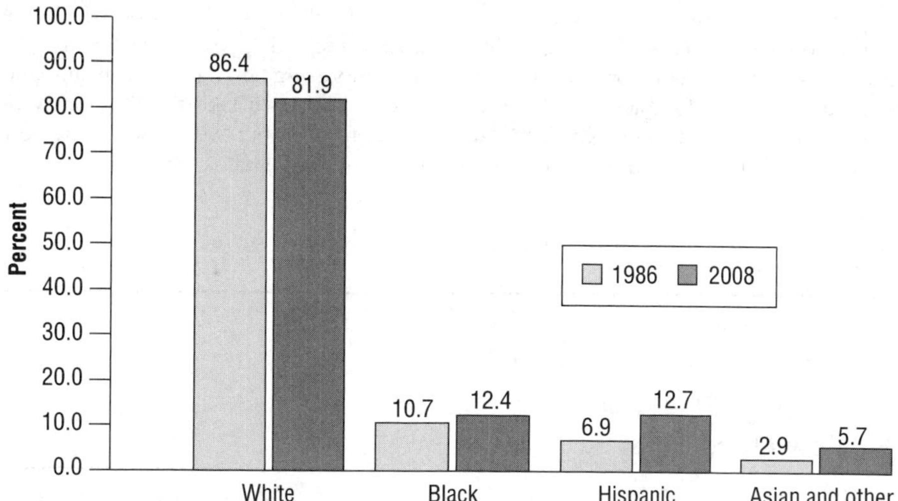

Figure 6.2 Racial and Ethnic Composition of the Labor Force, 1986 and 2008 (projection)
Source: H. Fullerton 1997:24, 1999:20.

but overall 20 percent of the entrants to the labor force are immigrants (*Migration News* 2000).

The workforce more and more reflects the diversity of the population as ethnic minorities enter the labor force and as immigrants and their children move from marginal jobs or employment in the informal economy (see Chapter 3) to positions of greater visibility and responsibility. The impact of this changing workforce is not merely statistical. It will affect whom we supervise, who supervises us, and who sets the direction of the organizations in which we function. This more diverse workforce means that social relationships between workers are more likely to cross gender, racial, religious, and ethnic lines. The kaleidoscope of the Untied States may be no further from us than our place of employment.

Conclusion

Joe Muskrat (1972), while working for the United States Commission on Civil Rights, declared that Native Americans could either assimilate or remain Indian and starve. Judy Syfers (1972), after reviewing all that a woman does for her partner, concluded that she would like a wife, too. Martin Luther King, Jr., told the thousands assembled before the Lincoln Memorial that he had a dream of a day when all people could work, play, and live together.

Assimilation, even when strictly followed, does not necessarily bring with it acceptance as an equal, nor does it mean even that one will be tolerated. Segregation persists. Efforts toward pluralism can be identified, but we can also easily see the counterefforts, whether they be the legal efforts to make English the official language or acts of intimidation by Klansmen, skinheads, and others. However, the sheer changing population of the Untied States guarantees that we will learn, work, and play in a more diverse society.

The task of making this kaleidoscope image of diverse cultures, languages, colors, and religions into a picture of harmony is overwhelming. But the images of failure in this task, some of which we have witnessed in our news media, are even more frightening. We can applaud success and even take time to congratulate ourselves, but we must also review the unfinished agenda.

Key Term

model or ideal minority 179

Review Questions

1. What contributes to the changing image of diversity in the United States?
2. Pose views of some issue facing contemporary society that takes the position of "half full" and then "half empty."

3. Why is it harmful to be viewed as a model minority?
4. Is just one view of racism the correct one?
5. Is the change in the workforce one of gender or race or ethnicity?

Critical Thinking

1. Toni Morrison feels that African Americans may view the monuments of Washington, D.C., differently from the way Whites may. With that approach in mind, how might different groups view the Constitution? The campaign to become president of the United States? The current best-seller list of books or current box office hits in movie theaters?
2. Consider conversations that you have had with people who are very different from yourself. Why do you feel that those people are very different? To what degree did you talk to them or past them? To what degree did they talk to you or past you?
3. How have places where you worked, even part-time, been different from those of your parents or grandparents in terms of diversity of the workforce? What explains these changes?

Internet Exercise

1. The chapter ends with a hope for harmony of diversity. This, too, is the hope of Many Faces, Many Voices, a PBS web site (http://www.pbs.org/manyfaces/home.html). Visit each of the six sections on the site, watching the video experiences of people from a variety of backgrounds, reflecting upon comments by other visitors, and reviewing statistics. What are the experiences and opinions of Pedro, Johnny, Carl, Sloan, and Sophara? How are each person's experiences unique? How are they similar to one another? What opinions do other visitors to the site offer of the videos of Pedro and the rest? What is your perspective on the videos? Which video did you find the most compelling or interesting and why? How many people in the United States speak English only? How many speak Spanish, French, German, Urdu, Hebrew, and Japanese? How many Americans live in rural areas? How many in urban? What is the state with the highest income level? The lowest? Spend time if you wish creating your own profile in the "Identity" section. Which questions were the hardest to answer? Why? How might your profile have been different ten years ago? How might it be different ten years from now? What are some answers that will never change? What suggestions does the site offer for "supporting diversity" in the home, at school, at work, and as an individual? Which suggestions do you find the most promising? Can you think of any others to add to the list?

Glossary

Parenthetical numbers refer to the pages in which the term is introduced.

absolute deprivation The minimum level of subsistence below which families or individuals should not be expected to exist. (76)

affirmative action Positive efforts to recruit subordinate group members including women for jobs, promotions, and educational opportunities. (93)

Afrocentric perspective An emphasis on the customs of African cultures and the way that they have penetrated the history, culture, and behavior of Blacks in the United States and around the world. (34)

amalgamation The process by which a dominant group and a subordinate group combine through intermarriage to form a new group. (27)

assimilation The process by which an individual forsakes his or her own cultural tradition to become part of a different culture. (27)

authoritarian personality A psychological construct of a personality type likely to be prejudiced and to use others as scapegoats. (48)

bilingualism The use of two or more languages in places of work or education and the treatment of each language as legitimate. (30)

biological race The mistaken notion of a genetically isolated human group. (9)

Bogardus scale Technique to measure social distance toward different racial and ethnic groups. (55)

brain drain Immigration to the United States of skilled workers, professionals, and technicians who are desperately needed by their home countries. (122)

caste approach An approach that views race and social class as synonymous, with disadvantaged minorities occupying the lowest social class and having little, if any, opportunity to improve their social position. (49)

civil religion The religious dimension in American life that merges the state with sacred beliefs. (158)

class As defined by Max Weber, persons who share similar levels of wealth. (15)

colonialism A foreign power's maintenance of political, social, economic, and cultural dominance over people for an extended period. (22)

conflict perspective A sociological approach that assumes that the social structure is best understood in terms of conflict or tension among competing groups. (18)

contact hypothesis An interactionist perspective stating that intergroup contact between people of equal status in noncompetitive circumstances will reduce prejudice. (68)

creationists People who support a literal interpretation of the biblical book of Genesis regarding the origins of the universe and who argue that evolution should not be presented as established scientific thought. (166)

denomination A large, organized religion not officially linked with the state or government. (143)

discrimination The denial of opportunities and equal rights to individuals and groups because of prejudice or for other arbitrary reasons. (45, 76)

double jeopardy The subordinate status twice defined, as experienced by women of color. (86)

dual labor market Division of the economy into two areas of employment, the secondary one of which is populated primarily by minorities working at menial jobs. (82)

dysfunction An element of society that may disrupt a social system or lead to a decrease in its stability. (16)

emigration Leaving a country to settle in another. (21)

environmental justice Efforts to ensure that hazardous substances are controlled so that all communities receive protection regardless of race or socioeconomic circumstances. (92)

ethclass The merged ethnicity and class in a person's status. (157)

ethnic cleansing Policy of ethnic Serbs to eliminate Muslims from parts of Bosnia. (24)

ethnic group A group set apart from other groups because of its national origin or distinctive cultural patterns. (6)

ethnicity paradox The maintenance of one's ethnic ties in a way that can assist with assimilation in larger society. (149)

ethnocentrism The tendency to assume that one's culture and way of life are superior to all others. (42)

ethnophaulism Ethnic or racial slurs, including derisive nicknames. (44)

exploitation theory A Marxist theory that views racial subordination in the United States as a manifestation of the class system inherent in capitalism. (49)

functionalist perspective A sociological approach emphasizing how parts of a society are structured in the interest of maintaining the system as a whole. (16)

fusion A minority and a majority group combining to form a new group. (26)

genocide The deliberate, systematic killing of an entire people or nation. (24)

glass ceiling The barrier that blocks the promotion of a qualified worker because of gender or minority membership. (101)

glass wall A barrier to moving laterally in a business to positions that more likely lead to upward mobility. (103)

hate crime A criminal offense committed against a person, property, or society which is motivated, in whole or in part, by the offender's bias against a race, religion, sexual orientation, or ethnic/national origin group. (42)

immigration Coming into a new country as a permanent resident. (21)

informal economy Transfers of money, goods, or services that are not reported to the government. Common in inner-city neighborhoods and poverty-stricken rural areas. (81)

institutional discrimination A denial of opportunities and equal rights to individuals or groups resulting from the normal operations of a society. (78)

intelligence quotient (IQ) The ratio of an individual's mental age (as computed by an IQ test) divided by his or her chronological age and multiplied by 100. (9)

internal colonialism The treatment of subordinate peoples like colonial subjects by those in power. (23)

irregular economy *See* informal economy. (81)

labeling theory A sociological approach introduced by Howard Becker that attempts to explain why certain people are viewed as deviants and why others engaging in the same behavior are not. (19)

life chances People's opportunities to provide themselves with material goods, positive living conditions, and favorable life experiences. (156)

marginality The status of being between two cultures at the same time, such as the status of Jewish immigrants in the United States. (33)

melting pot Diverse racial or ethnic groups or both forming a new creation, a new cultural entity. (27)

migradollars (or **remittances)** The money that immigrant workers send back to families in their native societies. (130)

migration A general term that describes any transfer of population. (21)

minority group A subordinate group whose members have significantly less control or power over their own lives than that held by the members of a dominant or majority group. (4)

model or ideal minority A group that, despite past prejudice and discrimination, succeeds economically, socially, and educationally without resorting to political or violent confrontations with Whites. (179)

nativism Beliefs and policies favoring native-born citizens over immigrants. (112)

normative approach The view that prejudice is influenced by societal norms and situations that serve to encourage or discourage the tolerance of minorities. (50)

panethnicity The development of solidarity among ethnic subgroups as reflected in the terms *Hispanic* or *Asian American*. (32)

pluralism Mutual respect among the various groups in a society for one another's cultures, allowing minorities to express their own culture without experiencing prejudice or hostility. (29)

prejudice A negative attitude toward an entire category of people, such as a racial or an ethnic minority. (44)

principle of third-generation interest Marcus Hansen's contention that ethnic interest and awareness increase in the third generation, among the grandchildren of immigrants. (147)

racial formation A sociohistorical process by which racial categories are created, inhibited, transformed, and destroyed. (13)

racial group A group that is socially set apart from others because of obvious physical differences. (5)

racism A doctrine that one race is superior. (12)

refugees People living outside their country of citizenship for fear of political or religious persecution. (131)

relative deprivation The conscious experience of a negative discrepancy between legitimate expectations and present actualities. (76)

remittances (or **migradollars)** The monies that migrants return to their country of origin. (130)

respectable bigotry Michael Lerner's term for the social acceptance of prejudice against White ethnics, when intolerance against non-White minorities is regarded as unacceptable. (150)

reverse discrimination Actions that cause better qualified White males to be passed over for women and minority men. (98)

scapegoat A person or group blamed irrationally for another person's or group's problems or difficulties. (47)

secessionist minority Groups, such as the Amish, that reject both assimilation and coexistence. (165)

segregation The act of physically separating two groups; often imposed on a subordinate group by the dominant group. (25)

self-fulfilling prophecy The tendency of individuals to respond to and act on the basis of stereotypes, a predisposition that can lead to the validation of false definitions. (19)

sinophobes People with a fear of anything associated with China. (115)

sociology The systematic study of social behavior and human groups. (14)

states' rights The principle, reinvoked in the late 1940s, that holds that each state is sovereign and has the right to order its own affairs without interference by the federal government. (89)

stereotypes Unreliable generalizations about all members of a group that do not take into account individual differences within the group. (19)

stratification A structured ranking of entire groups of people that perpetuates unequal rewards and power in a society. (15)

symbolic ethnicity Herbert Gans's term that describes emphasis on ethnic food and ethnically associated political issues rather than on deeper ties to one's heritage. (148)

total discrimination The combination of current discrimination with past discrimination created by poor schools and menial jobs. (77)

underclass Lower-class members who are not a part of the regular economy and whose situation is not changed by conventional assistance programs. (83)

underground economy *See* informal economy. (81)

world systems analysis A view of the global economic system as divided between nations that control wealth and those that provide natural resources and labor. (23)

xenophobia The fear or hatred of strangers or foreigners. (112)

References

ACORN. 1999. *Disparity in Mortgage Lending Increases, Minorities Rejected Over Whites*. Washington, DC: ACORN.

ACLU. 1996a. *Briefing Paper: Church and State*. New York: American Civil Liberties Union.

———. 1996. *Racial Justice*. New York: American Civil Liberties Union.

Adorno, T. W., Frenkel-Brunswik, Else, Levinson, Daniel J., and Sanford, R. Nevitt. 1950. *The Authoritarian Personality*. New York: Wiley.

Alba, Richard D. 1985. *Italian Americans: Into the Twilight of Ethnicity*. Englewood Cliffs, NJ: Prentice-Hall.

———. 1990. *Ethnic Identity: The Transformation of White America*. New Haven: Yale University Press.

Alba, Richard D., and Moore, Gwen. 1982. Ethnicity in the American Elite. *American Sociological Review* 47 (June), pp. 373–382.

Allport, Gordon W. 1979. *The Nature of Prejudice, 25th Anniversary Edition*. Reading, MA: Addison-Wesley.

Anderson, Dennis. 1998. Judge Rules Rest of Prop. 187 is Unconstitutional. *USA Today* (March 19), p. 9A.

Anti-Defamation League. 1996. *The Web of Hate: Extremists Exploit the Internet*. New York: Anti-Defamation League.

Asante, Molefi Kete. 1987. *The Afrocentric Idea*. Philadelphia: Temple University Press.

———. 1992. Afrocentric Systematics. *Black Issues in Higher Education* 9 (August 13), pp. 16–17, 21–22.

———. 1996. Afrocentricity, Eurocentricity, and Multiculturalism: Toward the 21st Century. Address at Western Illinois University, Macomb, IL, February 13.

Atlanta Braves. 2000. Commissioner Suspends, Finds Rocker. Press Release (January 31). Atlanta: Atlanta Braves Major League Baseball.

Ayres, Ian. 1991. Fair Driving: Gender and Race Discrimination in Retail Car Negotiations. *Harvard Law Review* 104 (February), pp. 817–872.

Bacon, John. 1987. Court Ruling Hasn't Quieted School Prayer. *USA Today* (April 3), p. 3A.

Badgett, M. V. Lee, and Hartmann, Heidi I. 1995. The Effectiveness of Equal Employment Opportunity Policies. In Margaret C. Simms, ed., *Economic Perspectives in Affirmative Action*, pp. 55–83. Washington, DC: Joint Center for Political and Economic Studies.

Baltzell, E. Digby. 1964. *The Protestant Establishment: Aristocracy and Caste in America*. New York: Vintage Books.

Barbaro, Fred. 1974. Ethnic Resentment. *Society* 11 (March–April) pp. 67–75.

Barnes, Edward. 1996. Can't Get There from Here. *Time* 147 (February 19), p. 33.

Barrett, David B., and Johnson, Todd M. 1998. Religious Adherents in the United States of America, AD 1900–2000. In David R. Calhoun, ed. *Britannica Book of Year*, p. 314. Chicago: Encyclopedia Britannica.

Bash, Harry M. 1979. *Sociology, Race and Ethnicity*. New York: Gordon & Breach.

Baumann, Marty. 1992. Agreement on King. *USA Today* (May 11), p. 4A.

BBDO. 1996. *Report on Black TV Viewing*. New York: BBDO.

Bell, Daniel. 1953. Crime as an American Way of Life. *Antioch Review* 13 (Summer), pp. 131–154.

Bell, Derrick. 1994. The Freedom of Employment Act. *The Nation* 258 (May 23), p. 708, 710–714.

Bell, Wendell. 1991. Colonialism and Internal Colonialism. In Richard Lachmann, ed., *The Encyclopedic Dictionary of Sociology*, 4th ed., pp. 52–53. Guilford, CT: Dushkin Publishing Group.

Bellah, Robert. 1967. Civil Religion in America. *Daedalus* 96 (Winter), pp. 1–21.

———. 1968. Response to Commentaries on "Civil Religion in America." In Donald R. Cutler, ed., *The Religious Situation: 1968*, pp. 388–393. Boston: Beacon Press.

———. 1970. *Beyond Belief: Essays on Religion in a Post-Traditional World*. New York: Harper & Row.

———. 1989. Comment to Mathisen. *Sociological Analysis* 50 (Summer), p. 147.

Bennett, Phillip. 1993. Ethnic Labels Fail to Keep Up with Reality. *The Cincinnati Enquirer* (November 18), p. A10.

Bennett, Vanora. 1998. Staying True to Their Roots. *Los Angeles Times* (April 10), p. A5.

Berndt, Ronald M., and Berndt, Catherine. 1951. *From Black to White in South Australia*. Melbourne: F. W. Chesire.

Berreman, Gerald D. 1973. *Caste in the Modern World*. Morristown, NJ: General Learning Press.

Bettelheim, Bruno, and Janowitz, Morris. 1964. *Social Change and Prejudice*. New York: Free Press.

Beyette, Beverly. 1995. Honoring Forgotten Victims of WWII. *Los Angeles Times* (February 10), p. E1.

Billson, Janet Mancini. 1988. No Owner of Soil: The Concept of Marginality Revisited on Its Sixtieth Birthday. *International Review of Modern Sociology* 18 (Autumn), pp. 183–204.

Blanchard, Fletcher A., Terri, Lilly, and Leigh, Ann Vaughn. 1991. Reducing the Expression of Racial Prejudice. *Psychological Science 2* (March), pp. 101–105.

Blauner, Bob. 1989. *Black Lives, White Lies: Three Decades of Race Relations in America*. Berkeley: University of California Press.

———. 1992. The Two Languages of Race. *The American Prospect* (Summer), pp. 55–64.

Blauner, Robert. 1969. Internal Colonialism and Ghetto Revolt. *Social Problems* 16 (Spring), pp. 393–408.

———. 1972. *Racial Oppression in America*. New York: Harper & Row.

Bloch, Hannah. 1996. Cutting Off the Brains. *Time* 147 (February 5), p. 46.

Bobo, Lawrence. 1998. Race, Interests, and Beliefs about Affirmative Action: Unanswered Questions and New Directions. *American Behavioral Scientist* 41 (April), pp. 985–1003.

Bobo, Lawrence, Kluegel, James R., and Smith, Ryan A. 1997. Laissez-Faire Racism: The Crystallization of a Kinder, Gentler, Antiblack Ideology. In Steven A. Tuch and Jack K. Martin, eds., *Racial Attitudes in the 1990's: Continuity and Change,* pp. 15–42. Westport, CT: Praeger.

Bogardus, Emory. 1968. Comparing Racial Distance in Ethiopia, South Africa, and the United States. *Sociology and Social Research* 52 (January), pp. 149–156.

Bonacich, Edna. 1972. A Theory of Ethnic Antagonism: The Split Labor Market. *American Sociological Review* 37 (October), pp. 547–559.

———. 1976. Advanced Capitalism and Black/White Race Relations in the United States: A Split Labor Market Interpretation. *American Sociological Review* 41 (February), pp. 34–51.

Bonfante, Jordan. 1995. The Catholic Paradox. *Time* 146 (October 9), pp. 64–68.

Bonilla-Silva, Eduardo. 1996. Rethinking Racism: Toward a Structural Interpretation. *American Sociological Review* 62 (June), pp. 465–480.

Borjas, George. 1990. *Friends or Strangers: The Impact of Immigrants on the U.S. Economy*. New York: Basic Books.

Borjas, G., and Freeman, Richard B. 1997. Findings We Never Found. *New York Times* (December 10), p. A23.

Bork, Robert H. 1995. What to Do About the First Amendment. *Commentary* 99 (February), pp. 23–29.

Bouvier, Leon F., and Grant, Lindsay. 1994. *How Many Americans? Population, Immigration, and the Environment*. San Francisco: Sierra Club.

Bowman, Tom. 1998. Evangelicals Allege Bias in U.S. Navy, Marine Chaplain Corps. *Baltimore Sun* (August 23), p. A12.

Bowser, Benjamin, and Hurst, Raymond G., eds. 1996. *Impacts of Racism on White Americans*. Beverly Hills, CA: Sage Publications.

Boyer, Edward J. 1996. Life in a New Land: Illegal Immigrant Who Fled Deputies Reaches Goal: A Job in U.S. *Chicago Tribune* (May 7), p. 131, B8.

Bracey, John H., Meier, August, and Rudwick, Elliot, eds. 1970. *Black Nationalism in America*. Indianapolis: Bobbs-Merrill.

Bradley, Martin B., Green, Norman M., Jr., Jones, Dale E., Lynn, Mac, and McNeil, Lou. 1992. *Churches and Church Membership in the United States 1990*. Atlanta: Glenmary Research Center.

Branigin, William. 1995. Sweatshops Reborn. *Washington Post National Weekly Edition* 12 (September 18), pp. 8–9.

Braxton, Greg. 1999. A Mad Dash For Diversity, *Los Angeles Times* (August 9), pp. F1, F10.

Briggs, David. 1996. Greeley Poll Says Catholics Want Democratic Church. *Chicago Tribune* (May 31), sect. 2, p. 9.

Briggs, Kenneth A. 1976. Churches Found Still Largely Segregated. *New York Times* (November 14), p. 26.

———. 1978. Jewish Leader Urges a Program to Convert "Seekers" to Judaism. *New York Times* (December 3), pp. 1, 37.

Brimelow, Peter. 1996. *Alien Nation*. New York: Random House.

Brimmer, Andrew. 1995. The Economic Cost of Discrimination Against Black Americans. In Margaret C. Simms, ed., *Economic Perspectives in Affirmative Action,* pp. 9–29. Washington, DC: Joint Center for Political and Economic Studies.

Brooke, James. 1995. Attacks on U.S. Muslims Surge Even as Their Faith Holds. *New York Times* (August 28), pp. A1, B7.

———. 1997. After Silence, Italians Recall the Internment. *New York Times* (August 11), p. A8.

Brooks-Gunn, Jeanne, Klebanov, Pamela K., and Duncan, Greg J. 1996. Ethnic Differences in Children's Intelligence Test Scores: Role of Economic Deprivation, Home Environment, and Maternal Characteristics. *Child Development* 67 (April), pp. 396–408.

Broom, Leonard. 1965. *The Transformation of the American Negro*. New York: Harper & Row.

Brown, Christopher. 1990. Discrimination and Immigration Law. *Focus* 18 (August), pp. 3–4, 8.

Bullard, Robert D. 1990. Ecological Inequities and the New South: Black Communities Under Siege, *Journal of Ethnic Studies 17* (Winter): 101–115.

Bullard, Robert. 1993. *Dumping in Dixie: Race, Class, and Environmental Quality,* 2d ed. Boulder, CO: Western Press.

Butterfield, Fox. 1986. Bostonians Debating Drive to Carve Out a Black City. *New York Times* (October 12), p. 26.

Card, David, DiNardo, John, and Estes, Eugenia. 1998. The More Things Change: Immigrants and the Children of Immigrants in the 1940s, the 1970s, and the 1990s. Paper presented at the Joint Center for Poverty Research, Northwestern University of Chicago, April 9.

Carney, Dan. 1996. As White House Calls Shots, Illegal Alien Bill Clears. *Congressional Quarterly Weekly Report* 54 (October 5), pp. 2864–2866.

Carvajal, Doreen. 1996. Diversity Pays Off in a Babel of Yellow Pages. *New York Times* (December 3), pp. 1, 23.

Chalfant, H. Paul, Beckley, Robert E., and Palmar, C. Eddie. 1994. *Religion in Contemporary Society,* 3rd ed. Itasca, IL: F. E. Peacock.

Chandler, Susan. 1998. Companies' Views Widely Divergent on Need for Diversity in Directors. *Chicago Tribune* (May 3), sect. 5, p. 1.

Children Now. 1998. *A Different World: Children's Perceptions of Race, Class, and the Media.* Oakland.

Clark, Kenneth B., and Clark, Mamie P. 1947. Racial Identification and Preferences in Negro Children. In Theodore M. Newcomb and Eugene L. Hartley, eds., *Readings in Social Psychology,* pp. 169–178. New York: Holt, Rinehart & Winston.

Commission on Civil Rights. 1972. *The Excluded Student: Educational Practices Affecting Mexican Americans in the Southwest.* Washington, DC: U.S. Government Printing Office.

Commission on Civil Rights. 1975. *Twenty Years After Brown: Equality of Economic Opportunity.* Washington, DC: U.S. Government Printing Office.

———. 1977. *Window Dressing on the Set: Women and Minorities in Television.* Washington, DC: U.S. Government Printing Office.

———. 1980. *Characters in Textbooks: A Review of the Literature.* Washington, DC: U.S. Government Printing Office.

———. 1981. *Affirmative Action in the 1980s: Dismantling the Process of Discrimination.* Washington, DC: U.S. Government Printing Office.

———. 1995. *Briefing Paper from the U.S. Commission on Civil Rights Legislative, Executive and Judicial Development of Affirmative Action. Prepared by the Office of General Counsel, U.S. Commision on Civil Rights.* Washington, DC: U.S. Government Printing Office.

Cone, Marla. 1998. Sierra Club to Remain Neutral on Immigration. *Los Angeles Times* (April 26), pp. A1, A26.

Conforti, Joseph M. 1974. WASP in the Woodpile: Inequalities and Injustices of Ethnic Ecology. Paper presented at American Sociological Association Annual Meeting, Montreal.

Cornacchia, Eugene J., and Nelson, Dale C. 1992. Historical Differences in the Political Experiences of American Blacks and White Ethnics: Revisiting an Unresolved Controversy. *Ethnic and Racial Studies* 15 (January), pp. 102–124.

Cornelius, Wayne A. 1996. Economics, Culture, and the Politics of Restricting Immigration. *Chronicle of Higher Education* 43 (November), p. B4–B5.

Cose, Ellis. 1993. *The Rage of a Privileged Class.* New York: HarperCollins.

Cox, Oliver C. 1942. The Modern Caste School of Race Relations. *Social Forces* 21 (December), pp. 218–226.

Cross, William E., Jr. 1991. *Shades of Black: Diversity in African-American Identity.* Philadelphia: Temple University Press.

Crull, Sue R., and Bruton, Brent T. 1985. Possible Decline in Tolerance Toward Minorities: Social Distance on a Midwest Campus. *Sociology and Social Research* 70 (October), pp. 57–62.

Cullen, Frances T., Gendreau, Paul, Jarjoura, G. Roger, and Wright, John Paul. 1997. Crime and the Bell Curve: Lessons from Intelligent Criminology. *Crime and Delinquency* 43 (October) pp. 387–411.

Cushman, John H., Jr. 1998. Pollution Policy Is Unfair Burden, States Tell E.P.A. *New York Times* (May 10), pp. 1, 20.

Daniels, Roger. 1990. *Coming to America.* New York: HarperCollins.

Dart, Bob. 1998. Preserving America: Lancaster County, PA. *Atlanta Journal and Constitution* (June 28).

Dart, John. 1994. A Closer Look at Islam in the West. *Los Angeles Times* (December 10), p. B4.

Davidson, Robert C., and Lewis, Ernest L. 1997. Affirmative Action and Other Special Consideration Admissions at the University of California, Davis, School of Medicine. *Journal of American Medical Association* 278 (October 8), pp. 1153–1158.

Day, Jennifer Chesseman. 1996. Population Projections of the United States by Age, Sex, Race, and Hispanic Origin: 1995 to 2050. *Current Population Reports,* Ser. P–25, No. 1130. Washington, DC: U.S. Government Printing Office.

De la Garza, Rodolfo O., De Sipio, Louis, Garcia, F. Chris, Garcia, John, and Flacon, Angelo. 1992. *Latino Voice: Mexican, Puerto Rican, and Cuban Perspectives on American Politics.* Boulder, CO: Westview Press.

DeParle, Jason. 1991. New Rows to Hoe in the "Harvest of Shame." *New York Times* (July 28), p. E3.

Deutscher, Irwin, Pestello, Fred P., and Pestello, H. Frances. 1993. *Sentiments and Acts.* New York: Aldine de Gruyter.

Dillon, Sam. 1996. Mexico Drug Wars Advance Within Sight of U.S. Border. *New York Times* (October 10), p. A1, A6.

Dionne, Jr., E. J. 1995. Slandered White Men. *Washington Post National Weekly Edition* 12 (May 8), p. 28.

Domestic Council Committee on Illegal Aliens. 1976. *Preliminary Report of the Domestic Council.* Washington, DC: Immigration and Naturalization Service, Department of Justice.

Donovan, Robert J., and Levers, Susan. 1993. Using Paid Advertising to Modify Racial Stereotype Beliefs. *Public Opinion Quarterly* 57 (Summer), pp. 205–218.

Dublin, Thomas, ed. 1996. *Becoming American, Becoming Ethnic: College Students Explore Their Roots.* Philadelphia: Temple University Press.

Du Bois, W. E. B. 1903. *The Souls of Black Folks: Essays and Sketches.* Reprinted in 1961 in New York: Facade Publications.

———. 1969. *An ABC of Color.* New York: International Publications.

Du Brow, Rick. 1994. Portrayals of Latinos on TV Regressing. *Los Angeles Times* (September 7), p. A5.

Duff, John B. 1971. *The Irish in the United States.* Belmont, CA: Wadsworth.

Dugger, Celia W. 1996. A Tattered Crackdown on Illegal Workers. *New York Times* (June 3), pp. A1, B1.

Duke, Lynn. 1992. You See Color-Blindedness, I See Discrimination. *Washington Post National Weekly Edition* 9 (June 15), p. 33.

Dunn, Ashley. 1994. Southeast Asians Highly Dependent on Welfare in U.S. *New York Times* (May 19), pp. A1, A20.

Dworkin, Anthony Gary. 1965. Stereotypes and Self-Images Held by Native-Born and Foreign-Born Mexican Americans. *Sociology and Social Research* 49 (January), pp. 214–224.

Early, Gerald. 1994. Defining Afrocentrism. *Journal of Blacks in Higher Education* 1 (Winter), p. 46.

El Nasser, Haya. 1996. Census Predicts California Will Grow 56% by 2025. *USA Today* (October 23), p. 7A.

Eng, Monica. 1998. Chinese-Americans Have Their Own Ways Of Paying Respect. *Chicago Tribune* (May 25), sec. 5, p. 1, 2.

Espiritu, Yen Le. 1992. *Asian American Panethnicity: Bridging Institutions and Identities.* Philadelphia: Temple University Press.

Farber, M. A. 1975. Immigration Service Inquiry Ending; Results in Dispute. *New York Times* (April 27), p. 47.

Feagin, Joe R., and Vera, Hernan. 1995. *White Racism: The Basics.* New York: Routledge.

Fermi, Laura. 1971. *Illustrious Immigrants,* rev. ed. Chicago: University of Chicago Press.

Fishman, Joshua A., Hayden, Robert G., and Warshaver, Mary E. 1966. The Non-English and the Ethnic Group Press, 1910–1960. In Joshua A. Fishman, ed., *Language Loyalty in the United States,* pp. 51–74. London and The Hague: Mouton.

Fix, Michael and Jeffrey S. Passel. 1999. *Trends in Noncitizens' and Citizens' Use of Public Benefits Following Welfare Reform: 1994–97.* Washington, D.C.: Urban Institute.

Ford, W. Scott. 1986. Favorable Intergroup Contact May Not Reduce Prejudice: Inconclusive Journal Evidence, 1960–1984. *Sociology and Social Research* 70 (July), pp. 256–258.

Fox, Stephen. 1990. *The Unknown Internment.* Boston: Twayne.

Fullerton, Jr., Howard N. 1997. Labor Force 2006: Slowing Down and Changing Composition. *Monthly Labor Review* (November), pp. 23–28.

———. 1999. Labor force projections to 2008: study growth and changing composition. *Monthly Labor Review* (November), pp. 19–32.

Gallup, Alec, and Moore, David W. 1995. Americans Favor Constitutional Amendment to Permit Spoken Prayer in Schools. *Gallup Poll* 358 (July), pp. 14–16.

Gallup Poll Monthly. 1998. Brief Questions. 388 (January), pp. 37–42.

Gambino, Richard. 1974a. *Blood of My Blood.* Garden City, NY: Doubleday.

Gambino, Richard. 1974b. The Italian Americans. *Chicago Tribune Magazine* (May 5), pp. 56–58.

Gans, Herbert J. 1979. Symbolic Ethnicity: The Future of Ethnic Groups and Cultures in America. *Ethnic and Racial Studies* 2 (January), pp. 1–20.

Gerber, David A. 1993. *Nativism, Anti-Catholicism, and Anti-Semitism.* New York: Scribner's.

Gerth, H. H., and Mills, C. Wright. 1958. *From Max Weber: Essays in Sociology.* New York: Galaxy Books.

Gilens, Martin. 1996. "Race Coding" and White Opposition to Welfare. *American Political Science Review* 90 (September), pp. 593–604.

Giles, Michael W., Gatlin, Douglas S., and Cataldo, Everette F. 1976. Racial and Class Prejudice: Their Relative Effects on Protest Against School Desegregation. *American Sociological Review* 41 (April), pp. 280–288.

Glancy, Diane. 1998. When the Boats Arrived. *Hungry Mind Review. The National Book Magazine* (Spring), p. 7.

Glaser, James M., and Gilens, Martin. 1997. Interregional Migration and Political Resocialization: A Study of Racial Attitudes under Pressure. *Public Opinion Quarterly* 61 (Spring), pp. 72–86.

Glazer, Nathan. 1971. The Issue of Cultural Pluralism in America Today. In *Pluralism Beyond Frontier: Report of the San Francisco Consultation on Ethnicity,* pp. 2–8. San Francisco: American Jewish Committee.

———. 1990. American Jewry or American Judaism? *Society* 28 (November–December), pp. 14–20.

Glazer, Nathan, and Moynihan, Daniel Patrick. 1963. *Beyond the Melting Pot: The Negroes, Puerto Ricans, Jews, Italians, and Irish of New York City.* Cambridge: MIT Press.

Glazer, Nathan, and Moynihan, Daniel Patrick. 1970. *Beyond the Melting Pot: The Negroes, Puerto Ricans, Jews, Italians, and Irish of New York City.* 2d ed. Cambridge, MA: MIT Press.

Gleason, Philip. 1980. American Identity and Americanization. In Stephen Therstromm, ed., *Harvard Encyclopedia of American Ethnic Groups,* pp. 31–58. Cambridge, MA: Belknap Press of Harvard University Press.

Glock, Charles Y. and Rodney Stark. 1965. Is There an American Protestantism? *Transaction* (November/December): 8–13 ff.

Goering, John M. 1971. The Emergence of Ethnic Interests: A Case of Serendipity. *Social Forces* 48 (March), pp. 379–384.

Gompers, Samuel, and Gustadt, Herman. 1908. *Meat vs. Rice: American Manhood Against Asiatic Coolieism: Which Shall Survive?* San Francisco: Asiatic Exclusion League.

Goozner, Merrill. Immigration tide helps keep U.S. wage inflation in check. *Chicago Tribune* (June 28), pp. 1,9.

Gordon, Milton M. 1964. *Assimilation in American Life: The Role of Race, Religion, and National Origins*. New York: Oxford University Press.

———. 1978. *Human Nature, Class, and Ethnicity*. New York: Oxford University Press.

———. 1996. Liberal versus Corporate Pluralism. *Society* 33 (March/April), pp. 37–40.

Graham, Lawrence Otis. 1995. *Member of the Club: Reflections on Life in a Racially Polarized World*. New York: HarperCollins.

Greeley, Andrew M. 1974a. *Ethnicity in the United States: A Preliminary Reconnaissance*. New York: Wiley.

———. 1974b. Political Participation among Ethnic Groups in the United States: A Preliminary Reconnaissance. *American Journal of Sociology* 80 (July), pp. 170–204.

———. 1977. *The American Catholic*. New York: Basic Books.

Greenhouse, Linda. 1989. Court Bars a Plan Set up to Provide Jobs to Minorities. *New York Times* (January 24), pp. A1, A19.

———. 1993a. Court, Citing Religious Freedom, Voids a Ban on Animal Sacrifice. *New York Times* (June 12), pp. 1, 8.

———. 1993b. High Court Backs Policy of Halting Haitian Refugees. *New York Times* (June 22), pp. 1, 8.

———. 1996. Case on Government Interface in Religion Tied to Separation of Powers. *New York Times* (October 16), p. C23.

Handlin, Oscar. 1951. *The Uprooted: The Epic Story of the Great Migrations That Made the American People*. New York: Grossett & Dunlap.

———. 1957. *Race and Nationality in American Life*. Boston: Little, Brown.

Hansen, Marcus Lee. 1952. The Third Generation in America. *Commentary* 14 (November), pp. 493–500.

Harvard Law Review. 1995. Unenforced Boundaries: Illegal Immigration and the Limits of Judicial Federalism. 108 (May), pp. 1643–1660.

Herberg, Will. 1983. *Protestant-Catholic-Jew: An Essay in American Religious Sociology*, rev. ed. Chicago: University of Chicago Press.

Herring, Cedric, and Amissah, Charles. 1997. Advance and Retreat: Racially Based Attitudes and Public Policy. In Steven A. Tuch and Jack K. Martin, eds., *Racial Attitudes in the 1990s: Continuity and Change*, pp. 121–143. Westport, CT: Praeger.

Herrnstein, Richard J., and Murray, Charles. 1994. *The Bell Curve: Intelligence and Class Structure in American Life*. New York: Free Press.

Herskovits, Melville J. 1930. *The Anthropormetry of the American Negro*. New York: Columbia University Press.

Hill, Herbert. 1967. The Racial Practices of Organized Labor—The Age of Gompers and After. In Arthur M. Ross and Herbert Hill, eds. *Employment, Race and Poverty*, pp. 365–402. New York: Harcourt, Brace and World.

Hirschman, Charles. 1983. America's Melting Pot Reconsidered. In Ralph H. Turner, ed., *Annual Review of Sociology 1983*, pp. 397–423. Palo Alto, CA: Annual Reviews.

Hirsley, Michael. 1991. Religious Display Needs Firm Court. *Chicago Tribune* (December 20), sect. 2, p. 10.

Hochschild, Jennifer L. 1995. *Facing Up to the American Dream: Race, Class, and the Soul of the Nation*. Princeton, NJ: Rutgers University Press.

Hoffman, Adonis. 1997. Through an Accurate Prism. *Los Angeles Times* (August 8), p. M1.

Hughes, Michael. 1998. Symbolic Racism, Old-Fashioned Racism and Whites: Opposition to Affirmative Action. In Steven A. Tuch and Jack K. Martin, eds., *Racial Attitudes in the 1990s: Continuity and Change*, pp. 45–75. Westport, Connecticut: Praeger.

Hughes, Michael, and Demo, David H. 1989. Self-Perceptions of Black Americans: Self-Esteem and Personal Efficacy. *American Journal of Sociology* 95 (July), pp. 132–159.

Hurh, Won Moo, and Kim, Kwang Chung. 1989. The "Success" Image of Asian Americans: Its Validity, and Its Practical and Theoretical Implications. *Ethnic and Racial Studies* 12 (October), pp. 512–538.

Ignatiev, Noel. 1994. Treason to Whiteness Is Loyalty to Humanity. Interview with Noel Ignatiev. *Utne Reader* (November/December), pp. 83–86.

———. 1995. *How the Irish Became White*. New York: Routledge.

Jacobs, James B., and Potter, Kimberly. 1998. Proposed Hate Crimes Bill Isn't Needed. *Los Angeles Times* (July 27), p. B5.

Jencks, Christopher, and Phillips, Meredith, eds. 1998. *The Black-White Test Score Gap*. Washington, DC: Brookings Institution.

Jenness, Valerie. 1995. Hate Crimes in the United States: The Transformation of Injured Persons into Victims and the Extension of Victim Status to Multiple Constituencies. In Joel Best, ed., *Images of Issues: Typifying Contemporary Social Problems*, 2d ed., pp. 213–237. New York: Aldine de Gruyter.

Johnson, Kevin. 1992. German Ancestry Is Strong Beneath Milwaukee Surface. *USA Today* (August 4), p. 9A.

Johnson, Thomas. Faith in a Box. Entertainment Television on Religion—1997. Media Research Center.

Accessed on July 17, 1998 at http://www.mrc.org/specialreports/ent/sr041998.html.

Joint Center for Political Studies. 1996. Affirmative Action Myths and Realities. *Focus* 24 (August), pp. 7–8.

Jones, Charisse. 1997. A World of Students. *USA Today* (September 24), pp. A1–A2.

Journal of Blacks in Higher Education. 1994. Are Nonresident Asian Students Displacing Black Ph.D.s in Science and Engineering? 1 (No. 2), p. 15.

Kagan, Jerome. 1971. The Magical Aura of the IQ. *Saturday Review of Literature* 4 (December 4), pp. 92–93.

Kahng, Anthony. 1978. EEO in America. *Equal Opportunity Forum* 5 (July), pp. 22–23.

Kalish, Susan. 1995. Multiracial Births Increase as U.S. Ponders Racial Definitions. *Population Today* 24 (April), pp. 1–2.

Kennedy, John F. 1964. *A Nation of Immigrants*. New York: Harper & Row.

Kilson, Martin. 1995. Affirmative Action. *Dissent* 42 (Fall), pp. 469–470.

King, Ursula, ed. 1995. *Religion and Gender*. Oxford: Blackwell.

Kinloch, Graham C. 1974. *The Dynamics of Race Relations: A Sociological Analysis*. New York: McGraw-Hill.

Kornblum, William. 1991. Who Is the Underclass? *Dissent* 38 (Spring), pp. 202–211.

Kosmin, Barry A., and Lachman, Seymour P. 1993. *One Nation Under God*. New York: Harmony Books.

Kraybill, Donald R. 1989. *The Riddle of Amish America*. Baltimore, MD: Johns Hopkins Press.

Kraybill, Donald R., and Nolt, Steven M. 1995. *Amish Enterprises: From Plows to Profits*. Baltimore: Johns Hopkins Press.

Kunen, James S. 1996. The End of Integration. *Time* 147 (April 29), pp. 39–45.

Lal, Barbara Ballis. 1995. Symbolic Interaction Theories. *American Behavorial Scientist* 38 (January), pp. 421–441

LaPiere, Richard T. 1934. Attitudes vs. Actions. *Social Forces* 13 (October), pp. 230–237.

———. 1969. Comment on Irwin Deutscher's "Looking Backward." *American Sociologist* 4 (February), pp. 41–42.

Lauter, David. 1995. Affirmative Action Poised to Become Political Divide. *Los Angeles Times* (February 21), pp. A1, A15.

Lederman, Douglas, and Burd, Stephen. 1996. High Court Refuses to Hear Appeal of Ruling That Barred Considering Race in Admissions. *Chronicle of Higher Education* 43 (July 12), pp. A25, A29.

Lee, Don. 1992. A Sense of Identity. *Kansas City Star* (April 4), pp. E1, E7.

———. 1998. Asian Americans Finding Cracks in the Glass Ceiling. *Los Angeles Times* (July 15), pp. A1, A12–113.

Lee, Elisa. 1993. Silicon Valley Study Finds Asian Americans Hitting the Glass Ceiling. *AsianWeek* (October 8), p. 21.

Lee, Felicia R. 1991. 'Model Minority' Label Taxes Asian Youths. *New York Times* (March 30), pp. B1, B4.

Leehotz, Robert. 1995. Is Concept of Race a Relic? *Los Angeles Times* (April 15), pp. A1, A14.

Lehman, Edward C., Jr. 1993. *Gender and Work: The Case of the Clergy*. Albany: State University of New York.

Lerner, Michael. 1969. Respectable Bigotry. *American Scholar* 38 (August), pp. 606–617.

———. 1993. Jews Are Not White. *Village Voice* 38 (May 18), pp. 33–34.

Levin, Gary. 1999. Your set has lost its color. *USA Today* (July 20), pp. D1, D2.

Levin, Jack, and Levin, William C. 1982. *The Functions of Prejudice,* 2d ed. New York: Harper & Row.

Lichtenberg, Judith. 1992. Racism in the Head, Racism in the World. *Report from the Institute for Philosophy and Public Policy* 12 (Spring–Summer), pp. 3–5.

Lichter, S. Robert, and Lichter, Linda S. 1988. *Television's Impact in Ethnic and Racial Images*. New York: American Jewish Committee.

Lind, Michael. 1998. The Beige and the Black. *New York Times Magazine* (August 18), pp. 38–39.

Lindner, Eileen W. (ed.) 2000. *Yearbook of American and Canadian Churches 2000*. Nashville: Abingdon Press.

Lopez, David, and Espiritu, Yen. 1990. Panethnicity in the United States: A Theoretical Framework. *Ethnic and Racial Studies* 13 (April), pp. 198–224.

Lopez, Julie Amparano. 1992. Study Says Women Face Glass Walls as Well as Ceilings. *Wall Street Journal* (March 3), pp. B1–B2.

Love, Spencie. 1996. *One Blood: The Death and Resurrection of Charles R. Drew*. Chapel Hill, NC: University of North Carolina Press.

Lowry, Brian, Jensen, Elizabeth, and Braxton, Greg. 1999. Networks Decide Diversity Doesn't Pay. *Los Angeles Times* (July 20), p. A1.

Lupsha, Peter A. 1981. Individual Choice, Material Culture, and Organized Crime. *Criminology* 19 (May), pp. 3–24.

Mack, Raymond W. 1996. Whose Affirmative Action? *Society* 33 (March/April), pp. 41–43.

MacRae, C. Neil, Stangor, Charles, and Hewstone, Miles. 1996. *Stereotypes and Stereotyping*. New York: Guilford Press.

Maning, Anita. 1997. Troubled Waters: Environmental Racism Suit Makes Waves. *USA Today* (July 31), p. A1.

Manning, Robert D. 1995. Multiculturalism in the United States: Clashing Concepts, Changing Demographics, and Competing Cultures. *International Journal of Group Tensions* (Summer), pp. 117–168.

Martin, Philip, and Midgley, Elizabeth. Immigration to the United States, *Population Bulletin* 54 (June).

Martin, Philip, and Widgren, Jonas. 1996. International Migration: A Global Challenge. *Population Bulletin* 5 (April).

Martin, Susan E. 1991. The Effectiveness of Affirmative Action: The Case of Women in Policing. *Justice Quarterly* 8, pp. 489–504.

Martinez, Rubén, and Dukes, Richard L. 1991. Ethnic and Gender Differences in Self-Esteem. *Youth and Society* 32 (March), pp. 318–338.

Marty, Martin E. 1976. *A Nation of Behaviors*. Chicago: University of Chicago Press.

———. 1985. Transpositions: American Religion in the 1980s. *Annals* 480 (July), pp. 11–23.

Marx, Karl, and Engels, Friedrich. 1955. *Selected Works in Two Volumes*. Moscow: Foreign Languages Publishing House.

Massey, Douglas S., and Denton, Nancy A. 1993. *American Apartheid: Segregation and the Making of the Underclass*. Cambridge, MA: Harvard University Press.

Mathisen, James A. 1989. Twenty Years After Bellah: Whatever Happened to American Civil Rights? *Sociological Analysis* 50 (Summer), pp. 129–146.

Matza, David. 1964. *Delinquency and Drift*. New York: Wiley.

Mauro, Tony. 1995. Ruling Helps Communities Set Guidelines. *USA Today* (December 21), pp. A1–A2.

———. 1996. English-only Debate Lost in Legalese. *USA Today* (December 5), p. 4A.

McCollom, Susana. 1996. Hispanic Immigrant Attitude Towards African Americans: A Study of Intergroup Contact. Paper presented at the Annual Meeting of the American Sociological Association, New York City.

McConahay, John B., and Hough, Jr., J. C. 1976. Symbolic Racism. *Journal of Social Issues* 32 (No. 1), pp. 23–45.

McCormick, John, and Begley, Sharon. 1996. How to Raise a Tiger. *Newsweek* 126 (December 9), pp. 52–59.

McCully, Bruce T. 1940. *English Education and Origins of Indian Nationalism*. New York: Columbia University.

Merl, Jean. 1997. City Still Viewed as Racially Split. *Los Angeles Times* (April 29), pp. A1, A18.

Merton, Robert K. 1949. Discrimination and the American Creed. In Robert M. MacIver, ed., *Discrimination and National Welfare*, pp. 99–126. New York: Harper & Row.

———. 1968. *Social Theory and Social Structure*. New York: Free Press.

———. 1976. *Sociological Ambivalence and Other Essays*. New York: Free Press.

Migration News. 2000. AFL-CIO: End Sanctions. (March):2–3.

Miles, Jack. 1992. Blacks vs. Browns. *The Atlantic Monthly* (October), pp. 41–68.

Miller, David and Richard Schaefer 1998. Promise Keepers and Race: The Stand in the Gap Rally, Washington, DC, 1997. Paper presented at the annual meeting of the Midwest Sociological Society, Kansas City, MO, April.

Miller, Donald E. 1997. *Reinventing American Protestantism*. Berkeley: University of California Press.

Moffat, Susan. 1995. Minorities Found More Likely to Live Near Toxic Sites. *Los Angeles Times* (August 30), pp. B1, B3.

Montagu, Ashley. 1972. *Statement on Race*. New York: Oxford University Press.

———. 1975. *Race and IQ*. London: Oxford University Press.

Moore, Stephen. 1998. *A Fiscal Report of the Newest Americans*. Washington, DC: National Immigration Forum and Cato Institute.

Morrison, Toni. 1989. A Bench by the Side of the Road. *The World: The Journal of the Unitarian Universalist Association* 3 (January/February).

Morse, Samuel F. B. 1835. *Foreign Conspiracy Against the Liberties of United States*. New York: Leavitt, Lord.

Moulder, Frances V. 1996. Teaching about Race and Ethnicity: A Message of Despair or a Message of Hope? Paper presented at the Annual Meeting of the American Sociological Association, New York City.

Muskrat, Joe. 1971. Assimilate-or Starve? *Civil Rights Digest* 5 (October), pp. 27–34.

Myrdal, Gunnar. 1944. *An American Dilemma: The Negro Problem and Modern Democracy*. With the assistance of Richard Steiner and Arnold Rose. New York: Harper.

Nash, Manning. 1962. Race and the Ideology of Race. *Current Anthropology* 3 (June), pp. 285–288.

National Asian Pacific American Legal Consortium. 1996. *1995 Audit of Violence Against Asian Pacific Americans*. Washington, DC: NAPALC.

National Conference of Christians and Jews (NCCJ). 1994. *Taking America's Pulse*. New York: NCCJ.

National Gay and Lesbian Task Force. Hate Crime Laws in the United States—April 2000. Accessed May 7, 2000 at http://www.ngltf.org.

Navarro, Mireya. 1998. With a Vote for "None of the Above," Puerto Ricans Endorse Island's Status Quo. *New York Times* (December 14), p. A12.

NBC News. 1998. *Shopping Malls*. NBC Dateline, August 31.

Newman, William M. 1973. *American Pluralism: A Study of Minority Groups and Social Theory*. New York: Harper & Row.

Newsweek. 1999. Feeling Better About the Future (June 7), p. 35.

New York Times. 1917a. Illiteracy Is Not All Alike. (February 8), p. 12.

———. 1917b. The Immigration Bill Veto. (January 31), p. 210.

———. 1991. For 2, an Answer to Years of Doubt on Use of Peyote in Religious Rite. (July 9), p. A14.

Neibuhr, Gustav. 1998. Southern Baptists Declare Wife Should "Submit" to Her Husband. *New York Times* (June 10), pp. A1, A20.

Nie, Norman H., Currie, Barbara, and Greeley, Andrew M. 1974. Political Attitudes Among American

Ethnics: A Study of Perceptual Distortion. *Ethnicity* 1 (December), pp. 317–343.

Novak, Michael. 1996. *Unmeltable Ethnics: Politics and Culture in American Life,* 2d. ed. New Brunswick, NJ: Transaction Books.

O'Connor, Anne-Marie. 1998. Church's New Wave of Change. *Los Angeles Times* (March 25), pp. A1, A16.

O'Hare, William P., and Curry-White, Brenda. 1992. Is There a Rural Underclass? *Population Today* 20 (March), pp. 6–8.

O'Hare, William P., and Felt, Judy C. 1991. *Asian Americans: America's Fastest Growing Minority Group*. Washington, DC: Population Reference Bureau.

Ohnuma, Keiko. 1991. Study Finds Asians Unhappy at CSU. *AsianWeek* 12 (August 8), p. 5.

Ojito, Mirta. 1998. A Record Backlog to Get Citizenship Stymies 2 Million. *New York Times* (April 20), pp. A1, A16.

O'Kane, James M. 1992. *The Crooked Ladder: Gangsters, Ethnicity, and the American Dream.* New Brunswick, NJ: Transaction Books.

Omi, Michael, and Winant, Howard. 1994. *Racial Formation in the United States.* 2d ed. New York: Routledge.

Onishi, Normitsu. 1996. New Sense of Race Arises Among Asian-Americans. *New York Times* (May 30), pp. A1, B6.

Owen, Carolyn A., Eisner, Howard C., and McFaul, Thomas R. 1981. A Half-Century of Social Distance Research: National Replication of the Bogardus Studies. *Sociology and Social Research* 66 (October), pp. 80–97.

Paral, Rob. 1996. *Estimated Costs of Providing Welfare and Education Services to the Native Born and to Immigrants in Illinois.* Chicago: Latino Institute.

Park, Robert E. 1928. Human Migration and the Marginal Man. *American Journal of Sociology* 33 (May), pp. 881–893.

———. 1950. *Race and Culture: Essays in the Sociology of Contemporary Man.* New York: Free Press.

Park, Robert E., and Burgess, Ernest W. 1921. *Introduction to the Science of Sociology.* Chicago: University of Chicago Press.

Passel, Jeffrey S., and Clark, Rebecca L. 1996. *Taxes Paid by Immigrants in Illinois.* Washington, DC: The Urban Institute.

Pearlman, Jeff. At Full Blast. *Sports Illustrated* (December 7), pp. 60–62, 64.

Pease, John, and Martin, Lee. 1997. Want Ads and Jobs for the Poor: A Glaring Mismatch. *Sociological Forum* 12 (No. 4), pp. 545–564.

Pedder, Sophie. 1991. Social Isolation and the Labour Market: Black Americans in Chicago. Paper presented at the Chicago Urban Poverty and Family Life Conference, Chicago.

———. 1959. Regional Differences in Anti-Negro Prejudice. *Journal of Abnormal and Social Psychology* 59 (July), pp. 28–36.

Pettigrew, Thomas F., and Martin, Joanne. 1987. Shaping the Organizational Context for Black American Inclusion. *Journal of Social Issues* 43 (No. 1), pp. 41–78.

Pileggi, Nicolas. 1971. Risorgimento: The Red, White, and Greening of New York. *New York Times Magazine* (June 7), pp. 26–36.

Piller, Charles. 1998. The Gender Gap Goes High Tech. *Los Angeles Times* (August 25), p. A1.

Porter, Jack Nusan. 1985. Self-Hatred and Self-Esteem. *The Jewish Spectator* (Fall), pp. 51–55.

Portes, Alejandro, and MacLeod, Dag. 1996. What Shall I Call Myself? Hispanic Identity Formation in the Second Generation. *Ethnic and Racial Studies* 19 (July), pp. 523–547.

Powell-Hopson, Darlene, and Hopson, Derek. 1988. Implications of Doll Color Preferences Among Black Preschool Children and White Preschool Children. *Journal of Black Psychology* 14 (February), pp. 57–63.

Princeton Survey Research Associates. 1997. *State of the Union.* Washington, DC: Pew Research Center for the People and the Press.

Price, David Andrew. 1996. English-Only Rules: EEOC Has Gone Too Far. *USA Today* (March 28), p. 13A.

Public Broadcasting System. 1998. Weekend Edition: National Public Radio with Eric Westervelt and Scott Simon. May 30.

Puente, Maria. 1996. Naturalization at All-Time High. *USA Today* (July 5), p. 3A.

Qian, Zhenchao. 1997. Breaking the Racial Barriers: Variation in Interracial Marriage Between 1980 and 1990. *Demography* 34 (May), pp. 263–276.

Raymond, Chris. 1991. Cornell Scholar Attacks Key Psychological Studies Thought to Demonstrate Blacks' Self-Hatred. *Chronicle of Higher Education* 37 (May 8), pp. A5, A8, A11.

Religion Watch. 1995. Reform Synagogues Increasingly Adopting Orthodox Practices. 10 (March), p. 7.

Reskin, Barbara F. 1998. *The Realities of Affirmative Action in Employment.* Washington, DC: American Sociological Association.

Richman, Ruth. 1992. Glass Ceiling? Break It Yourselves, Federal Official Says. *Chicago Tribune* (August 16), sect. 6, pp. 1, 11.

Roberts, Bari-Ellen, and White, Jack. 1998. *Roberts vs. Texaco: A True Story of Race and Corporate America.* New York: Avon.

Roberts, D. F. The Dynamics of Racial Intermixture in the American Negro—Some Anthropological Considerations. *American Journal of Human Genetics* 7 (December), pp. 361–367.

Robles, Frances, and Casimir, Leslie. 1996. Legacies of a Shooting: Ethnic Tension, Boycott. *Miami Herald* (July 7), p. 1B.

Roediger, David R., ed. 1998. *Black on White: Black Writers on What It Means to Be White.* New York: Schocken Books.

Rohter, Larry. 1993. Rights Groups Fault Decision, As Do Haitians. *New York Times* (June 22), p. 18.

Rolle, Andrew F. 1972. *The American Indians: Their History and Culture*. Belmont, CA: Wadsworth.

Rose, Arnold. 1951. *The Roots of Prejudice*. Paris: UNESCO.

Rosenbaum, James E., and Meaden, Patricia. 1992. Harassment and Acceptance of Low-Income Black Youth in White Suburban Schools. Paper presented at the Annual Meeting of the American Sociological Association, Pittsburgh.

Rosenberg, Morris, and Simmons, Roberta G. 1971. *Black and White Self-Esteem: The Urban School Child*. Washington, DC: American Sociological Association.

Ross, Robert J. S. 1998. The New Sweatshops in the United States: How New, How Real, How Many, Why? Paper presented at the Annual Meeting of the American Sociological Association. San Francisco, CA, August.

Roth, Elizabeth. 1993. The Civil Rights History of "Sex." *Ms.* 3 (March–April), pp. 84–85.

Rothman, Stanley. 1996. Is God Really Dead in Beverly Hills? *American Scholar* 65 (Spring), pp. 272–278.

Rumbaut, Rubén G. 1998. Coming of Age in Immigrant America. *Research Perspectives on Migration* 1 (January/February), pp. 1, 3–14.

Ryan, William. 1976. *Blaming the Victim,* rev. ed. New York: Random House.

Saad, Lydia. 1995. Immigrants See U.S. As Land of Opportunity. *Gallup Poll Monthly* 358 (July), pp. 19–33.

———. 1998. America Divided Over Status of Puerto Rico. *Gallup Poll Monthly* 390 (March), p. 278.

Saad, Lydia, and McAneny, Leslie. 1994. Most Americans Think Religion Losing Clout in the 1990s. *Gallup Poll Monthly* (April), pp. 2–4.

Sanders, Irwin T., and Morawska, Ewa T. 1975. *Polish-American Community Life: A Survey of Research*. Boston: Community Sociology Training Program.

Schaefer, Richard T. 1976. *The Extent and Content of Racial Prejudice in Great Britain*. San Francisco: R & E Research Associates.

———. 1986. Racial Prejudice in a Capitalist State: What Has Happened to the American Creed? *Phylon* 47 (September), pp. 192–198.

———. 1992. People of Color: The "Kaleidoscope" May Be a Better Way to Describe America Than "The Melting Pot." *Peoria Journal Star* (January 19), p. A7.

———. 1996. Education and Prejudice: Unraveling the Relationship. *Sociological Quarterly* 37 (January), pp. 1–16.

Sears, David O., and Kinder, Donald R. 1971. Racial Tensions and Voting Behavior in Los Angeles. In Werner Z. Hirsch, ed., *Los Angeles: Viability and Prospects for Metropolitan Leadership*, pp. 51–88. New York: Praeger.

Sengupta, Somini. 1997. Asians' Advances Academically Are Found to Obscure a Need. *New York Times* (November 9), p. 17.

Severo, Richard. 1970. New York's Italians: A Question of Identity. *New York Times* (November 9), pp. 43, 50.

Shanklin, Eugenia. 1994. *Anthropology and Race*. Belmont, CA: Wadsworth.

Sherif, Musafer, and Sherif, Carolyn. 1969. *Social Psychology*. New York: Harper & Row.

Shuster, Beth. 1996. Consulate Takes Activist Role for Mexicans in U.S. *Los Angeles Times* (April 9), pp. A1, A18–A19.

Sigelman, Lee, Bledsoe, Timothy, Welch, Susan, and Combs, Michael W. 1996. Making Contact? Black-White Social Interaction in an Urban Setting. *American Journal of Sociology* 5 (March), pp. 1306–1332.

Sigelman, Lee, and Tuch, Steven A. 1997. Metastereotypes: Blacks' Perception of Whites' Stereotypes of Blacks. *Public Opinion Quarterly* 61 (Spring), pp. 87–101.

Silverstein, Stuart. 1996. Glass Ceiling Over Women Still Intact In Workplace. *Los Angeles Times* (October 18), pp. A1, A21.

Simpson, Jacqueline C. 1995. Pluralism: The Evolution of a Nebulous Concept. *American Behavioral Scientist* 38 (January), pp. 459–477.

Skrentny, John David. 1996. *The Ironies of Affirmative Action*. Chicago: University of Chicago Press.

Slavin, Robert E. 1985. Cooperative Learning: Applying Contact Theory in Desegregated Schools. *Journal of Social Issues* 41 (No. 3), pp. 45–62.

Smith, James P., and Edmonston, Barry, eds. 1997. *The New Americans: Economic, Demographic, and Fiscal Effects of Immigration*. Washington, DC: National Academy Press.

Song, Tae-Hyon. 1991. Social Contact and Ethnic Distance Between Koreans and the U.S. Whites in the United States. Paper, Western Illinois University, Macomb.

Sontag, Deborah. 1993. Émigrés in New York: Work off the Books. *New York Times* (June 13), pp. 1, 42.

Southern, David W. 1987. *Gunnar Myrdal and Black-White Relations*. Baton Rouge: Louisiana State University.

Stammer, Larry B. Pope: 1999. As He Comes to U.S., a study finds a decline in Catholics' commitment. *Los Angeles Times* (January 26), pp. A1, A17.

Stark, Rodney. 1987. Correcting Church Membership Rates: 1971 and 1980. *Review of Religious Research* 29 (September), pp. 69–77.

Stark, Rodney, and Glock, Charles. 1968. *American Piety: The Nature of Religious Commitment*. Berkeley: University of California Press.

Stonequist, Everett V. 1937. *The Marginal Man: A Study in Personality and Culture Conflict*. New York: Scribner's.

Swatos, William H. Jr., (ed.) 1994. *Gender and Religion*. New Brunswick, NJ: Transaction.

Syfers, Judy. 1972. I Want a Wife. *Ms.* (Spring Preview Issue), pp. 56–59.

Tachibana, Judy. 1990. Model Minority Myth Presents Unrepresentative Portrait of Asian Americans, Many Educators Say. *Black Issues in Higher Education* 6 (March 1), pp. 1, 11.

Takagi, Dana Y. 1992. *The Retreat from Race: Asian-American Admissions and Racial Politics.* New Brunswick, NJ: Rutgers University Press.

Takaki, Ronald. 1989. *Strangers from a Different Shore: A History of Asian Americans.* Boston: Little, Brown.

Tamaki, Julie. 1998. Cultural Balancing Act Adds to Teen Angst. *Los Angeles Times* (July 13), pp. A1, A8–A9.

Taylor, Stuart, Jr. 1987a. High Court Backs Basing Promotion on a Racial Quota. *New York Times* (February 26), pp. 1, 14.

———. 1987b. High Court Voids Curb on Teaching Evolution Theory. *New York Times* (June 20), pp. 1, 7.

———. 1988. Justices Back New York Law Ending Sex Bias by Big Clubs. *New York Times* (June 21), pp. A1, A18.

Terry, Clifford. 1975. Chicagoans—Pro Soccer. *Chicago Tribune Magazine* (May 5), p. 26.

Thomas, William Isaac. 1923. *The Unadjusted Girl.* Boston: Little, Brown.

Tilove, Jonathan. 1998. Face of the Nation. *Fort Lauderdale Sun-Sentinel* (July 12), sect. G, pp. 1, 2.

Thornton, Russell. 1987. Demographic Antecedents of the 1890 Ghost Dance. *American Sociological Review* 46 (February), pp. 88–96.

Ture, Kwame, and Hamilton, Charles. 1992. *Black Power: The Politics of Liberation.* New York: Vintage Books.

Tyler, Gus. 1972. White Worker/Blue Mood. *Dissent* 190 (Winter), pp. 190–196.

U.S. Committee for Refugees. 1996a. *World Refugee Summary 1996.* Washington, DC: Immigration and Refugee Services of America.

———. 1996b. 1996 Statistical Issue. *Refugee Reports* 17 (December 31):1–13.

USA Today. 1994. Urban League Urges a "Marshall Plan" (January 21), p. 3A.

U.S. Bureau of the Census. 1975. *Historical Statistics of the United States, Colonial Times to 1970.* Washington, D.C.: U.S. Government Printing Office.

U.S. Bureau of the Census. 1992. *Statistical Abstract of the United States, 1992.* Washington, DC: U.S. Government Printing Office.

———. 1993a. *Statistical Abstract of the United States 1993.* Washington DC: U.S. Government Printing Office.

———. 1996. *Statistical Abstract of the United States 1996.* Washington, DC: U.S. Government Printing Office.

———. 1998a. *United States Census 2000. Dress Rehearsal.* Washington, DC: U.S. Government Printing Office.

———. 1998b. Money Income in the United States: 1997 (with separate data on valuation of noncash benefits). *Current Population Reports*, pp. 60–200. Washington, DC: U.S. Government Printing Office.

———. 1998c. *Statistical Abstract of the United States 1998.* Washington, DC: U.S. Government Printing Office.

———. 1998d. Young Adults Boost Asian College-Completion Levels. *Census Bureau Reports.* Press Release. June 29.

———. 1998e. Asians and Pacific Islanders Have Nation's Highest Median Household Income in 1997. *Census Bureau Reports.* Press Release. August 24.

———. 1999a. *Statistical Abstract of the United States 1999.* Washington, DC: U.S. Government Printing Office.

———. 1999b. Nearly 1 in 10 U.S. Residents Are Foreign-Born, Census Bureau Reports. Press release. Washington, D.C.: Census Bureau. August 17.

———. 1999i. Current Money Income in the United States 1998. *Current Population Reports.* Ser. P60. No. 206. Washington, DC: U.S. Government Printing Office.

———. 2000. National Population Projections. Internet Release Date: January 13, 2000. Accessed on May 11, 2000 at http://www.census.gov/population/www/projection/natsum-T3.html.

U.S. Department of Justice. 1999. *Crime in the United States, 1999.* Washington, DC: U.S. Government Printing Office.

U.S. Department of Labor. 1993. *Breaking the Glass Ceiling.* Washington, DC: U.S. Government Printing Office.

———. 1995a. *Good for Business: Making Full Use of the Nation's Capital.* Washington, DC: U.S. Government Printing Office.

———. 1995b. *A Solid Investment: Making Full Use of the Nation's Human Capital.* Washington, DC: U.S. Government Printing Office.

U.S. Immigration and Naturalization Service. 1997. *1996 Statistical Yearbook of the Immigration and Naturalization Service.* Washington, DC: U.S. Government Printing Office.

———. 1999a. *Legal Immigration, Fiscal Year 1998.* Washington, D.C.: U.S. Government Printing Office.

———. 1999b. *1997 Statistical Yearbook of the Immigration and Naturalization Service.* Washington, DC: U.S. Government Printing Office.

Usdansky, Margaret L. 1992a. Old Ethnic Influences Still Play in Cities. *USA Today* (August 4), p. 9A.

———. 1992b. Asian Immigrants Changing Face of Rural USA. *USA Today* (September 10), p. 10A.

———. 1993. Census: Languages Not Foreign at Home. *USA Today* (April 28), pp. A1, A2.

Verhovek, Sam Hove. 1995. Mother Scolded by Judge for Speaking in Spanish. *New York Times* (August 30), p. A12.

———. 1999. Record for Women in Washington Legislature. *New York Times* (February 4), p. A14.

Wagley, Charles, and Harris, Marvin. 1958. *Minorities in the New World: Six Case Studies.* New York: Columbia University Press.

Wallerstein, Immanuel. 1974. *The Modern World System*. New York: Academic Press.

———. 1979. *The Capitalist World-Economy*. Cambridge, Eng.: Cambridge University Press.

———. 1996. Social Change? Change Is Eternal. Nothing Ever Changes. Paper presented at the III Congresso Português de Sociologia, Lisbon, Portugal.

———. 1996b. The ANC and South Africa: The Past and Future of Liberation Movements in the World-System. Paper presented at the annual meeting of the South African Sociological Association, Durban, South Africa.

Warner, Sam Bass Jr. 1968. *The Private City: Philadelphia in Three Periods of Its Growth*. Philadelphia: University of Pennsylvania Press.

Warner, W. Lloyd, and Srole, Leo. 1945. *The Social Systems of American Ethnic Groups*. New Haven: Yale University Press.

Waters, Mary. 1990. *Ethnic Options. Choosing Identities in America*. Berkeley: University of California Press.

Weitz, Rose. 1992. College Students' Images of African American, Mexican American, and Jewish American Women. Paper presented at the Annual Meeting of the American Sociological Association, Pittsburgh.

Wernick, Robert. 1996. The Rise, and Fall, of a Fervid Third Party. *Smithsonian* 27 (November), pp. 150–152, 154–158.

White, Jack E. 1997. I'm Just Who I Am. *Time* 149 (May 5), pp. 32–34, 36.

Wickham, DeWayne. 1993. Subtle Racism Thrives. *USA Today* (October 25), p. 2A.

Williams, Patricia J. 1997. Of Race and Risk. *The Nation* (December 29).

Wilson, James Q., and Banfield, Edward C. 1964. Public Regardingness as a Value Premise in Voting Behavior. *American Political Science Review* 58 (December), pp. 876–887.

Wilson, William J. 1987. *The Truly Disadvantaged: The Inner City, The Underclass, and Public Policy*. Chicago: University of Chicago Press.

———. 1988. The Ghetto Underclass and the Social Transformation of the Inner City. *The Black Scholar* 19 (May–June), pp. 10–17.

———. 1996. *When Work Disappears: The World of the New Urban Poor*. New York: Knopf.

Winant, Howard. 1994. *Racial Conditions: Politics, Theory, Comparisons*. Minneapolis: University of Minnesota Press.

Wood, Daniel B. 2000. Minorities hope TV deals don't just lead to 'tokenism.' *Christian Science Monitor* (January 19).

Wright, Robert. 1995. Who's Really to Blame? *Time* 146 (November 6), pp. 33–37.

Wright, Susan. 1993. Blaming the Victim, Blaming Society, or Blaming the Discipline: Fixing Responsibility for Poverty and Homelessness. *Sociological Quarterly* 34 (No. 1), pp. 1–16.

Wrong, Dennis H. 1972. How Important Is Social Class? *Dissent* 19 (Winter), pp. 278–285.

Wu, Shanlon. 1990. In Search of Bruce Lee's Grave, *New York Times Magazine* (April 15).

Wyman, Mark. 1990. *Round-Trip to America. The Immigrants Return to Europe, 1830–1930*. Ithaca, NY: Cornell University Press.

Yinger, John. 1995. *Closed Doors, Opportunities Lost: The Continuing Costs of Housing Discrimination*. New York: Russell Sage Foundation.

Yu, Henry. 1996. How Tiger Woods Lost His Stripes. *Los Angeles Times* (December 2), p. B5.

Zhou, Min, and Kamo, Yoshinori. 1994. An Analysis of Earnings Patterns for Chinese, Japanese, and Non-Hispanic White Males in the United States. *Sociological Quarterly* 35 (No. 4), pp. 581–602.

Photo Credits

CHAPTER 1 Page 1: Al Seib/Los Angeles Times Syndicate; **8:** Corbis; **10:** Tribune Media Services, Inc.; **17:** Karin Cooper/Liaison Agency, Inc.; **22:** AP/Wide World Photos; **26:** Mark C. Burnett/Stock Boston; **28:** Shelly Katz/Liaison Agency, Inc.; **31:** AP/Wide World Photos.

CHAPTER 2 Page 39: Jim Bourg/Liaison Agency, Inc.; **41:** The Phillips Collection; **53:** Bernard J. "Barney" Gallagher; **58:** Robert Cohen/St. Louis Post-Dispatch; **69:** Copley News Service/Cartoonist, Michael Ramirez.

CHAPTER 3 Page 73: Corbis; **75:** Ted Hardin; **79:** John F. Kelly; **82:** Michael Dwyer; **92:** Charles Kennard/Stock Boston; **97:** Louie Balukoff/AP/Wide World Photos; **99:** Milwaukee Journal Sentinel; **103:** Dayton Daily News.

CHAPTER 4 Page 108: Chromosohm/Sohm/Photo Researchers, Inc.; **114:** UPI/Corbis; **116:** George Eastman House; **119:** Raffi Ishkanian; **123:** Washington Post; **127:** Rex Babin; **129:** Denis Poroy/AP/Wide World Photos; **131:** Richard R. Renaldi/Impact Visuals Photo & Graphics, Inc.

CHAPTER 5 Page 137: J. Nordell/The Image Works; **141:** Dave Scheele/Diane Glancy; **149:** Robert Frerck/Stone; **153:** Philip Jon Bailey/Stock Boston; **157:** Jose R. Lopez/New York Times Pictures; **159:** Cartoonists & Writers Syndicate/Cartoon Archive; **164:** Karin Shamsi-Sasha/Corbis/Sygma; **166:** Mike Peters/Tribune Media Services, Inc.; **168:** Jack Kurtz/Impact Visuals Photo & Graphics, Inc.

CHAPTER 6 Page 175: Bill Anderson/Photo Researchers, Inc.; **180:** Oliver Chin; **183:** Bob Kramer/Index Stock Imagery, Inc.; **184:** Ulf Andersen/Liaison Agency, Inc.

NAME INDEX

SUBJECT INDEX